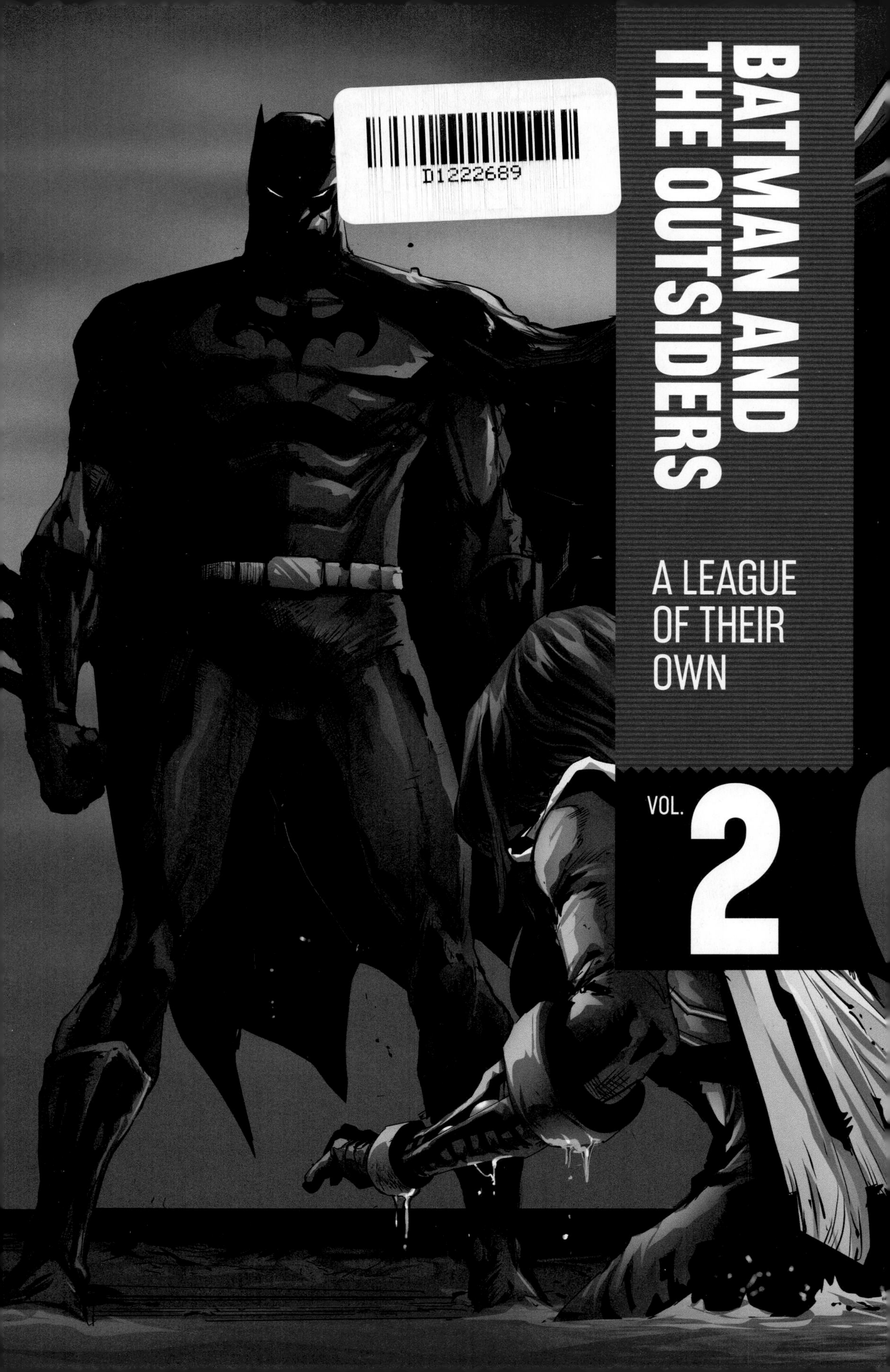

BATMAN AND THE OUTSIDERS

A LEAGUE OF THEIR OWN

VOL. 2

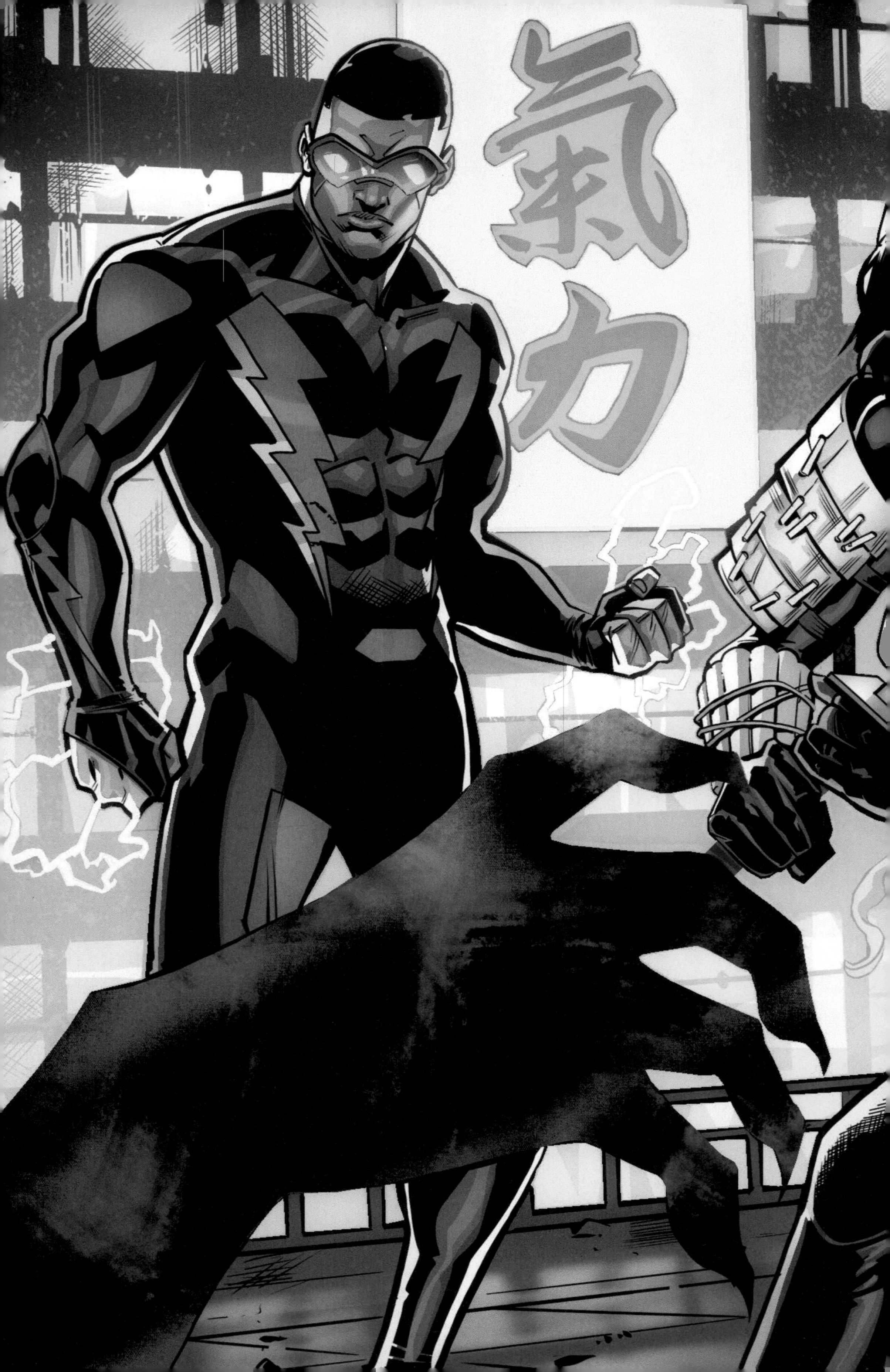
氣力

BATMAN AND THE OUTSIDERS

A LEAGUE OF THEIR OWN

writer
BRYAN HILL

artists
DEXTER SOY
MAX RAYNOR

colorists
VERONICA GANDINI
LUIS GUERRERO

letterers
CLAYTON COWLES
ALW STUDIOS' TROY PETERI

collection cover artist
MICHAEL GOLDEN

BATMAN created by BOB KANE with BILL FINGER

SUPERMAN created by JERRY SIEGEL and JOE SHUSTER
By special arrangement with the Jerry Siegel family

VOL.

2

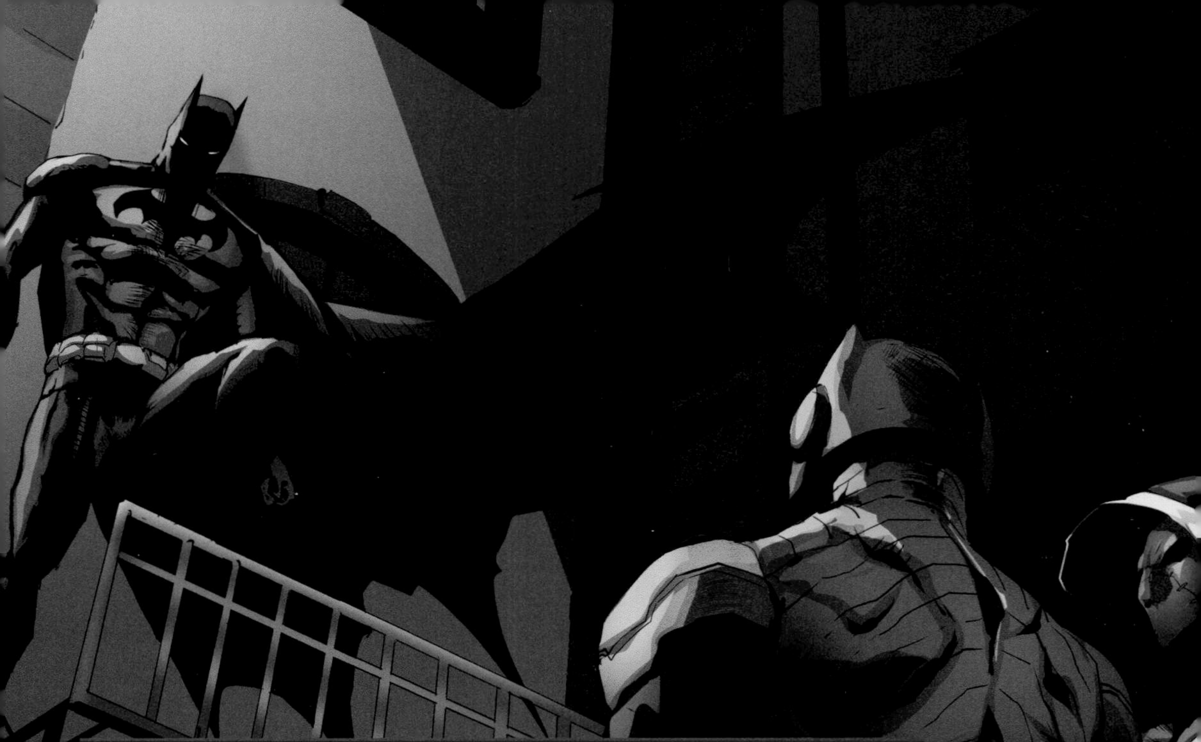

DAVE WIELGOSZ Editor – Original Series
JEB WOODARD Group Editor – Collected Editions
ERIKA ROTHBERG Editor – Collected Edition
STEVE COOK Design Director – Books
JOHN J. HILL Publication Design
CHRISTY SAWYER Publication Production

BOB HARRAS Senior VP – Editor-in-Chief, DC Comics

DAN DiDIO Publisher
JIM LEE Publisher & Chief Creative Officer
BOBBIE CHASE VP – New Publishing Initiatives
DON FALLETTI VP – Manufacturing Operations & Workflow Management
LAWRENCE GANEM VP – Talent Services
ALISON GILL Senior VP – Manufacturing & Operations
HANK KANALZ Senior VP – Publishing Strategy & Support Services
DAN MIRON VP – Publishing Operations
NICK J. NAPOLITANO VP – Manufacturing Administration & Design
NANCY SPEARS VP – Sales
JONAH WEILAND VP – Marketing & Creative Services
MICHELE R. WELLS VP & Executive Editor, Young Reader

BATMAN AND THE OUTSIDERS VOL. 2: A LEAGUE OF THEIR OWN

DC Comics, 2900 West Alameda Ave., Burbank, CA 91505
Printed by LSC Communications, Kendallville, IN, USA. 7/3/20. First Printing.
ISBN: 978-1-77950-286-5

Library of Congress Cataloging-in-Publication Data is available.

PEFC Certified
This product is from sustainably managed forests and controlled sources
PEFC
PEFC/29-31-337
www.pefc.org

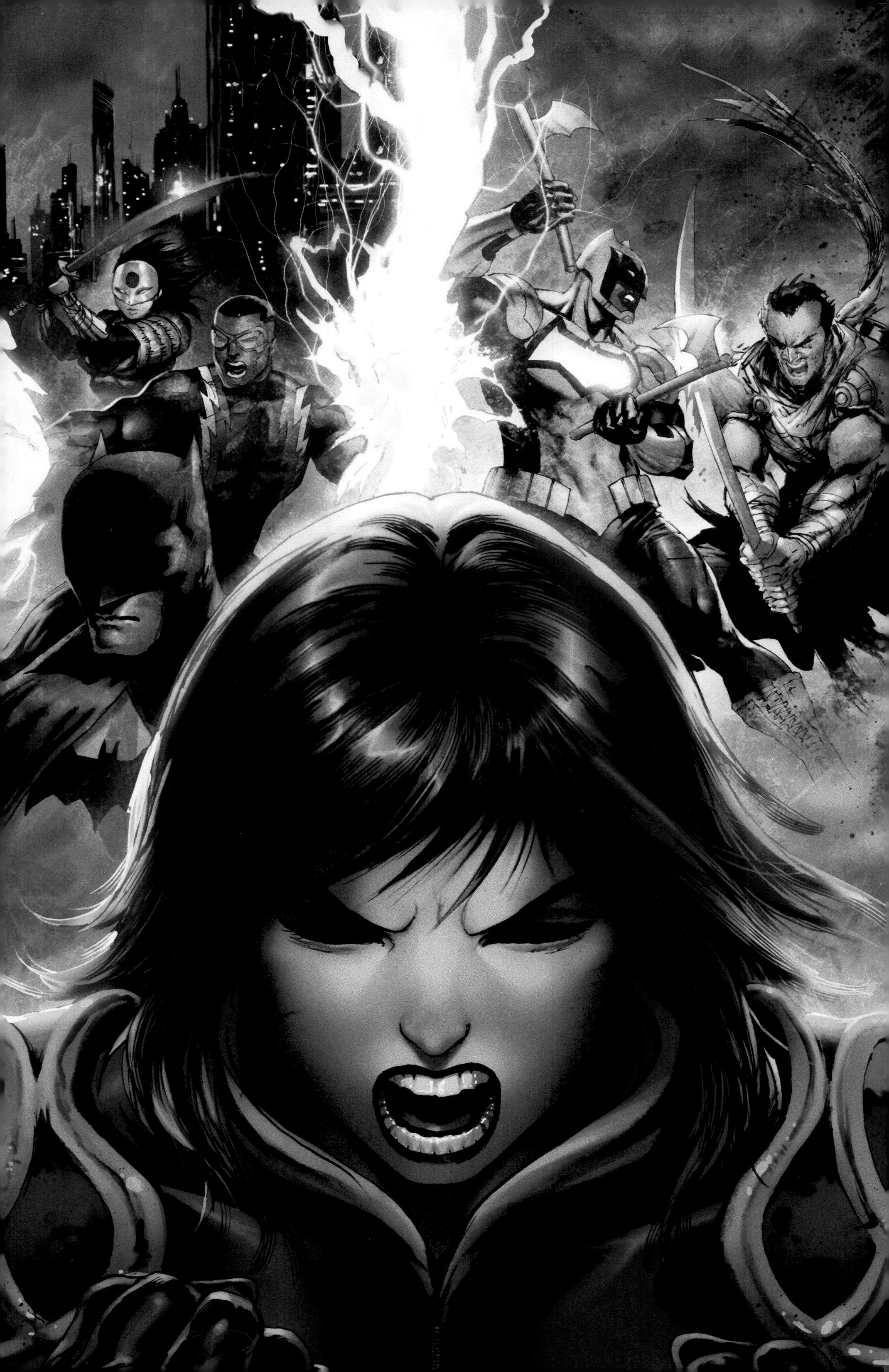

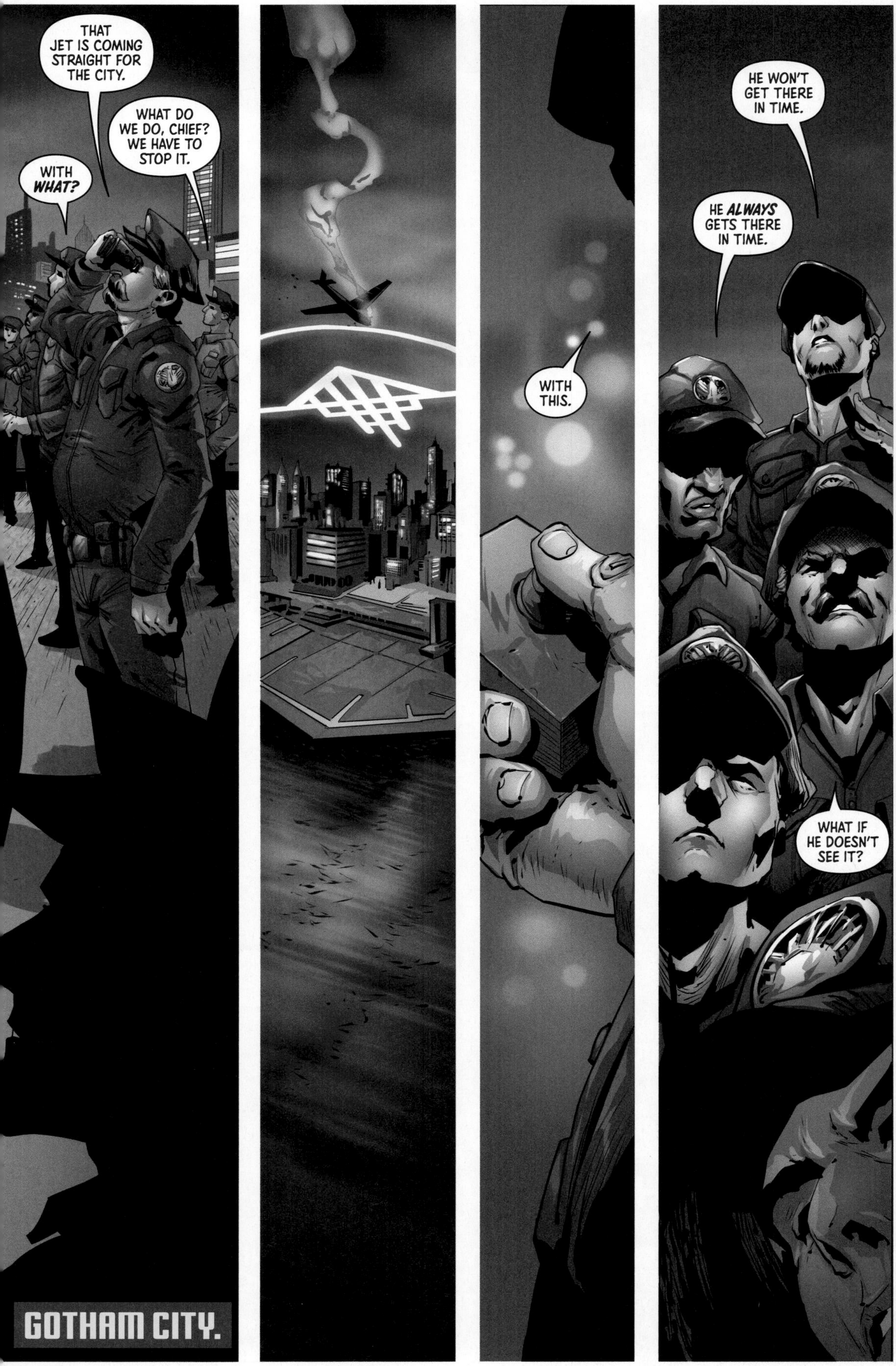
GOTHAM CITY.
THAT JET IS COMING STRAIGHT FOR THE CITY.
WHAT DO WE DO, CHIEF? WE HAVE TO STOP IT.
WITH *WHAT?*
WITH THIS.
HE WON'T GET THERE IN TIME.
HE *ALWAYS* GETS THERE IN TIME.
WHAT IF HE DOESN'T SEE IT?

SENTS
DERS IN

AGUE
EIR OWN part 1

ER SOY ARTIST VERONICA GANDINI COLO
RS TYLER KIRKHAM & NEI RUFFINO COV
BEN ABERNATHY GROUP EDITOR

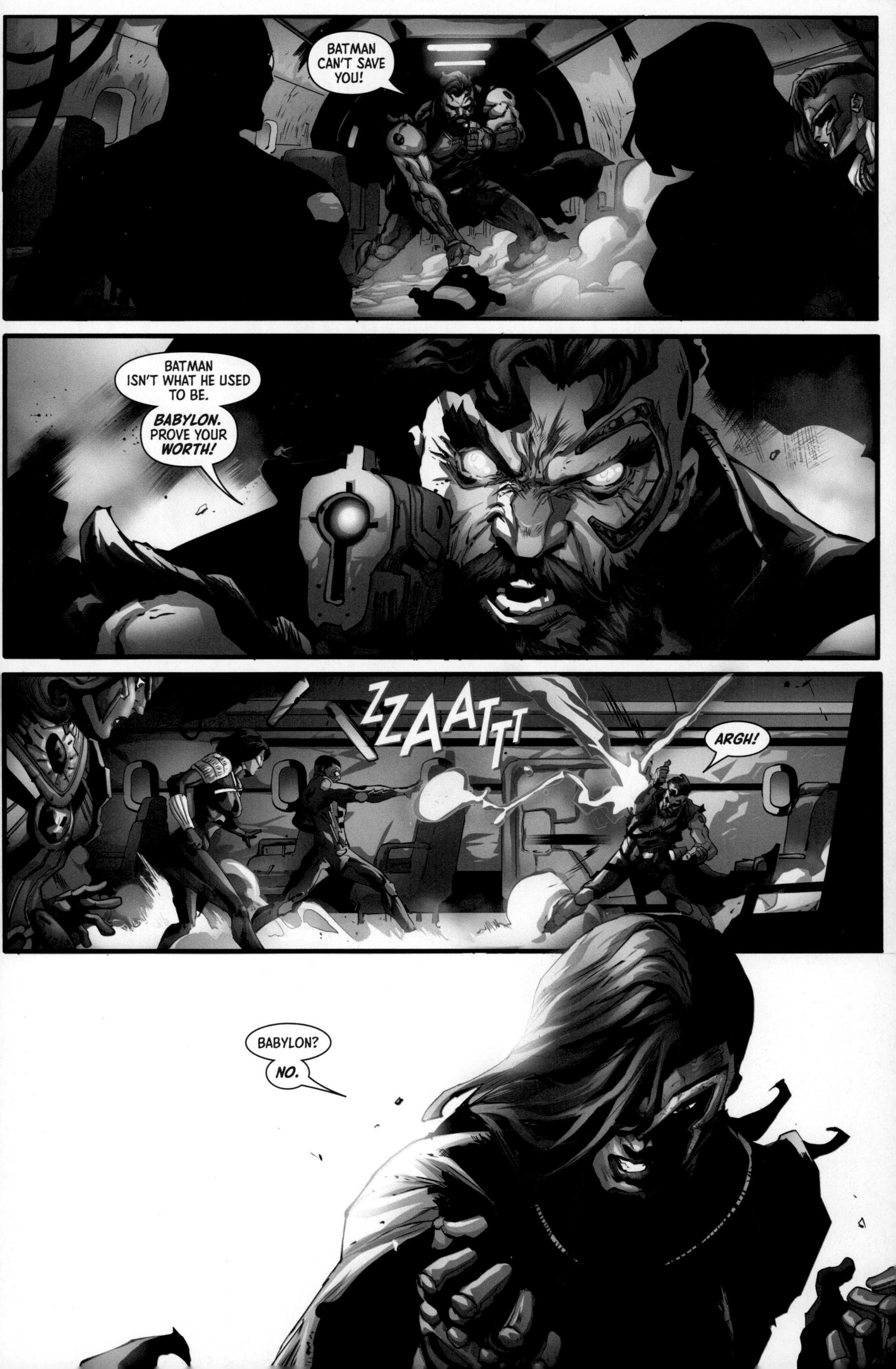
BATMAN CAN'T SAVE YOU!
BATMAN ISN'T WHAT HE USED TO BE. BABYLON. PROVE YOUR WORTH!
ZZAATTT
ARGH!
BABYLON? NO.

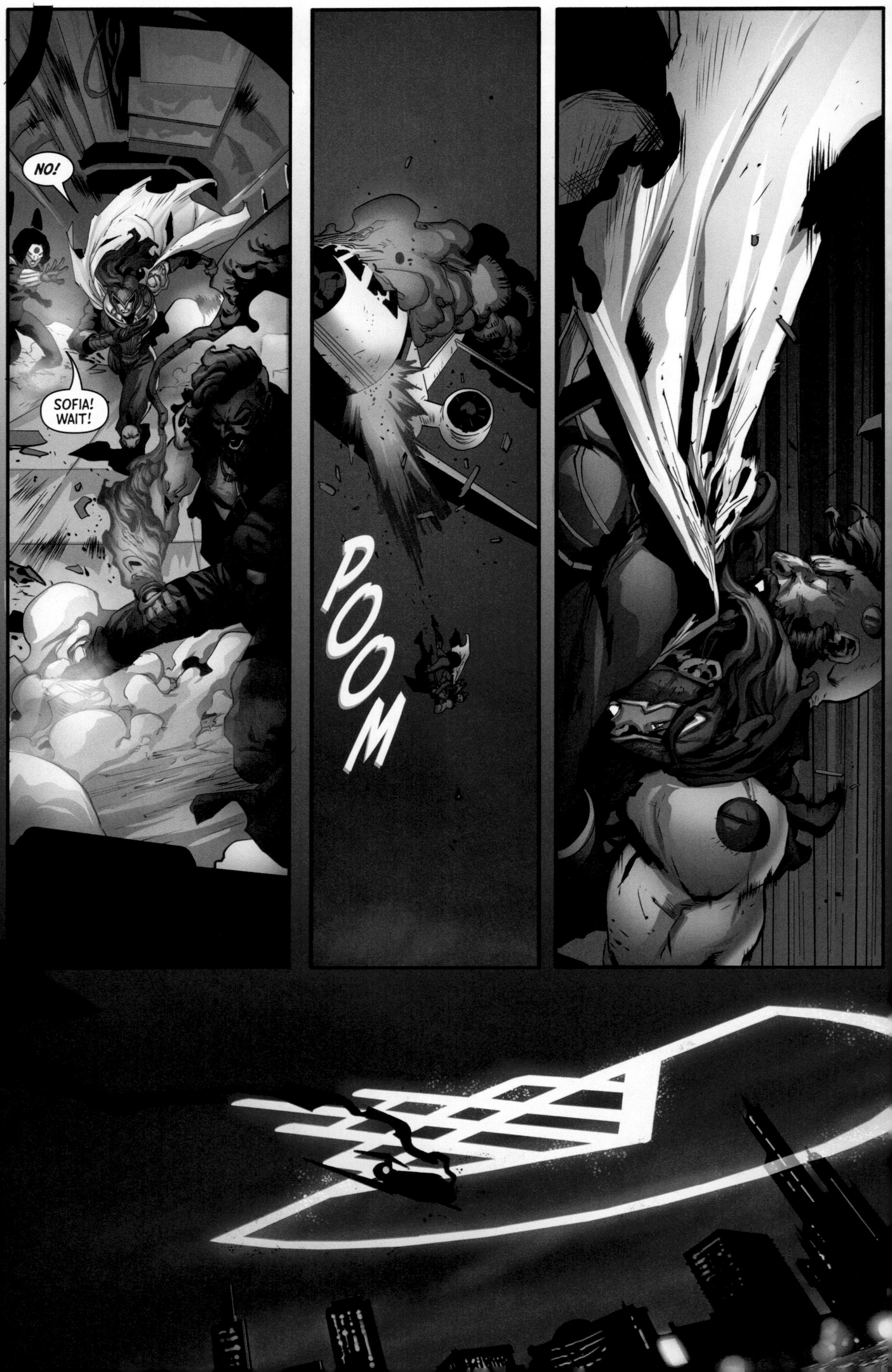
NO!
SOFIA! WAIT!
POOOM

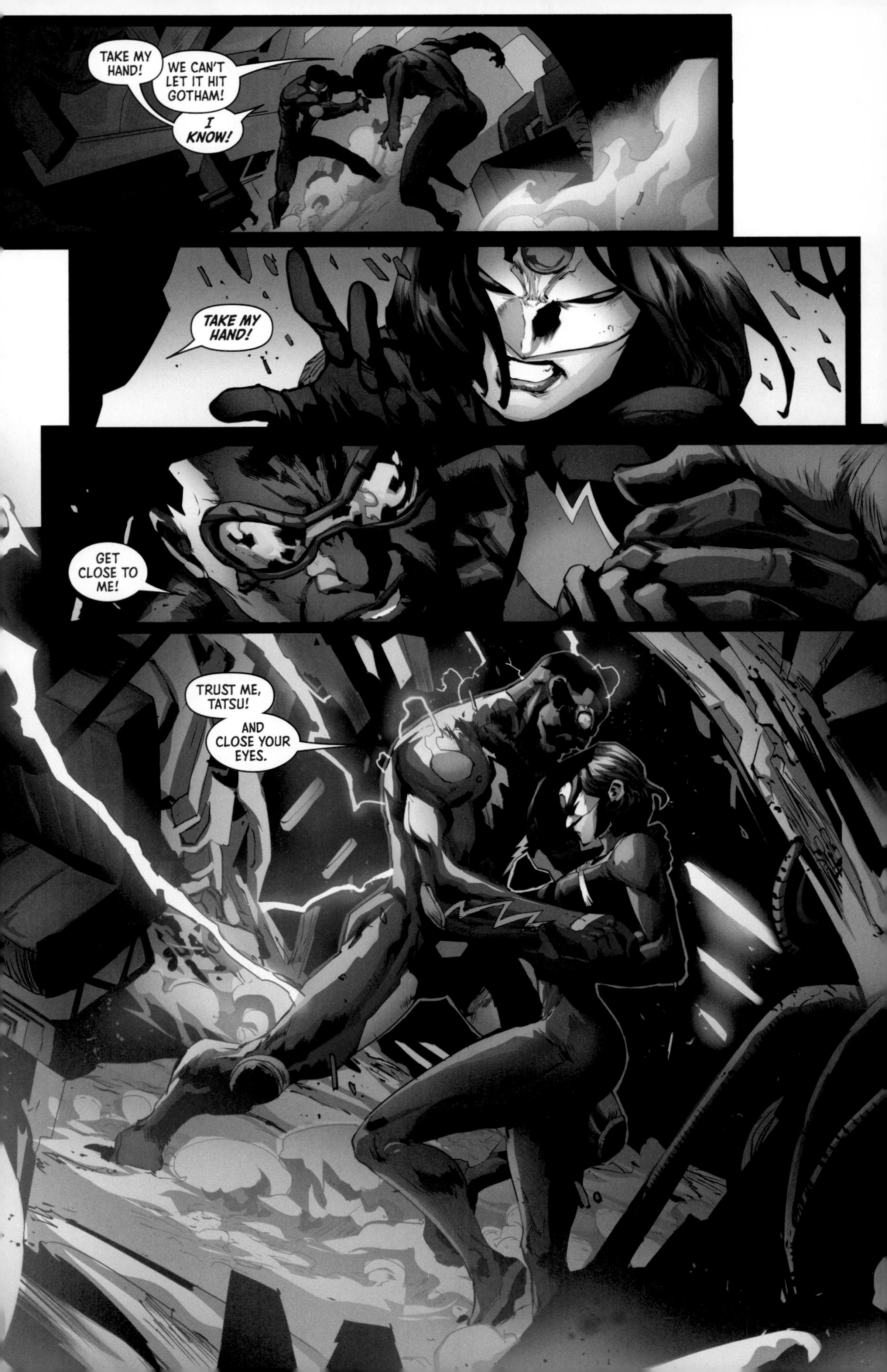
TAKE MY HAND!
WE CAN'T LET IT HIT GOTHAM!
I KNOW!
TAKE MY HAND!
GET CLOSE TO ME!
TRUST ME, TATSU!
AND CLOSE YOUR EYES.

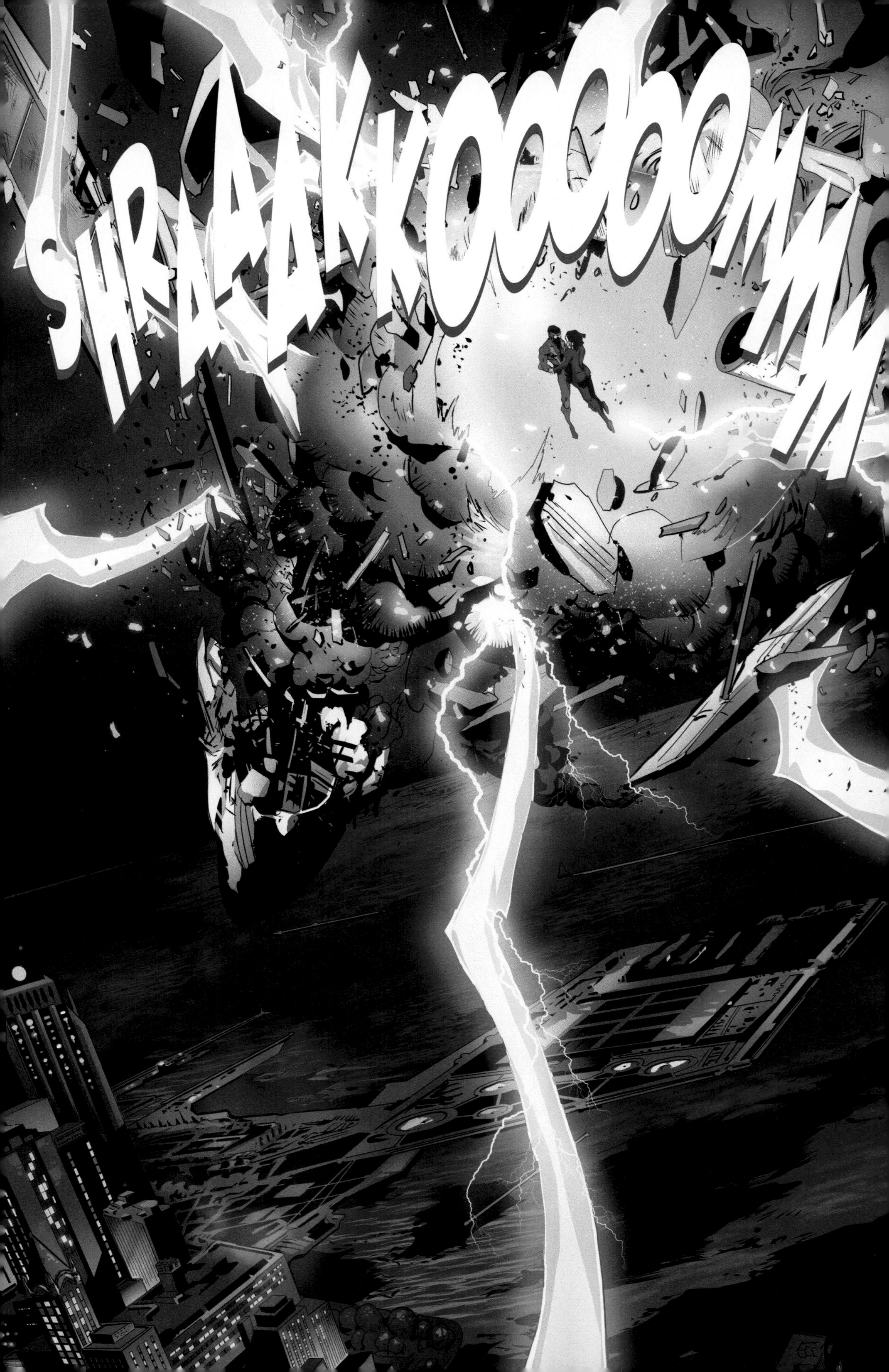
SHRAAKKOOOOOMMM

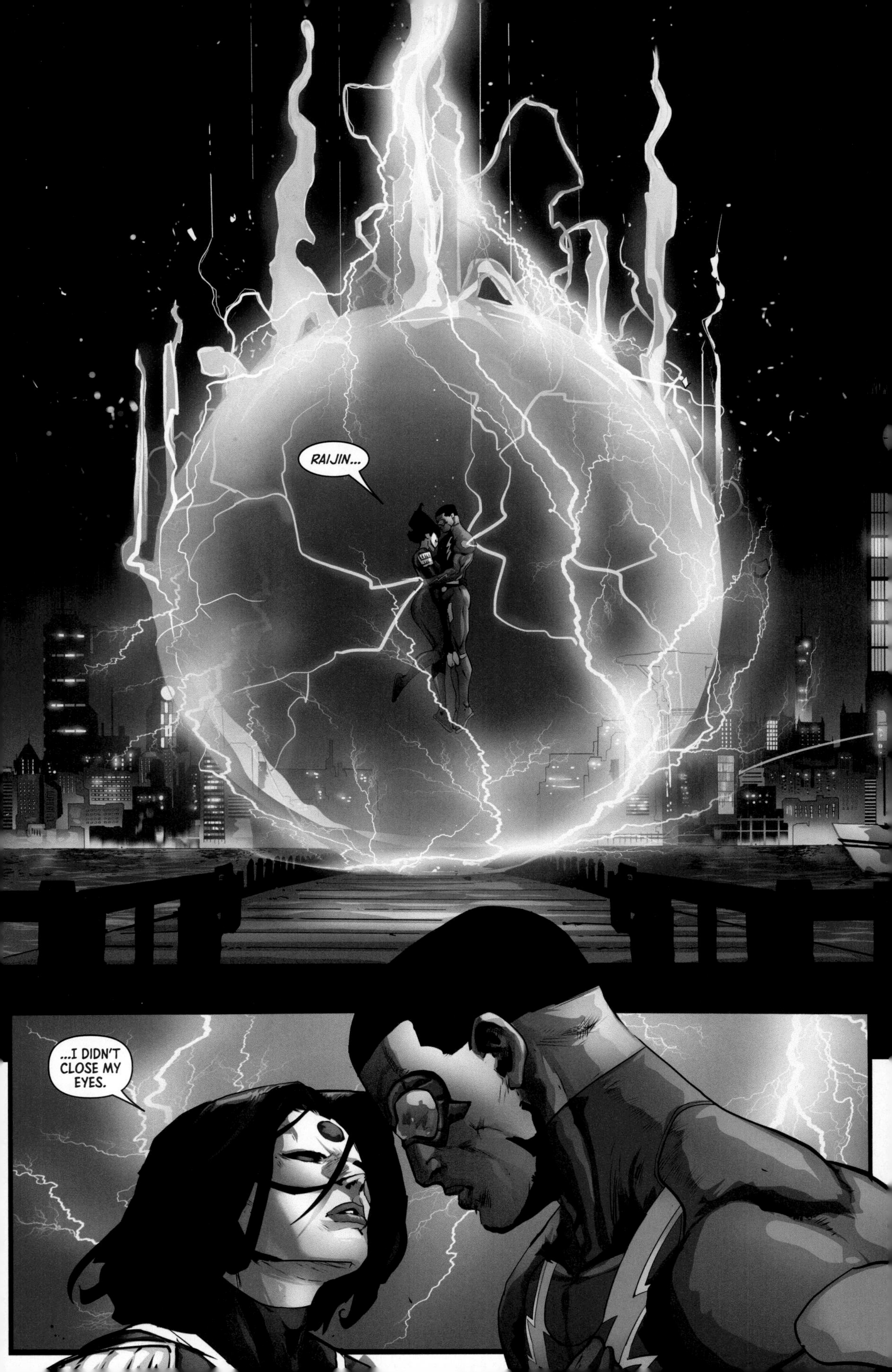
RAIJIN...
...I DIDN'T CLOSE MY EYES.

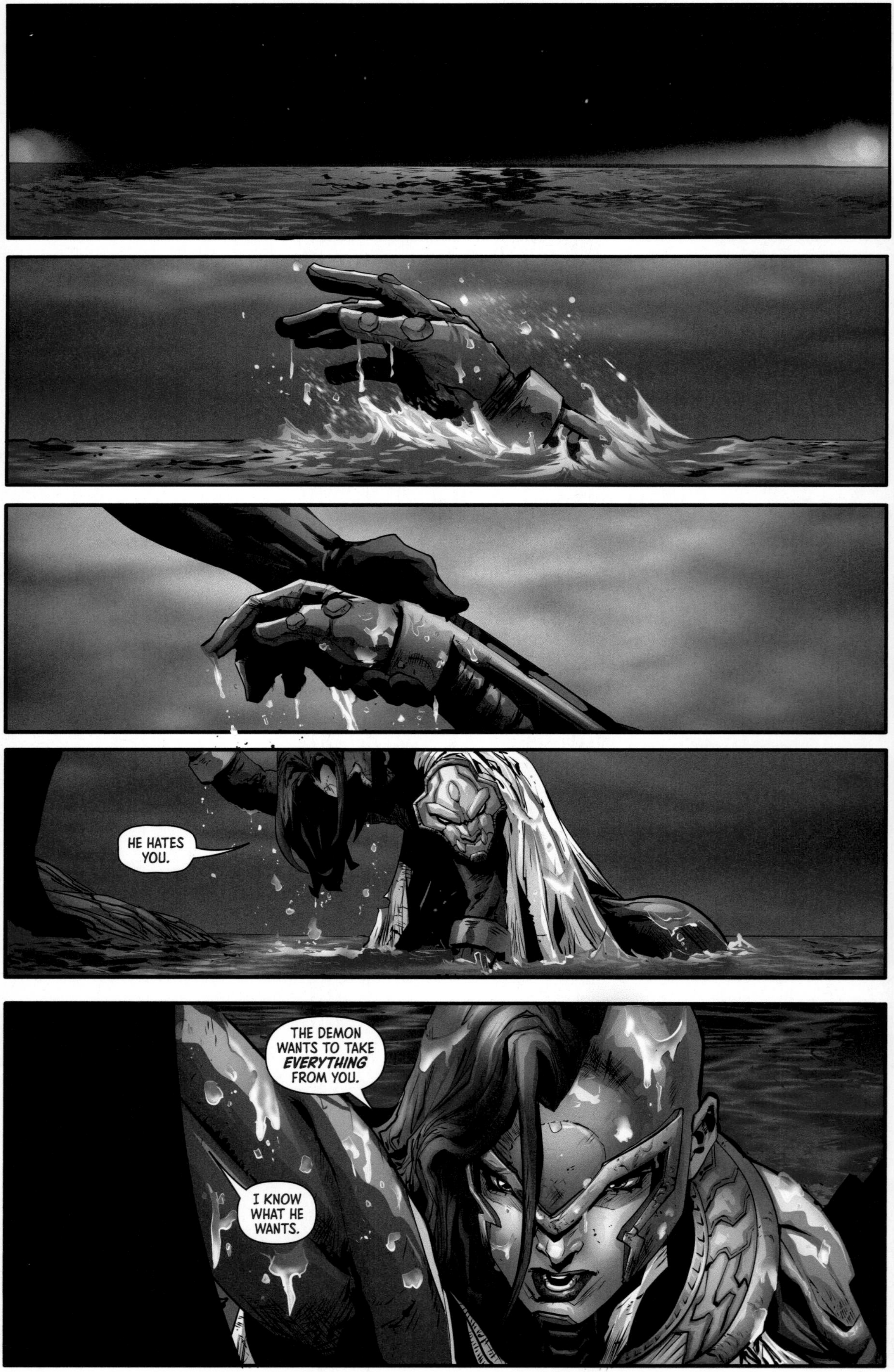
HE HATES YOU.
THE DEMON WANTS TO TAKE *EVERYTHING* FROM YOU.
I KNOW WHAT HE WANTS.

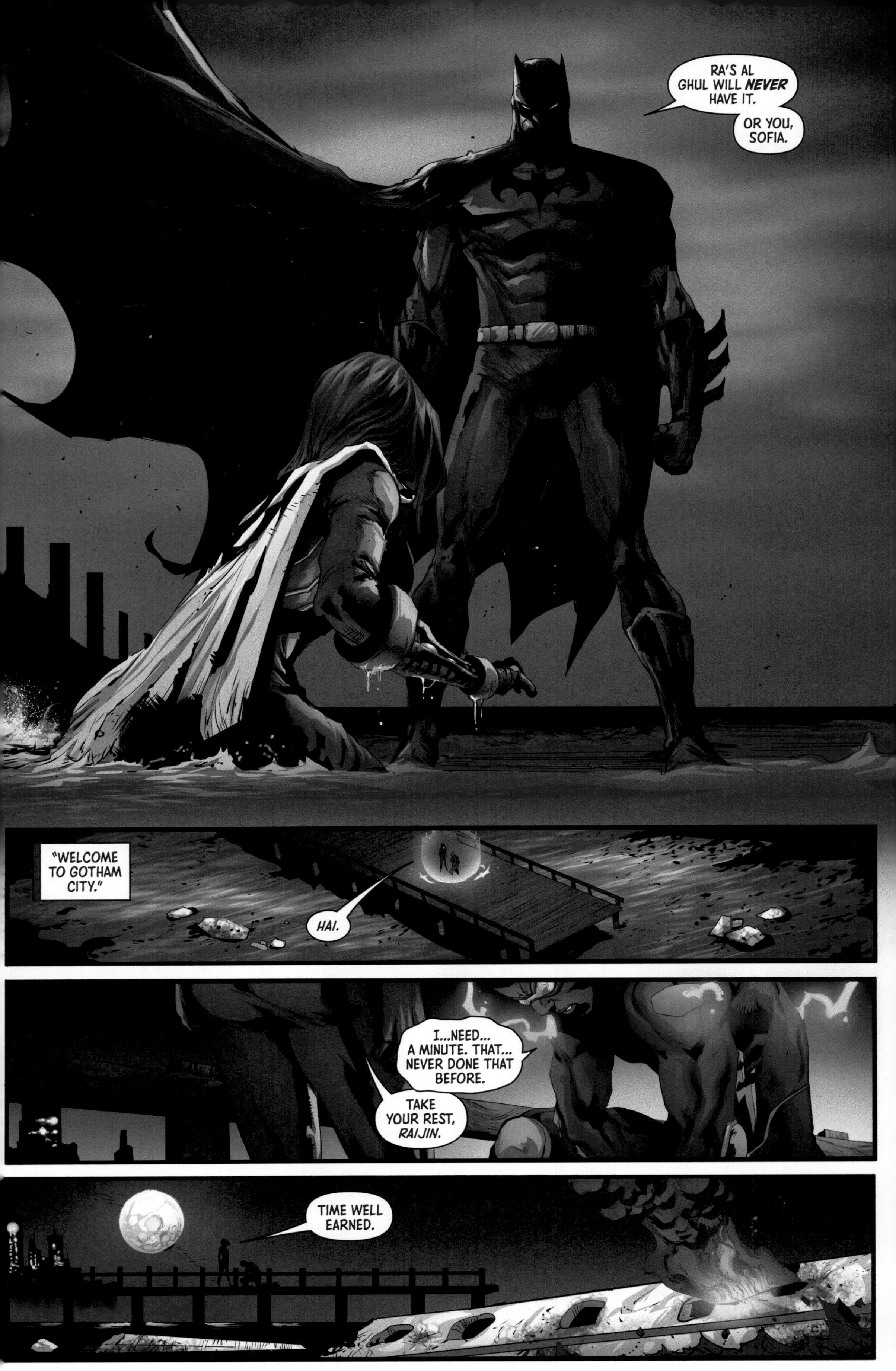
RA'S AL GHUL WILL **NEVER** HAVE IT.
OR YOU, SOFIA.
"WELCOME TO GOTHAM CITY."
HAI.
I...NEED... A MINUTE. THAT... NEVER DONE THAT BEFORE.
TAKE YOUR REST, *RAIJIN.*
TIME WELL EARNED.

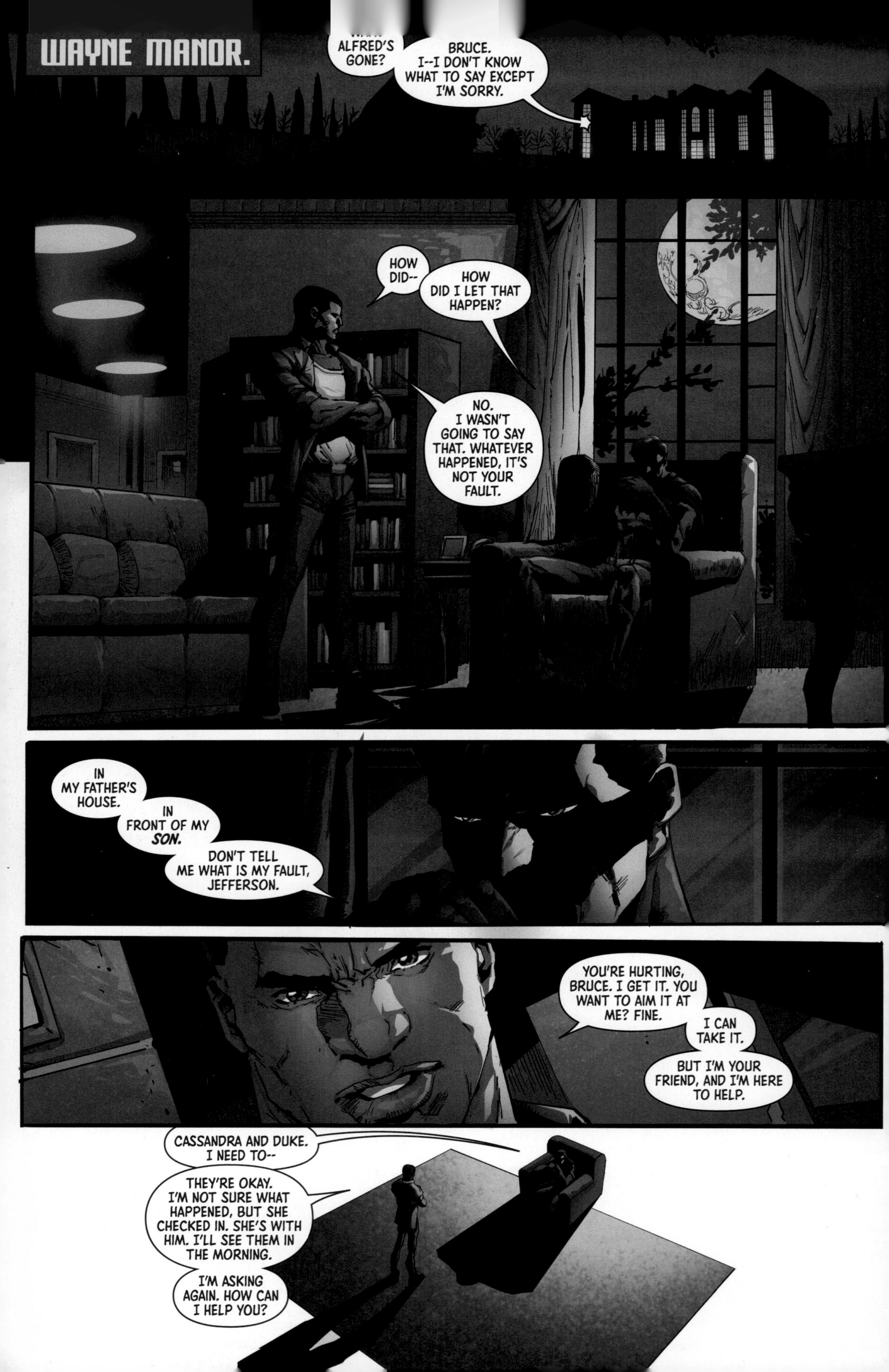
WAYNE MANOR.
ALFRED'S GONE?
BRUCE. I--I DON'T KNOW WHAT TO SAY EXCEPT I'M SORRY.
HOW DID--
HOW DID I LET THAT HAPPEN?
NO. I WASN'T GOING TO SAY THAT. WHATEVER HAPPENED, IT'S NOT YOUR FAULT.
IN MY FATHER'S HOUSE.
IN FRONT OF MY *SON.*
DON'T TELL ME WHAT IS MY FAULT, JEFFERSON.
YOU'RE HURTING, BRUCE. I GET IT. YOU WANT TO AIM IT AT ME? FINE.
I CAN TAKE IT.
BUT I'M YOUR FRIEND, AND I'M HERE TO HELP.
CASSANDRA AND DUKE. I NEED TO--
THEY'RE OKAY. I'M NOT SURE WHAT HAPPENED, BUT SHE CHECKED IN. SHE'S WITH HIM. I'LL SEE THEM IN THE MORNING.
I'M ASKING AGAIN. HOW CAN I HELP YOU?

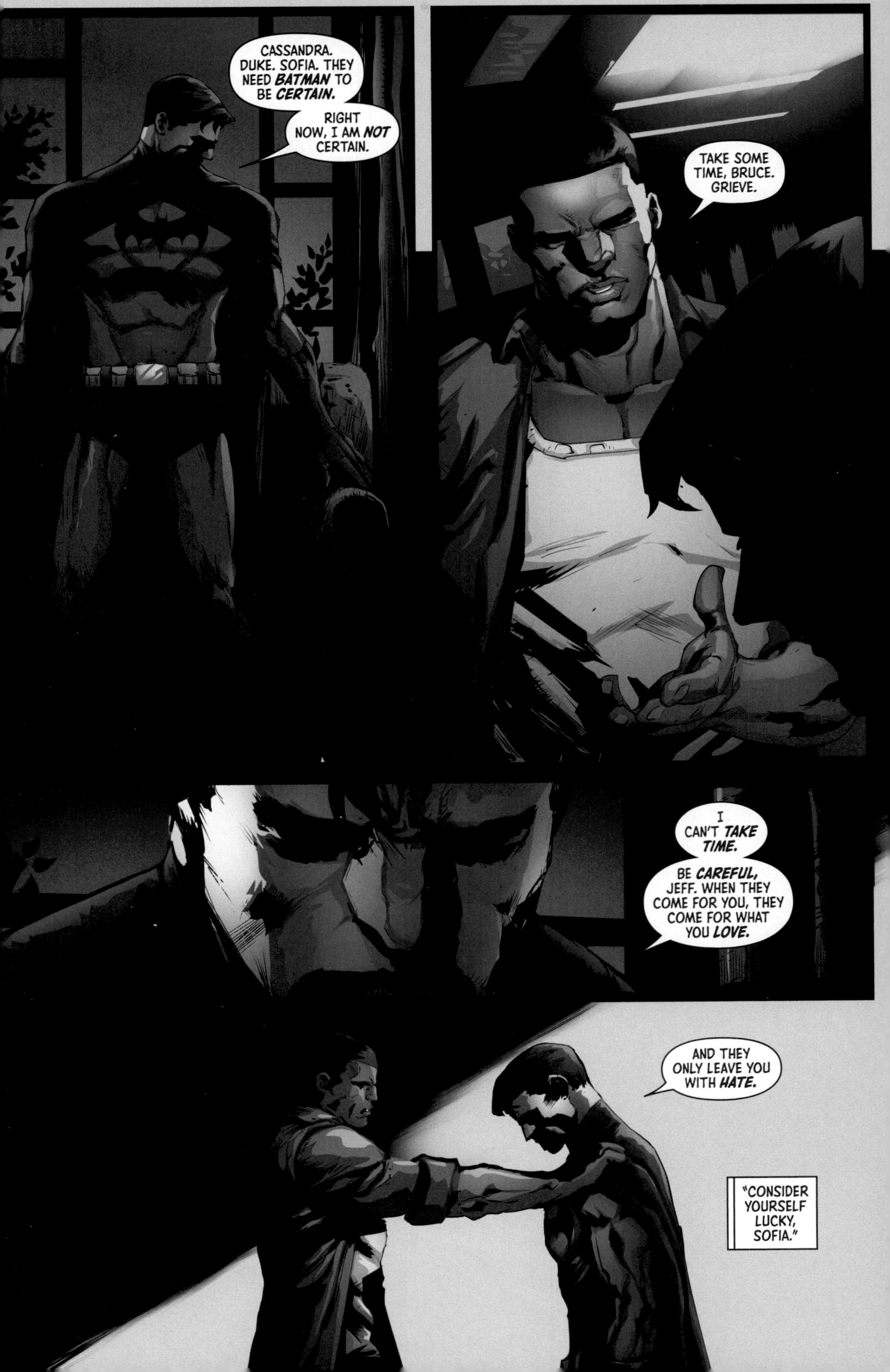
CASSANDRA. DUKE. SOFIA. THEY NEED **BATMAN** TO BE **CERTAIN.**
RIGHT NOW, I AM **NOT** CERTAIN.
TAKE SOME TIME, BRUCE. GRIEVE.
I CAN'T **TAKE TIME.**
BE **CAREFUL,** JEFF. WHEN THEY COME FOR YOU, THEY COME FOR WHAT YOU **LOVE.**
AND THEY ONLY LEAVE YOU WITH **HATE.**
"CONSIDER YOURSELF LUCKY, SOFIA."

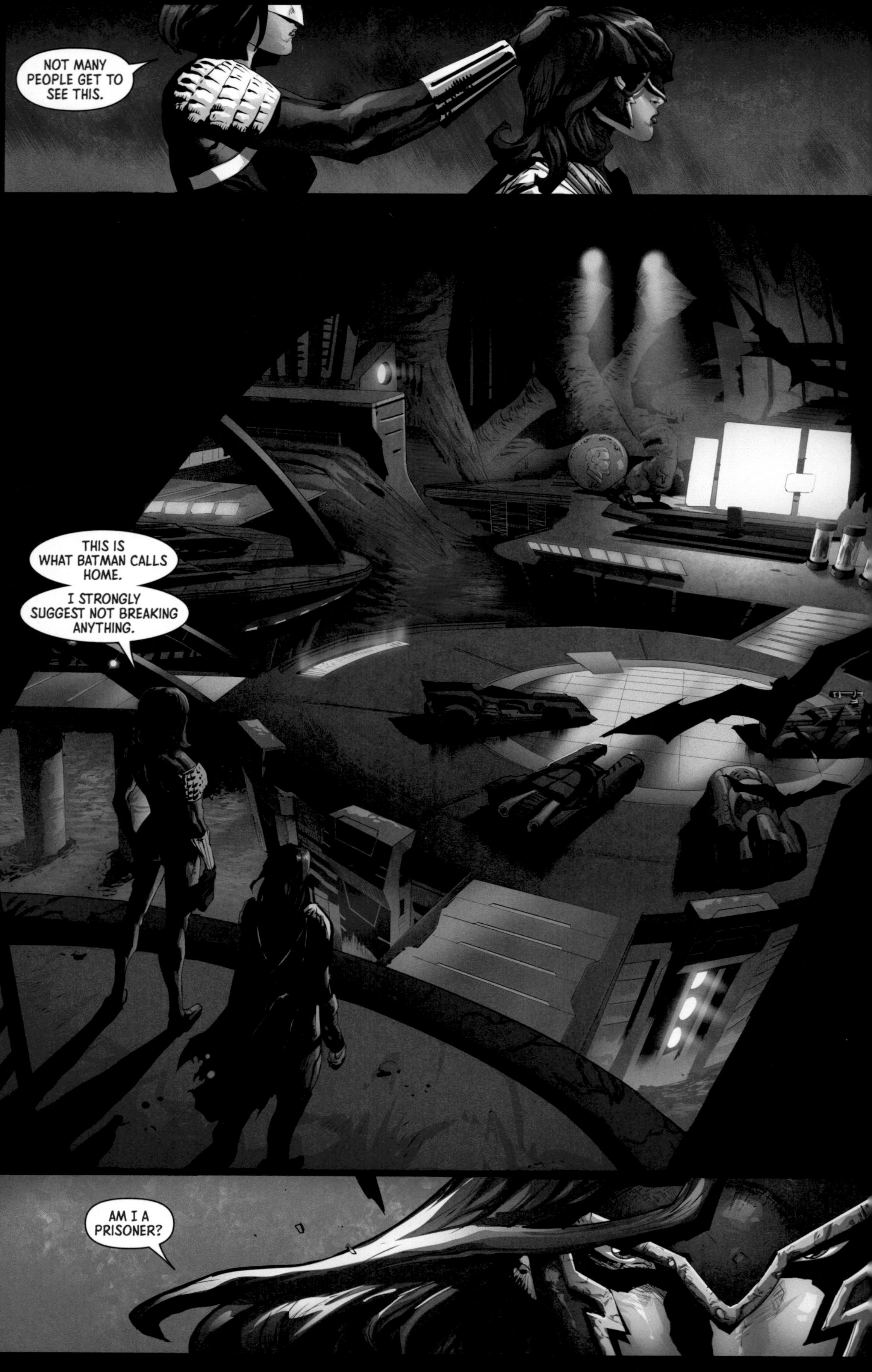
NOT MANY PEOPLE GET TO SEE THIS.
THIS IS WHAT BATMAN CALLS HOME.
I STRONGLY SUGGEST NOT BREAKING ANYTHING.
AM I A PRISONER?

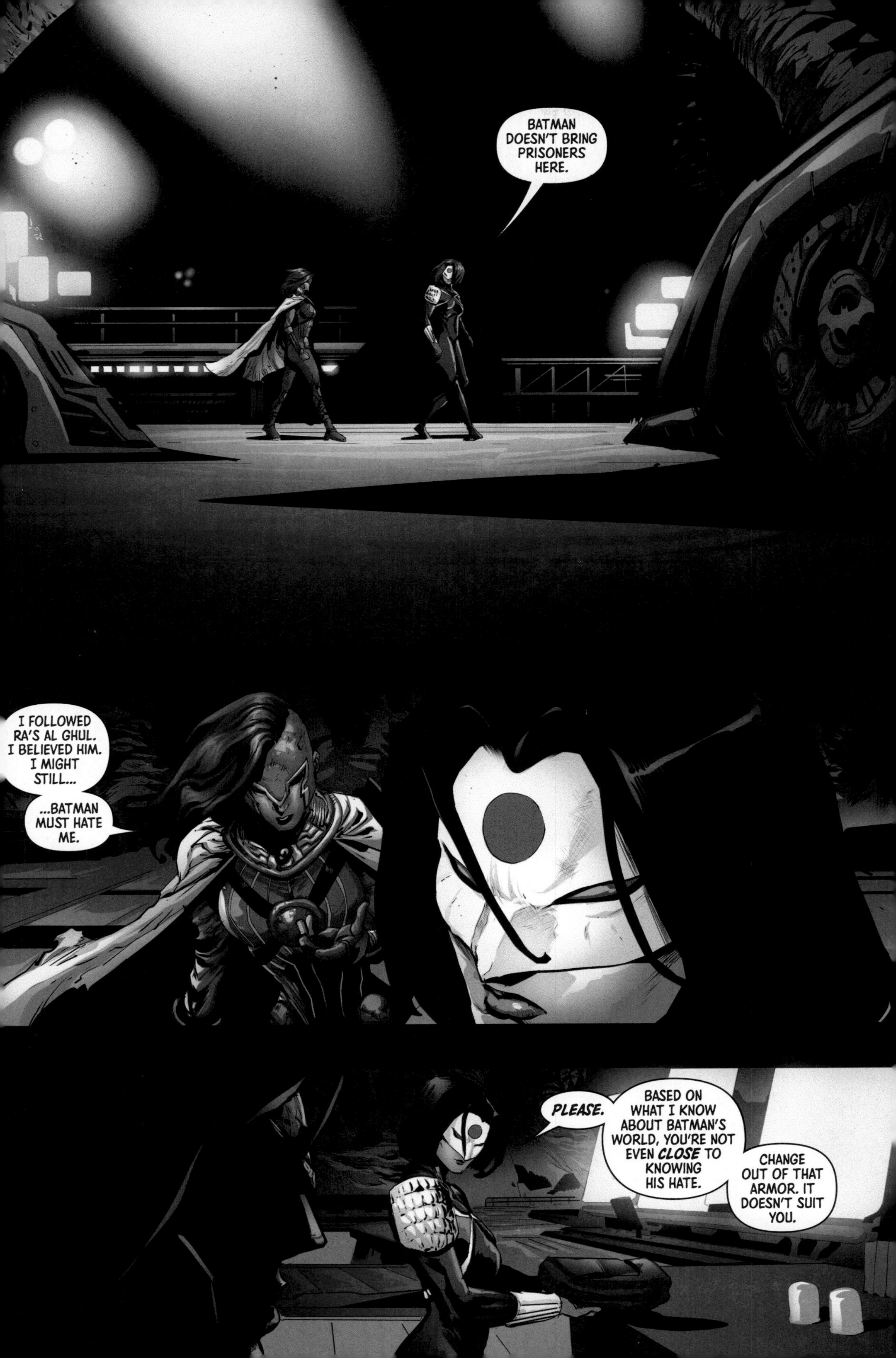
BATMAN DOESN'T BRING PRISONERS HERE.
I FOLLOWED RA'S AL GHUL. I BELIEVED HIM. I MIGHT STILL...
...BATMAN MUST HATE ME.
PLEASE.
BASED ON WHAT I KNOW ABOUT BATMAN'S WORLD, YOU'RE NOT EVEN CLOSE TO KNOWING HIS HATE.
CHANGE OUT OF THAT ARMOR. IT DOESN'T SUIT YOU.

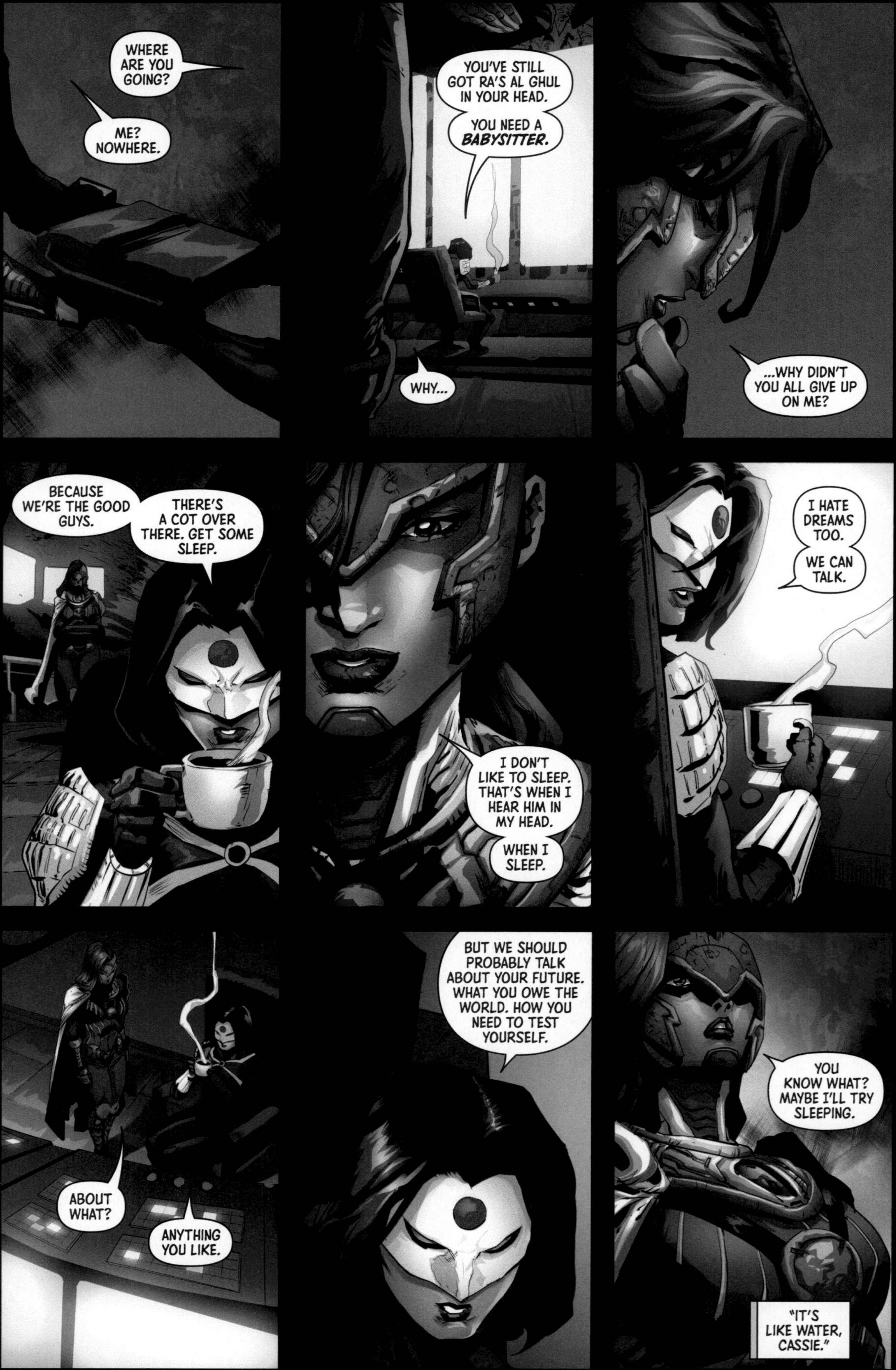
WHERE ARE YOU GOING?
ME? NOWHERE.
YOU'VE STILL GOT RA'S AL GHUL IN YOUR HEAD.
YOU NEED A *BABYSITTER.*
WHY...
...WHY DIDN'T YOU ALL GIVE UP ON ME?
BECAUSE WE'RE THE GOOD GUYS.
THERE'S A COT OVER THERE. GET SOME SLEEP.
I DON'T LIKE TO SLEEP. THAT'S WHEN I HEAR HIM IN MY HEAD.
WHEN I SLEEP.
I HATE DREAMS TOO.
WE CAN TALK.
ABOUT WHAT?
ANYTHING YOU LIKE.
BUT WE SHOULD PROBABLY TALK ABOUT YOUR FUTURE. WHAT YOU OWE THE WORLD. HOW YOU NEED TO TEST YOURSELF.
YOU KNOW WHAT? MAYBE I'LL TRY SLEEPING.
"IT'S LIKE WATER, CASSIE."

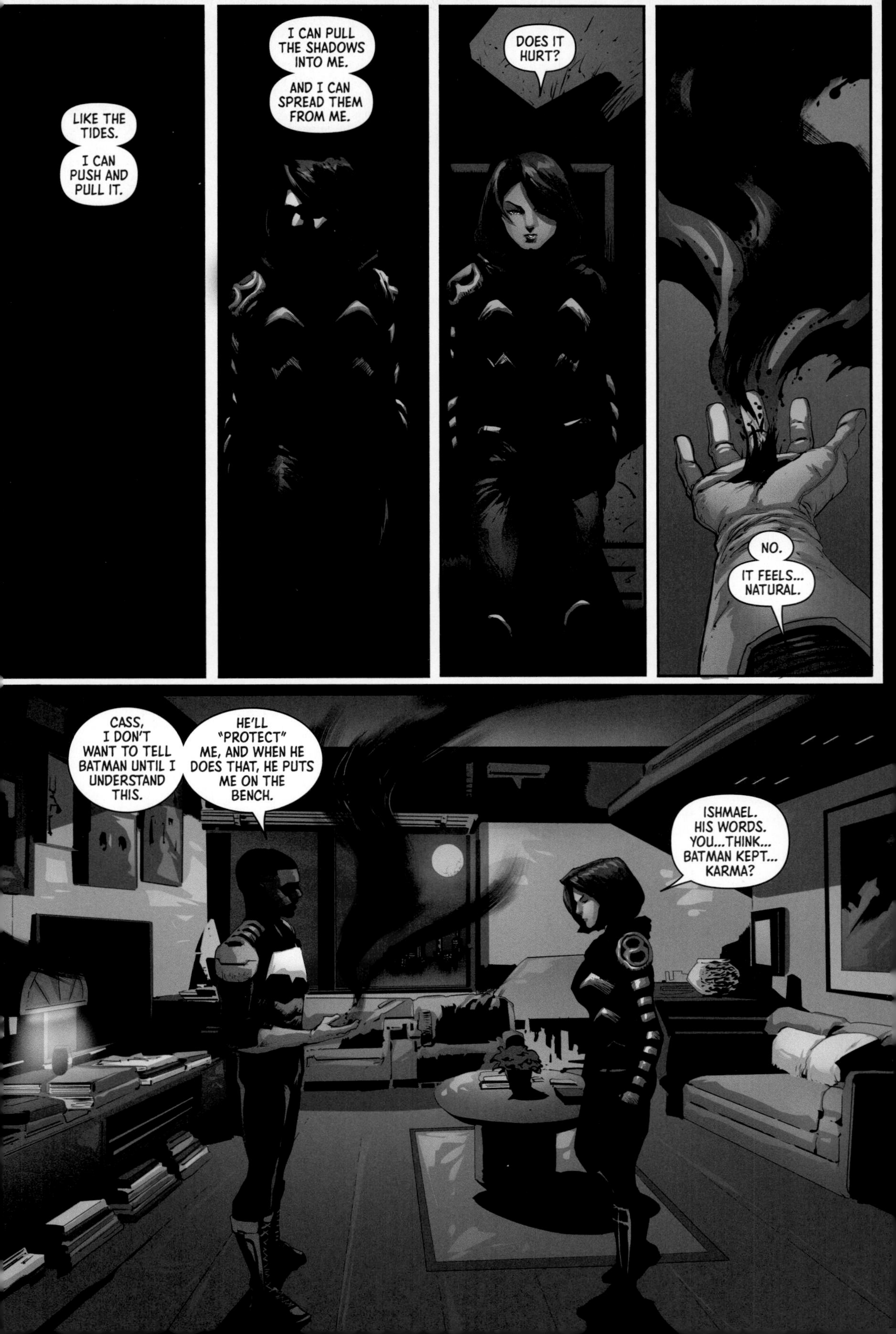
LIKE THE TIDES.
I CAN PUSH AND PULL IT.
I CAN PULL THE SHADOWS INTO ME.
AND I CAN SPREAD THEM FROM ME.
DOES IT HURT?
NO.
IT FEELS... NATURAL.
CASS, I DON'T WANT TO TELL BATMAN UNTIL I UNDERSTAND THIS.
HE'LL "PROTECT" ME, AND WHEN HE DOES THAT, HE PUTS ME ON THE BENCH.
ISHMAEL. HIS WORDS. YOU...THINK... BATMAN KEPT... KARMA?

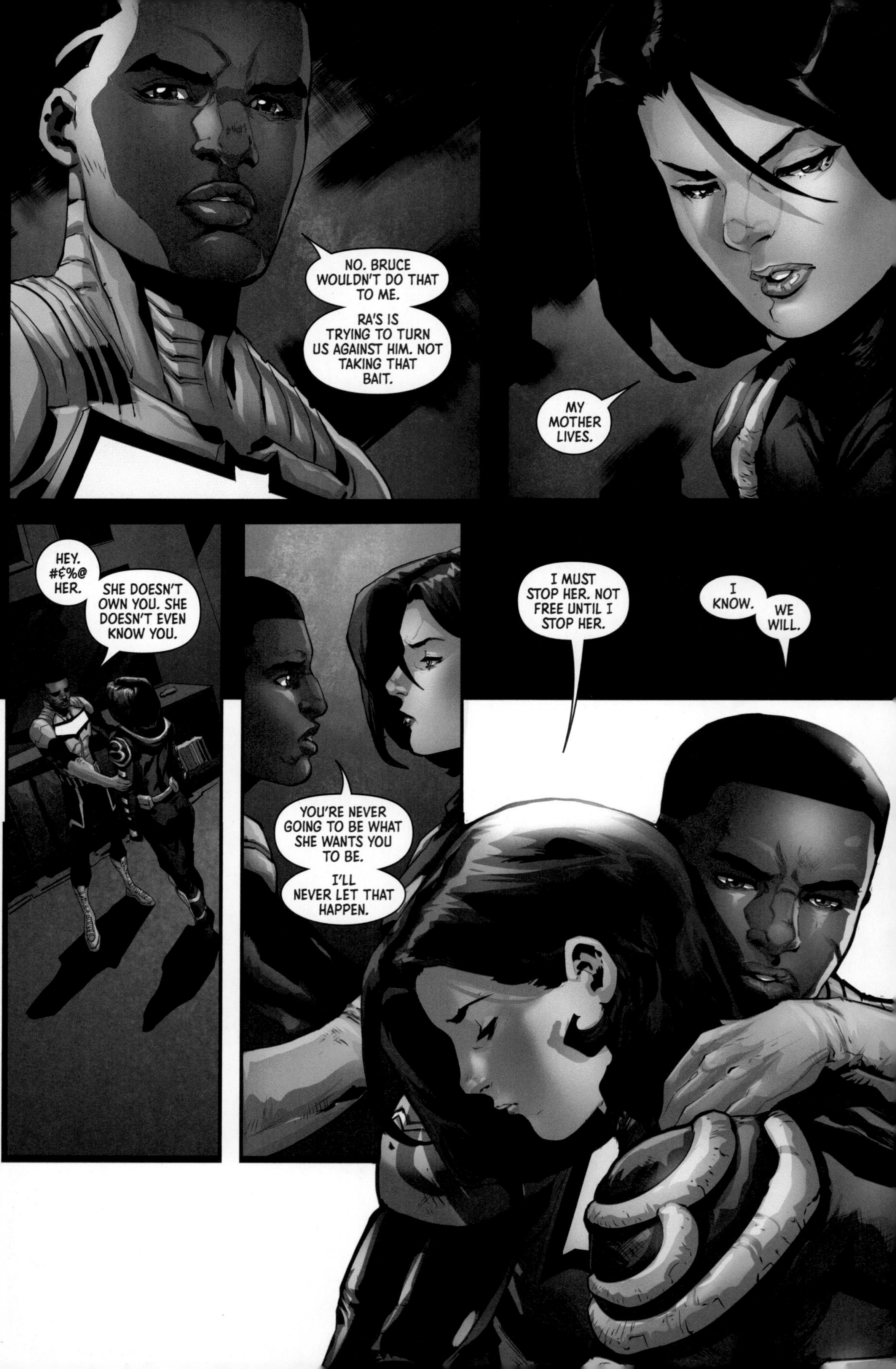
NO. BRUCE WOULDN'T DO THAT TO ME.
RA'S IS TRYING TO TURN US AGAINST HIM. NOT TAKING THAT BAIT.
MY MOTHER LIVES.
HEY. #¢%@ HER.
SHE DOESN'T OWN YOU. SHE DOESN'T EVEN KNOW YOU.
YOU'RE NEVER GOING TO BE WHAT SHE WANTS YOU TO BE.
I'LL NEVER LET THAT HAPPEN.
I MUST STOP HER. NOT FREE UNTIL I STOP HER.
I KNOW.
WE WILL.

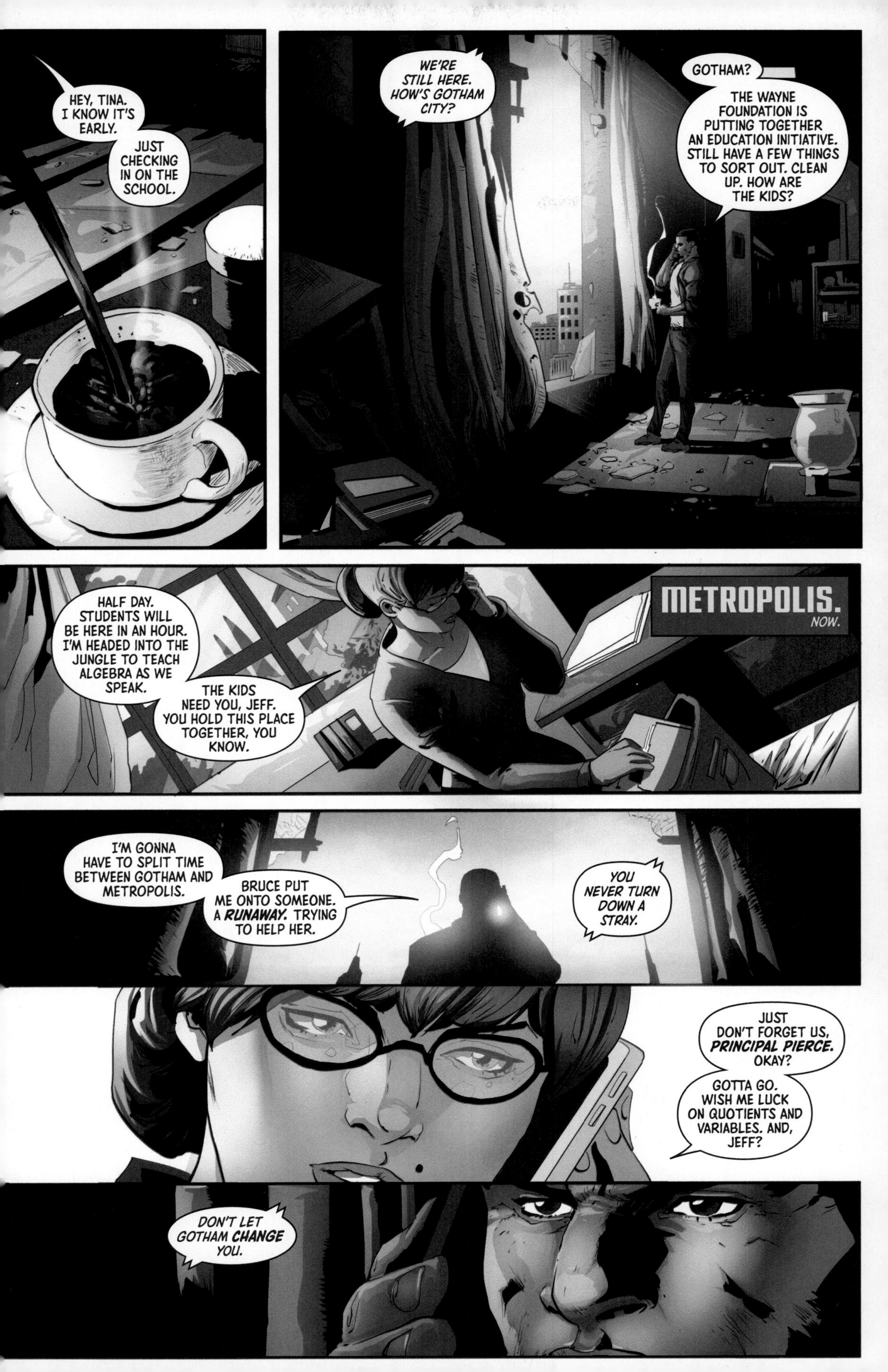
HEY, TINA. I KNOW IT'S EARLY.
JUST CHECKING IN ON THE SCHOOL.
WE'RE STILL HERE. HOW'S GOTHAM CITY?
GOTHAM?
THE WAYNE FOUNDATION IS PUTTING TOGETHER AN EDUCATION INITIATIVE. STILL HAVE A FEW THINGS TO SORT OUT. CLEAN UP. HOW ARE THE KIDS?
METROPOLIS. NOW.
HALF DAY. STUDENTS WILL BE HERE IN AN HOUR. I'M HEADED INTO THE JUNGLE TO TEACH ALGEBRA AS WE SPEAK.
THE KIDS NEED YOU, JEFF. YOU HOLD THIS PLACE TOGETHER, YOU KNOW.
I'M GONNA HAVE TO SPLIT TIME BETWEEN GOTHAM AND METROPOLIS.
BRUCE PUT ME ONTO SOMEONE. A RUNAWAY. TRYING TO HELP HER.
YOU NEVER TURN DOWN A STRAY.
JUST DON'T FORGET US, PRINCIPAL PIERCE. OKAY?
GOTTA GO. WISH ME LUCK ON QUOTIENTS AND VARIABLES. AND, JEFF?
DON'T LET GOTHAM CHANGE YOU.

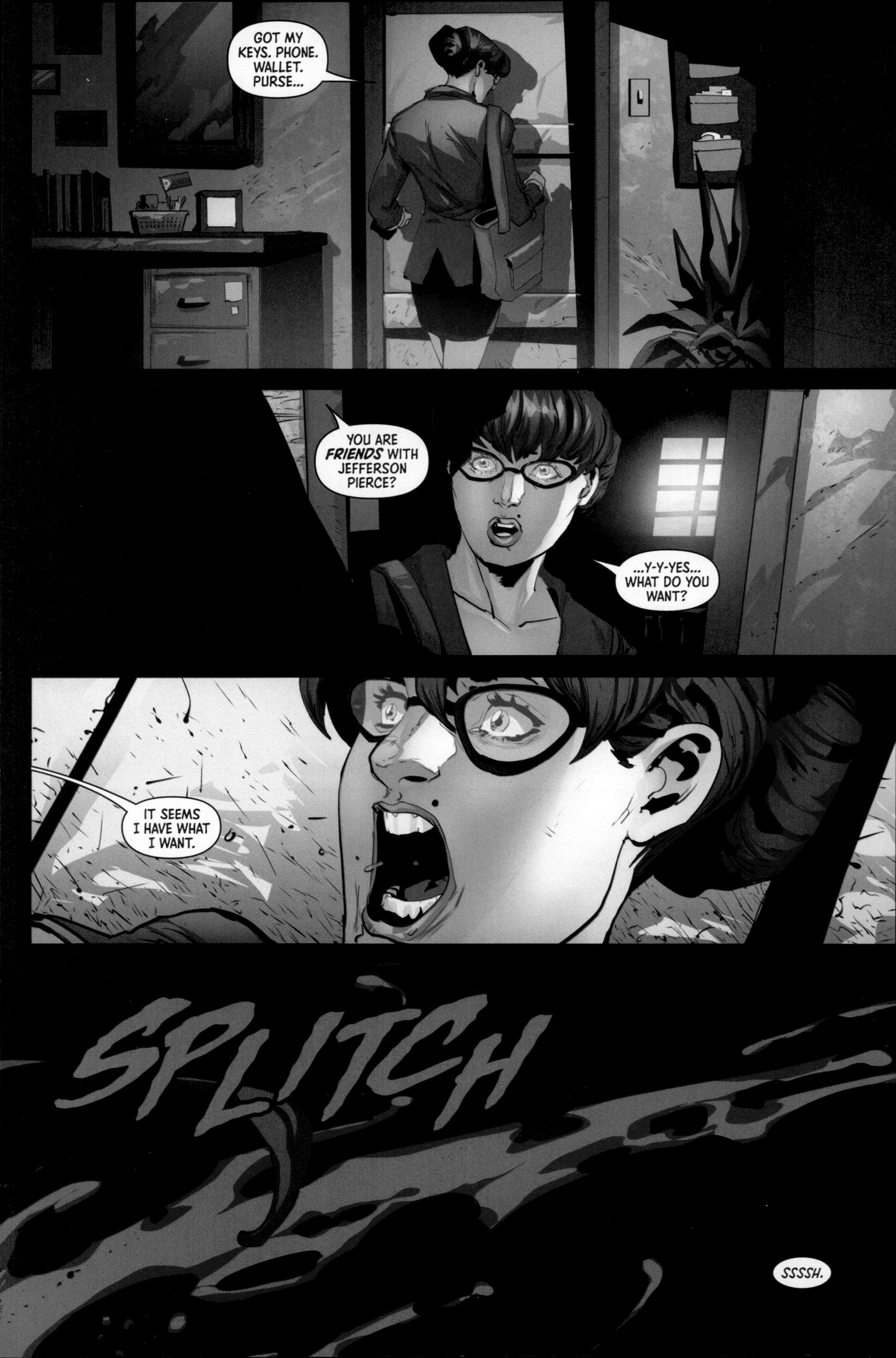
GOT MY KEYS. PHONE. WALLET. PURSE...
YOU ARE *FRIENDS* WITH JEFFERSON PIERCE?
...Y-Y-YES... WHAT DO YOU WANT?
IT SEEMS I HAVE WHAT I WANT.
SPLITCH
SSSSH.

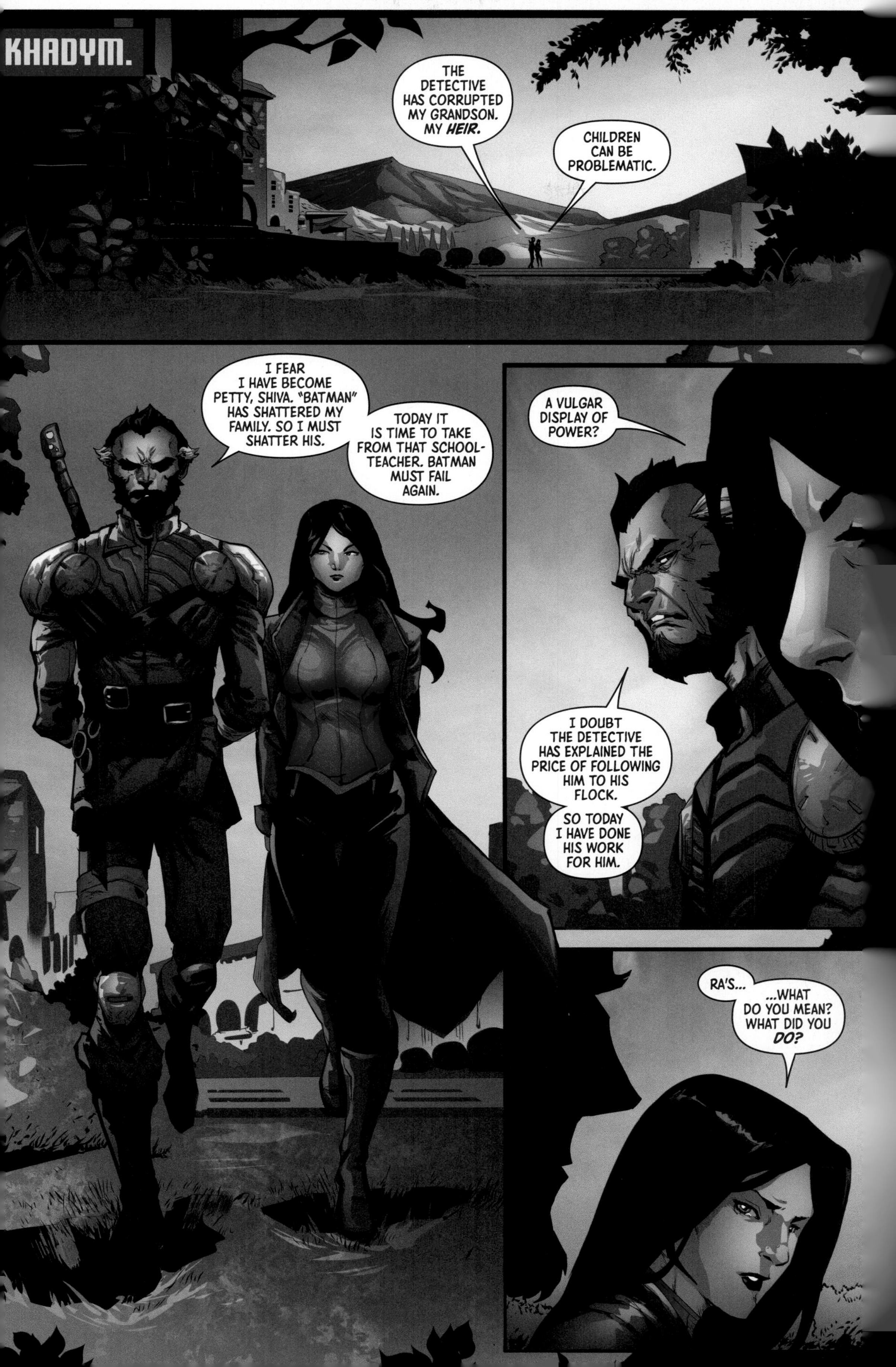
KHADYM.
THE DETECTIVE HAS CORRUPTED MY GRANDSON. MY HEIR.
CHILDREN CAN BE PROBLEMATIC.
I FEAR I HAVE BECOME PETTY, SHIVA. "BATMAN" HAS SHATTERED MY FAMILY. SO I MUST SHATTER HIS.
TODAY IT IS TIME TO TAKE FROM THAT SCHOOL-TEACHER. BATMAN MUST FAIL AGAIN.
A VULGAR DISPLAY OF POWER?
I DOUBT THE DETECTIVE HAS EXPLAINED THE PRICE OF FOLLOWING HIM TO HIS FLOCK.
SO TODAY I HAVE DONE HIS WORK FOR HIM.
RA'S...
...WHAT DO YOU MEAN? WHAT DID YOU DO?

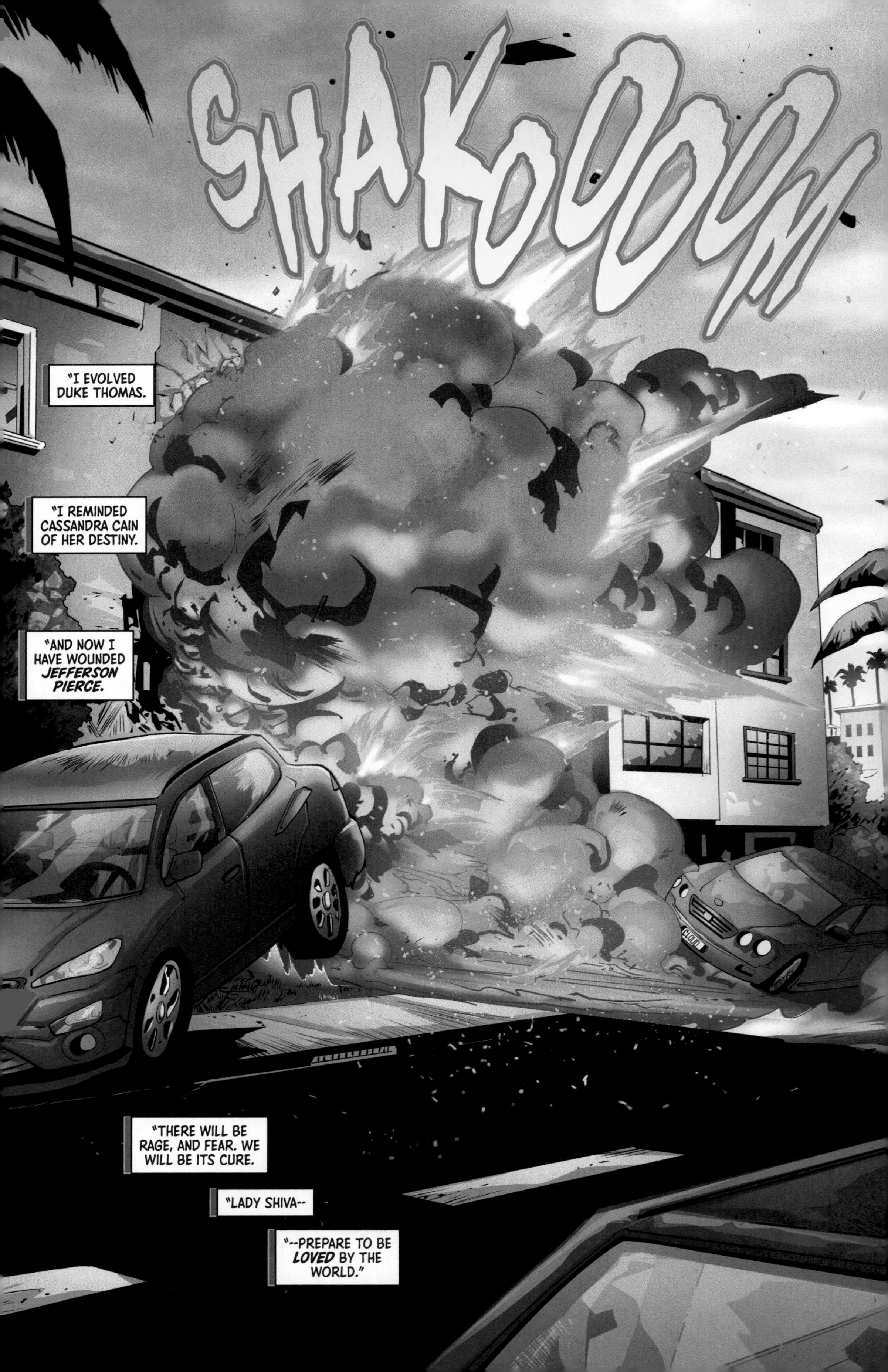
SHAKOOOM
"I EVOLVED DUKE THOMAS.
"I REMINDED CASSANDRA CAIN OF HER DESTINY.
"AND NOW I HAVE WOUNDED *JEFFERSON PIERCE.*
"THERE WILL BE RAGE, AND FEAR. WE WILL BE ITS CURE.
"LADY SHIVA--
"--PREPARE TO BE *LOVED* BY THE WORLD."

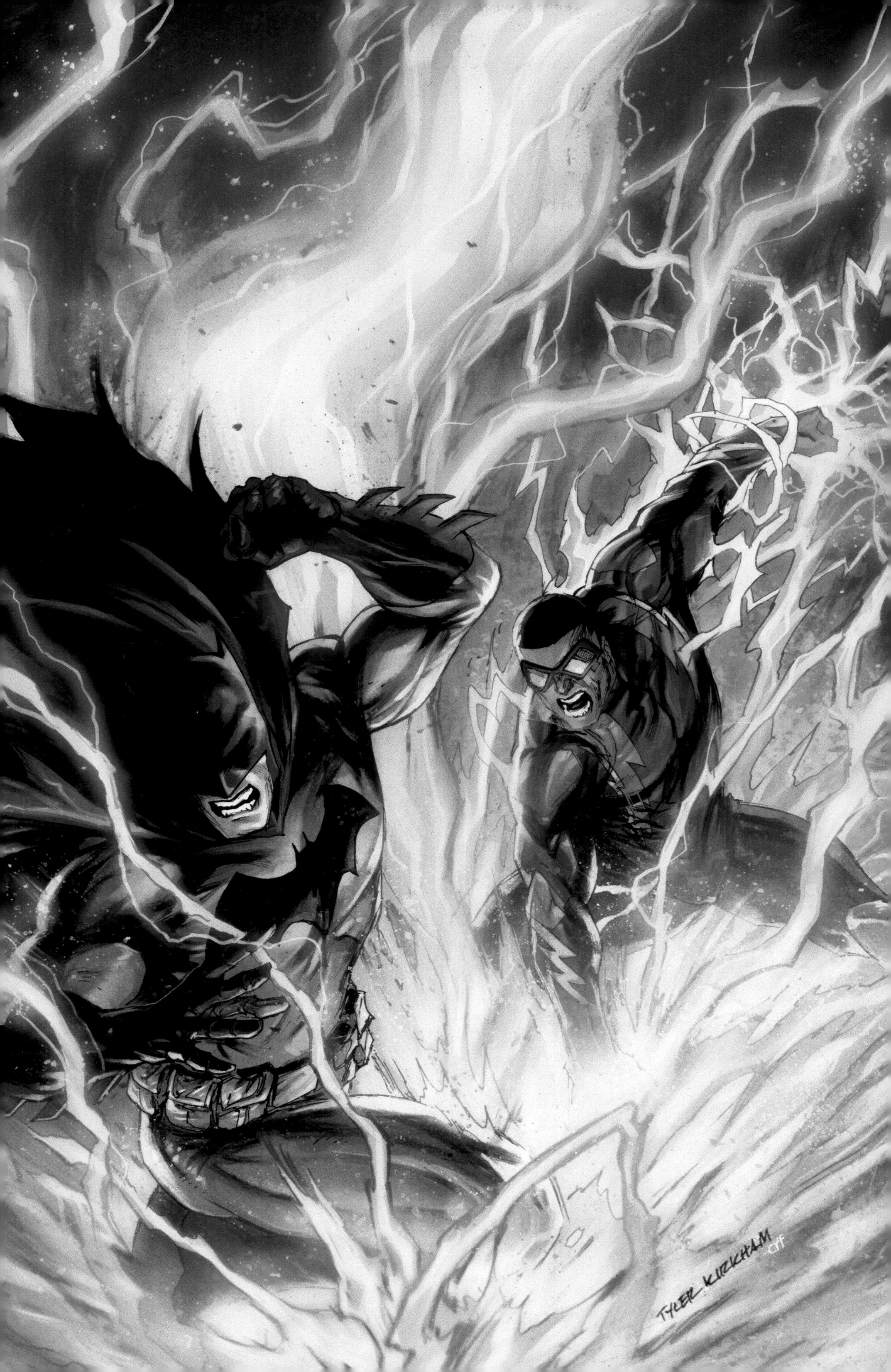
TYLER KIRKHAM

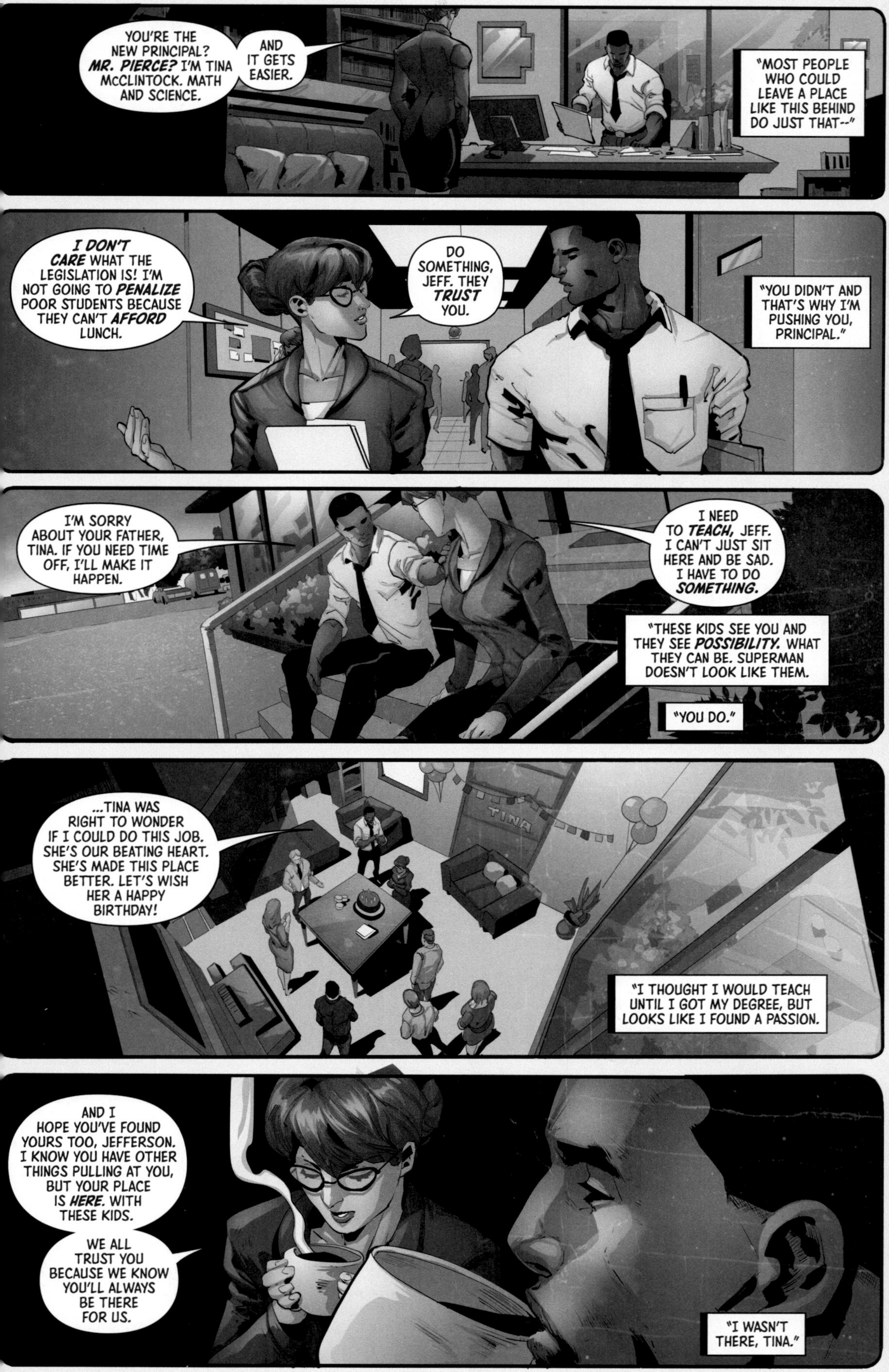

YOU'RE THE NEW PRINCIPAL? MR. PIERCE? I'M TINA McCLINTOCK. MATH AND SCIENCE.
AND IT GETS EASIER.
"MOST PEOPLE WHO COULD LEAVE A PLACE LIKE THIS BEHIND DO JUST THAT--"
I DON'T CARE WHAT THE LEGISLATION IS! I'M NOT GOING TO PENALIZE POOR STUDENTS BECAUSE THEY CAN'T AFFORD LUNCH.
DO SOMETHING, JEFF. THEY TRUST YOU.
"YOU DIDN'T AND THAT'S WHY I'M PUSHING YOU, PRINCIPAL."
I'M SORRY ABOUT YOUR FATHER, TINA. IF YOU NEED TIME OFF, I'LL MAKE IT HAPPEN.
I NEED TO TEACH, JEFF. I CAN'T JUST SIT HERE AND BE SAD. I HAVE TO DO SOMETHING.
"THESE KIDS SEE YOU AND THEY SEE POSSIBILITY. WHAT THEY CAN BE. SUPERMAN DOESN'T LOOK LIKE THEM.
"YOU DO."
TINA
...TINA WAS RIGHT TO WONDER IF I COULD DO THIS JOB. SHE'S OUR BEATING HEART. SHE'S MADE THIS PLACE BETTER. LET'S WISH HER A HAPPY BIRTHDAY!
"I THOUGHT I WOULD TEACH UNTIL I GOT MY DEGREE, BUT LOOKS LIKE I FOUND A PASSION.
AND I HOPE YOU'VE FOUND YOURS TOO, JEFFERSON. I KNOW YOU HAVE OTHER THINGS PULLING AT YOU, BUT YOUR PLACE IS HERE. WITH THESE KIDS.
WE ALL TRUST YOU BECAUSE WE KNOW YOU'LL ALWAYS BE THERE FOR US.
"I WASN'T THERE, TINA."

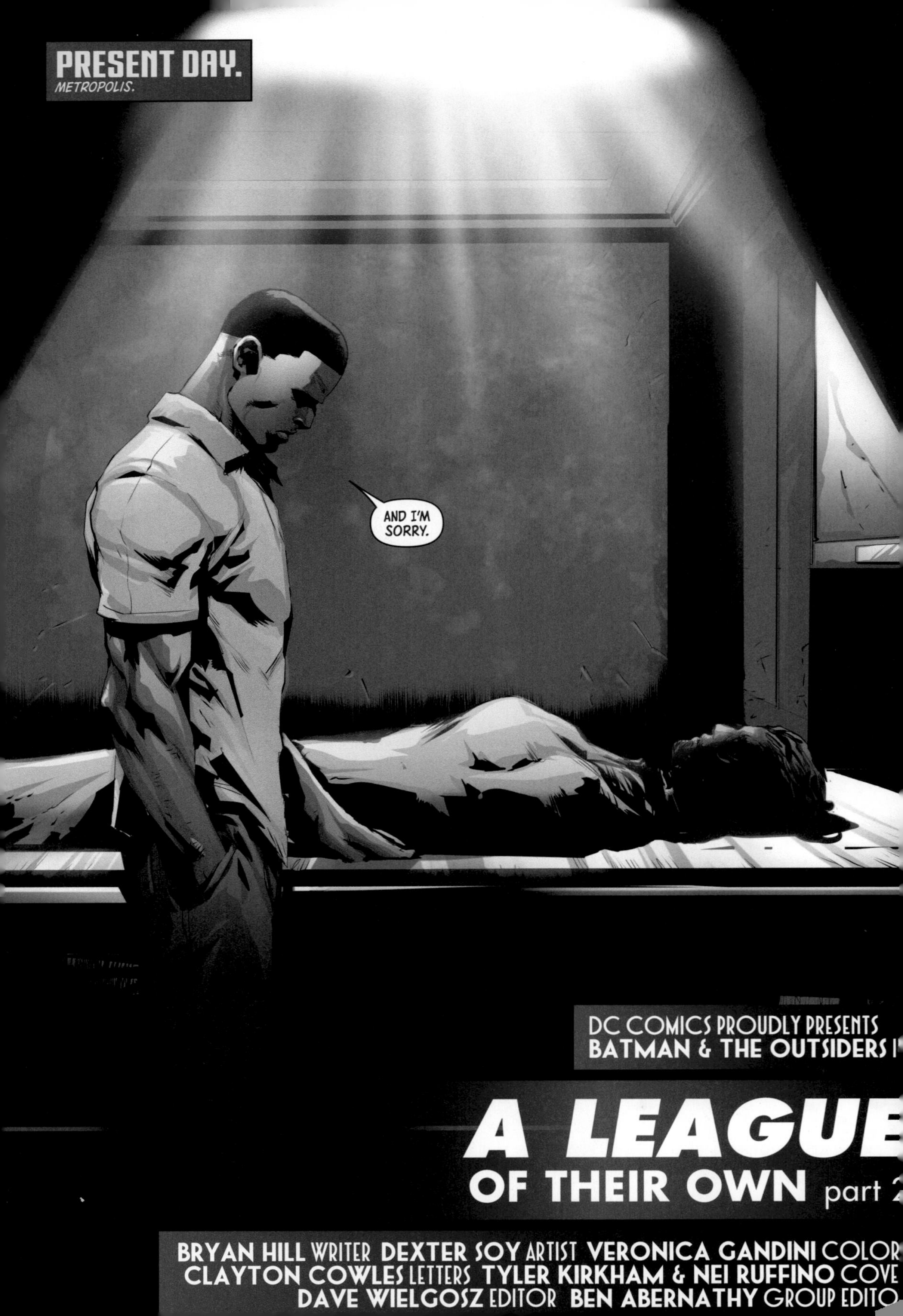
PRESENT DAY.
METROPOLIS.
AND I'M SORRY.
DC COMICS PROUDLY PRESENTS
BATMAN & THE OUTSIDERS
A LEAGUE
OF THEIR OWN part 2
BRYAN HILL WRITER DEXTER SOY ARTIST VERONICA GANDINI COLOR
CLAYTON COWLES LETTERS TYLER KIRKHAM & NEI RUFFINO COVE
DAVE WIELGOSZ EDITOR BEN ABERNATHY GROUP EDITO

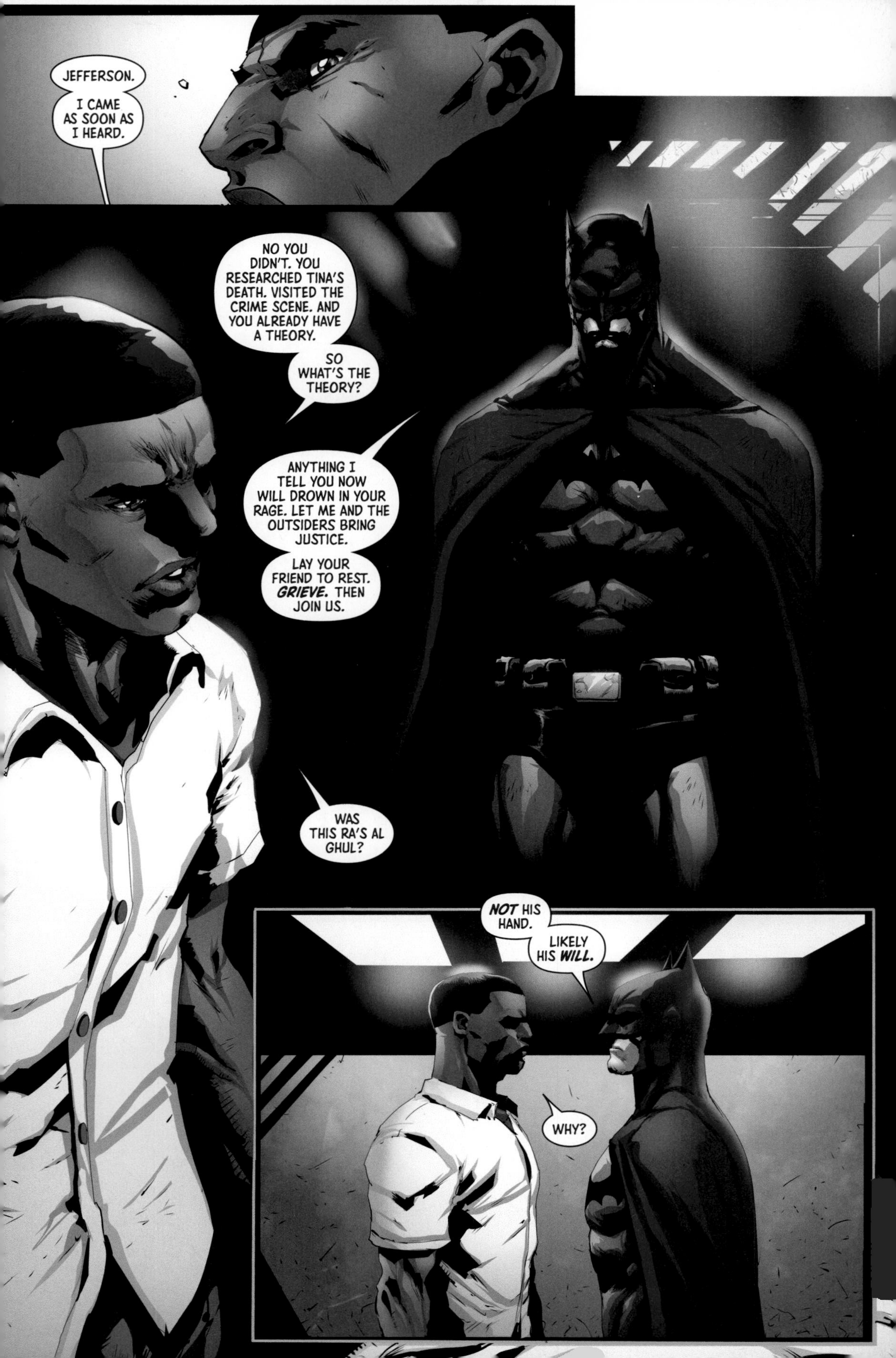
JEFFERSON.
I CAME AS SOON AS I HEARD.
NO YOU DIDN'T. YOU RESEARCHED TINA'S DEATH. VISITED THE CRIME SCENE. AND YOU ALREADY HAVE A THEORY.
SO WHAT'S THE THEORY?
ANYTHING I TELL YOU NOW WILL DROWN IN YOUR RAGE. LET ME AND THE OUTSIDERS BRING JUSTICE.
LAY YOUR FRIEND TO REST. GRIEVE. THEN JOIN US.
WAS THIS RA'S AL GHUL?
NOT HIS HAND.
LIKELY HIS WILL.
WHY?

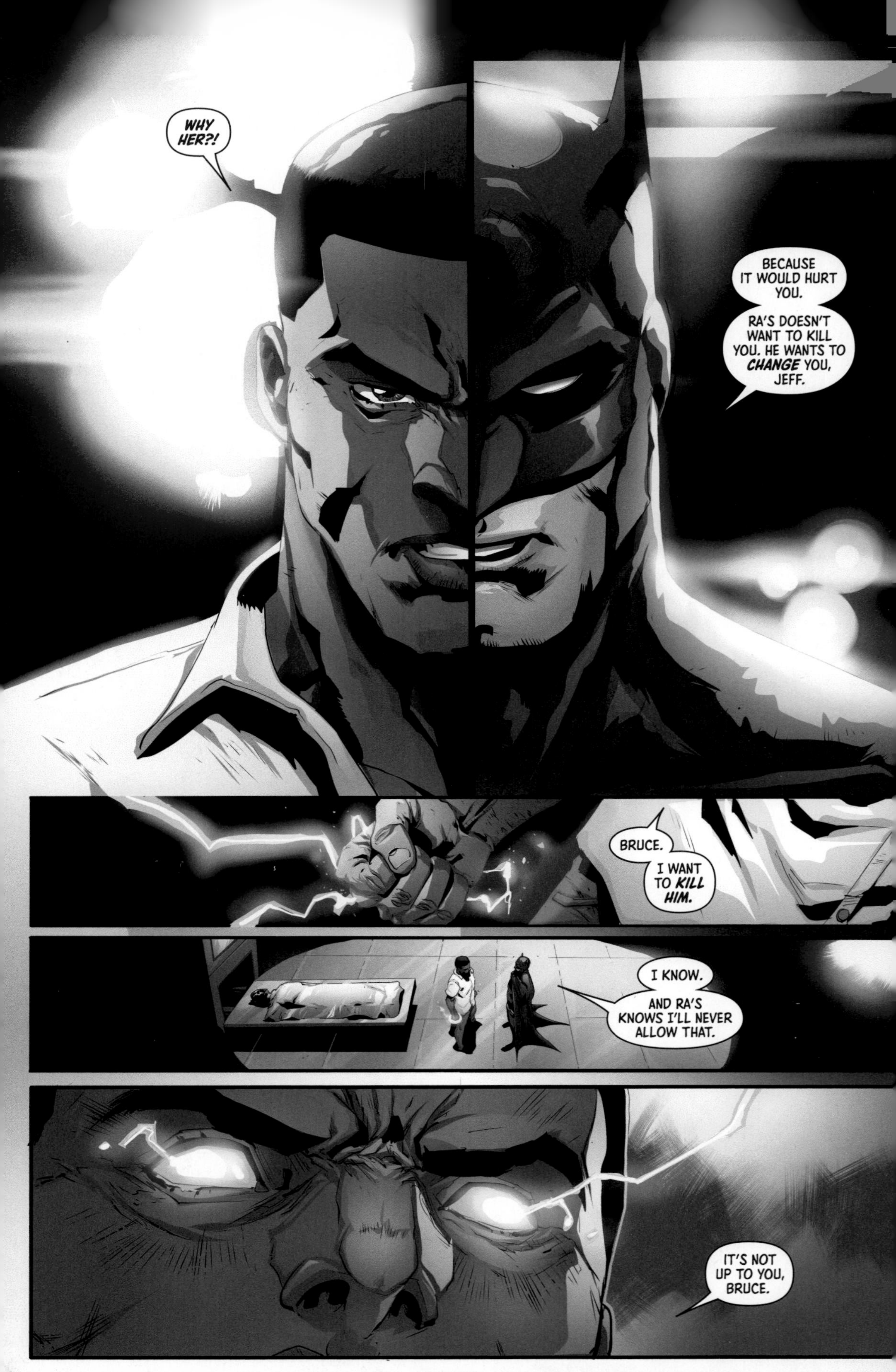
WHY HER?!
BECAUSE IT WOULD HURT YOU.
RA'S DOESN'T WANT TO KILL YOU. HE WANTS TO *CHANGE* YOU, JEFF.
BRUCE.
I WANT TO *KILL HIM.*
I KNOW.
AND RA'S KNOWS I'LL NEVER ALLOW THAT.
IT'S NOT UP TO YOU, BRUCE.

WHEN WE FIRST MET. AFTER KARMA.* DO YOU REMEMBER WHAT YOU TOLD ME ABOUT MY PARENTS?

I'M GOING TO TELL YOU THE SAME THING NOW.

*SEE DETECTIVE COMICS: ON THE OUTSIDE. -- DAVE

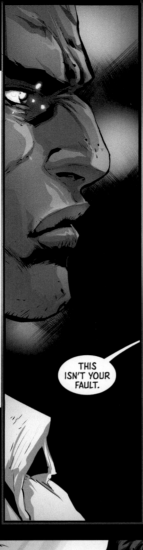

THIS ISN'T YOUR FAULT.

CONSIDER KATANA IN CHARGE OF WHATEVER TEAM YOU WANT TO HAVE.

I'M NOT USED TO THIS, BRUCE. NO ONE SHOULD BE USED TO THIS.

THE PROBLEM ISN'T THAT I'M ANGRY.

THE PROBLEM IS YOU AREN'T.

NO.

THE PROBLEM IS ANGER NEVER BRINGS THEM BACK.

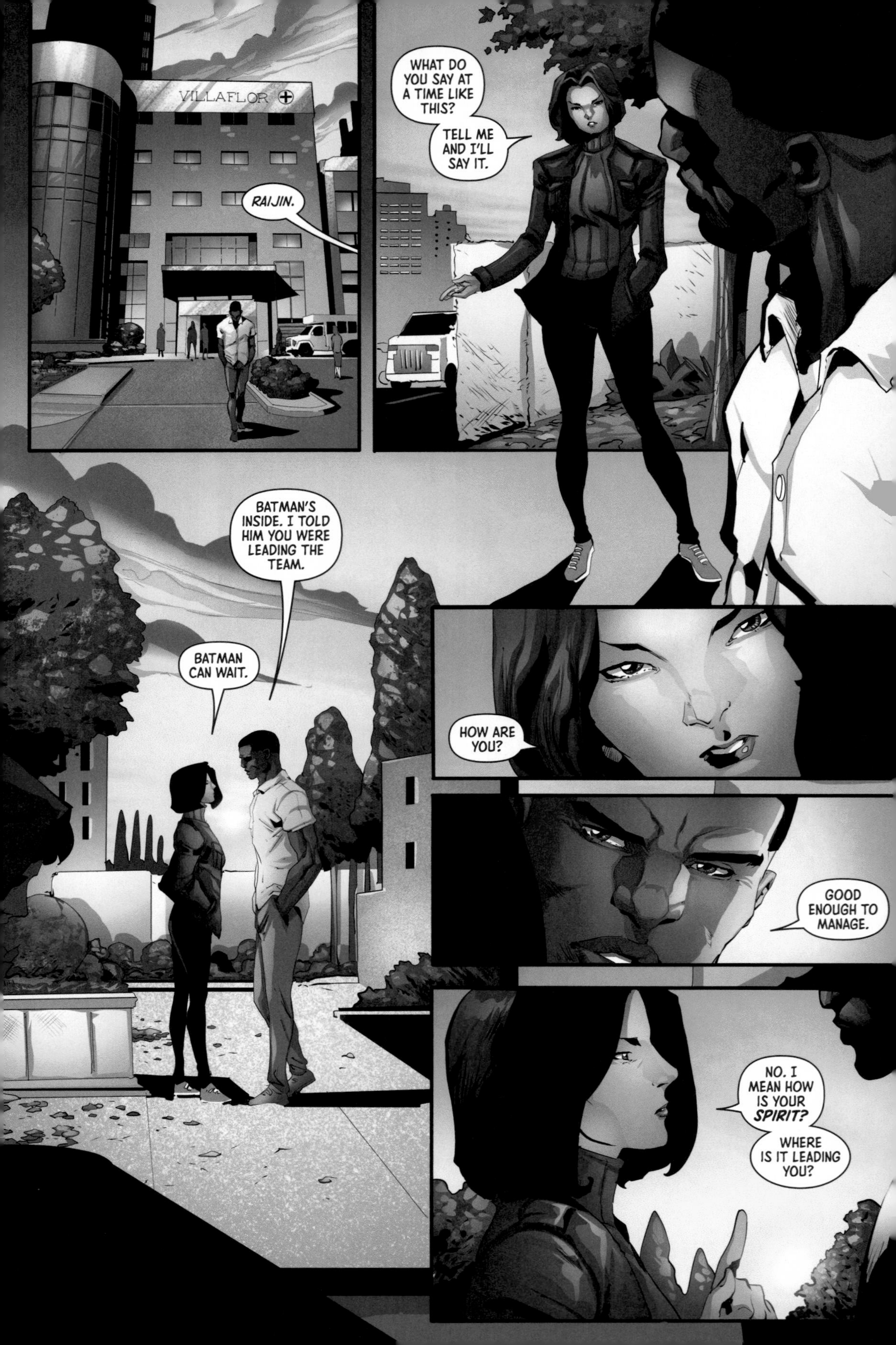
VILLAFLOR
RAIJIN.
WHAT DO YOU SAY AT A TIME LIKE THIS?
TELL ME AND I'LL SAY IT.
BATMAN'S INSIDE. I TOLD HIM YOU WERE LEADING THE TEAM.
BATMAN CAN WAIT.
HOW ARE YOU?
GOOD ENOUGH TO MANAGE.
NO. I MEAN HOW IS YOUR ***SPIRIT?***
WHERE IS IT LEADING YOU?

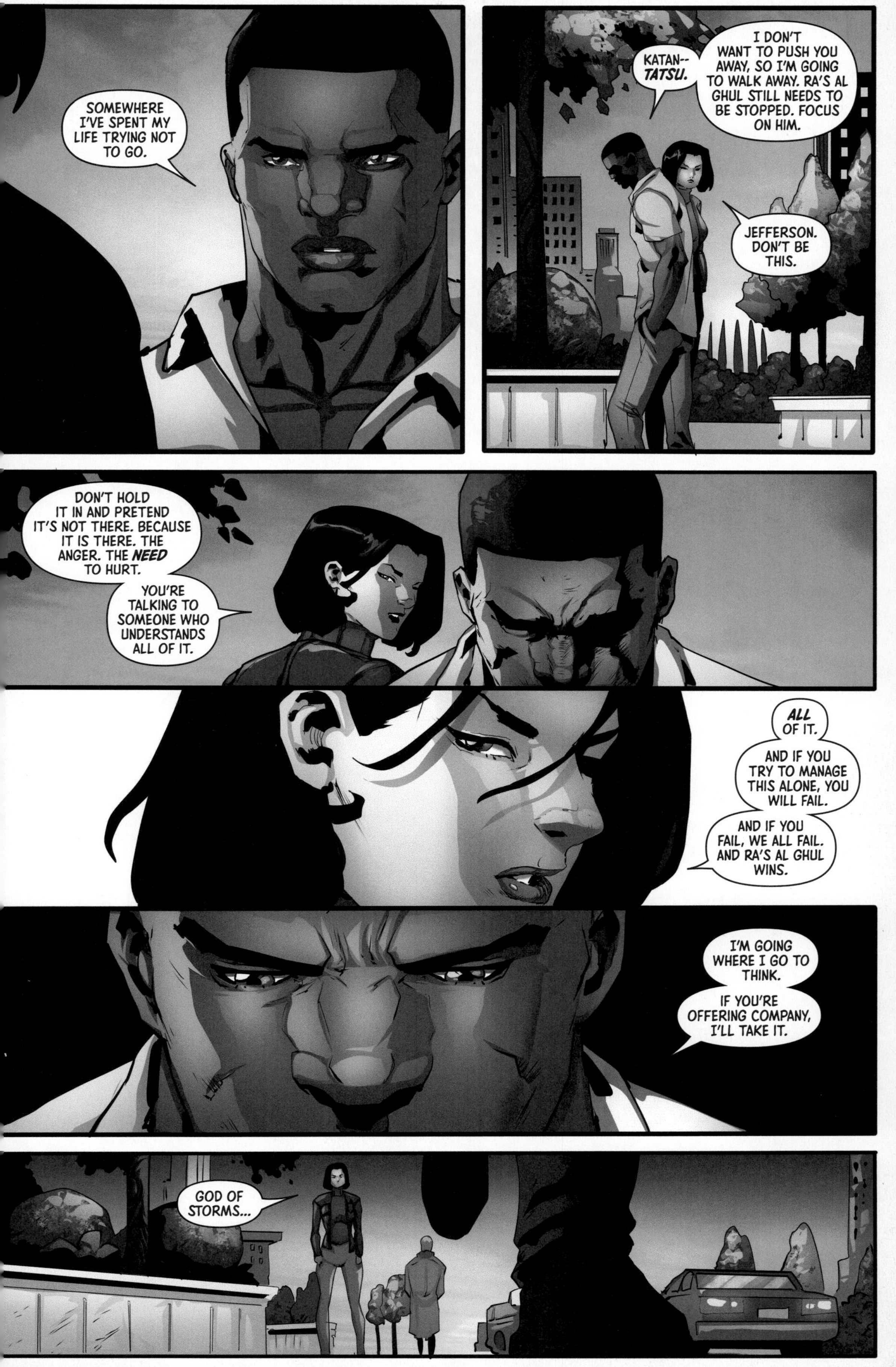
SOMEWHERE I'VE SPENT MY LIFE TRYING NOT TO GO.
KATAN-- *TATSU.*
I DON'T WANT TO PUSH YOU AWAY, SO I'M GOING TO WALK AWAY. RA'S AL GHUL STILL NEEDS TO BE STOPPED. FOCUS ON HIM.
JEFFERSON. DON'T BE THIS.
DON'T HOLD IT IN AND PRETEND IT'S NOT THERE. BECAUSE IT IS THERE. THE ANGER. THE *NEED* TO HURT.
YOU'RE TALKING TO SOMEONE WHO UNDERSTANDS ALL OF IT.
ALL OF IT.
AND IF YOU TRY TO MANAGE THIS ALONE, YOU WILL FAIL.
AND IF YOU FAIL, WE ALL FAIL. AND RA'S AL GHUL WINS.
I'M GOING WHERE I GO TO THINK.
IF YOU'RE OFFERING COMPANY, I'LL TAKE IT.
GOD OF STORMS...

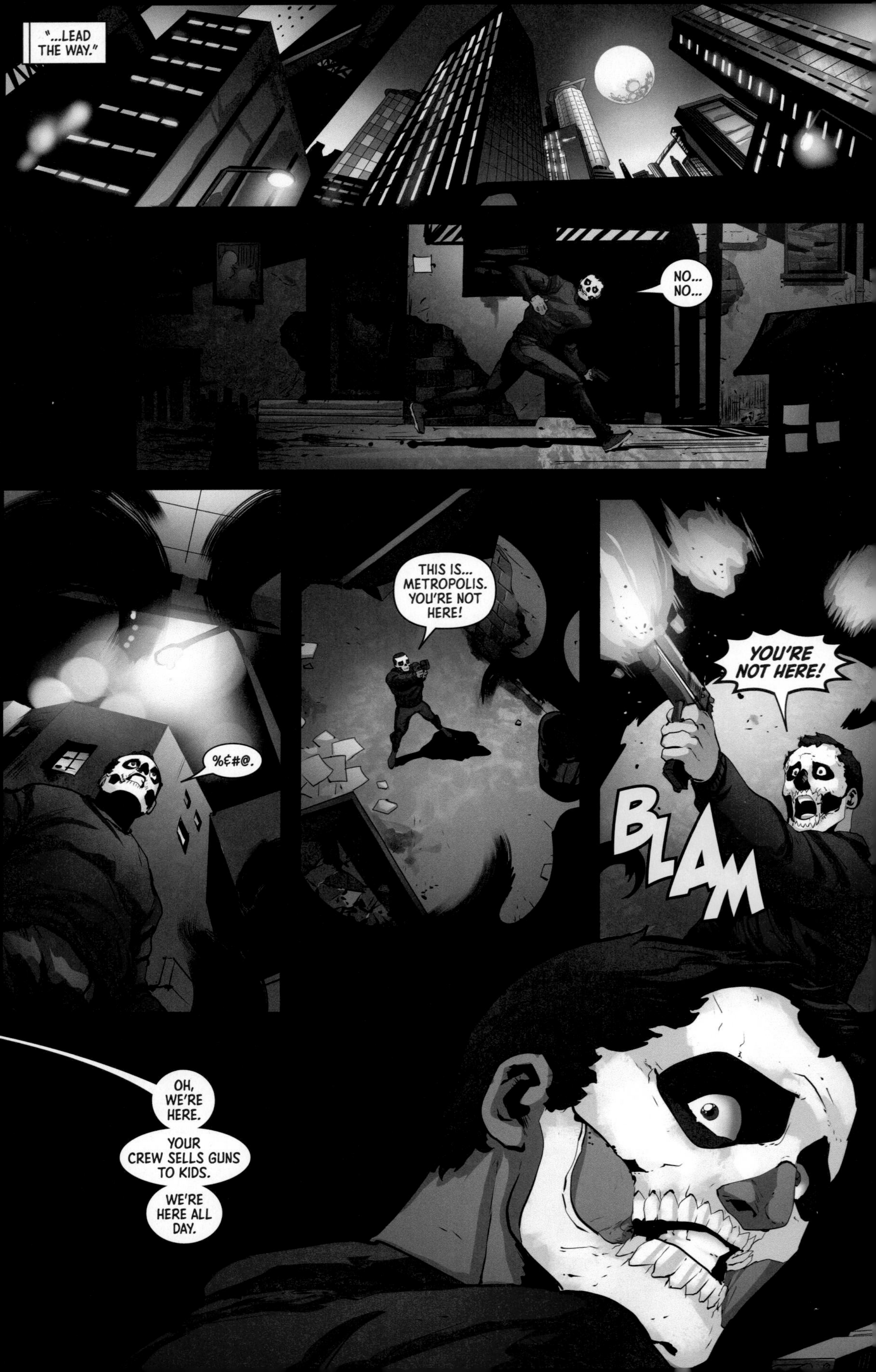
"...LEAD THE WAY."
NO... NO...
%&#@.
THIS IS... METROPOLIS. YOU'RE NOT HERE!
YOU'RE NOT HERE!
BLAM
OH, WE'RE HERE.
YOUR CREW SELLS GUNS TO KIDS.
WE'RE HERE ALL DAY.

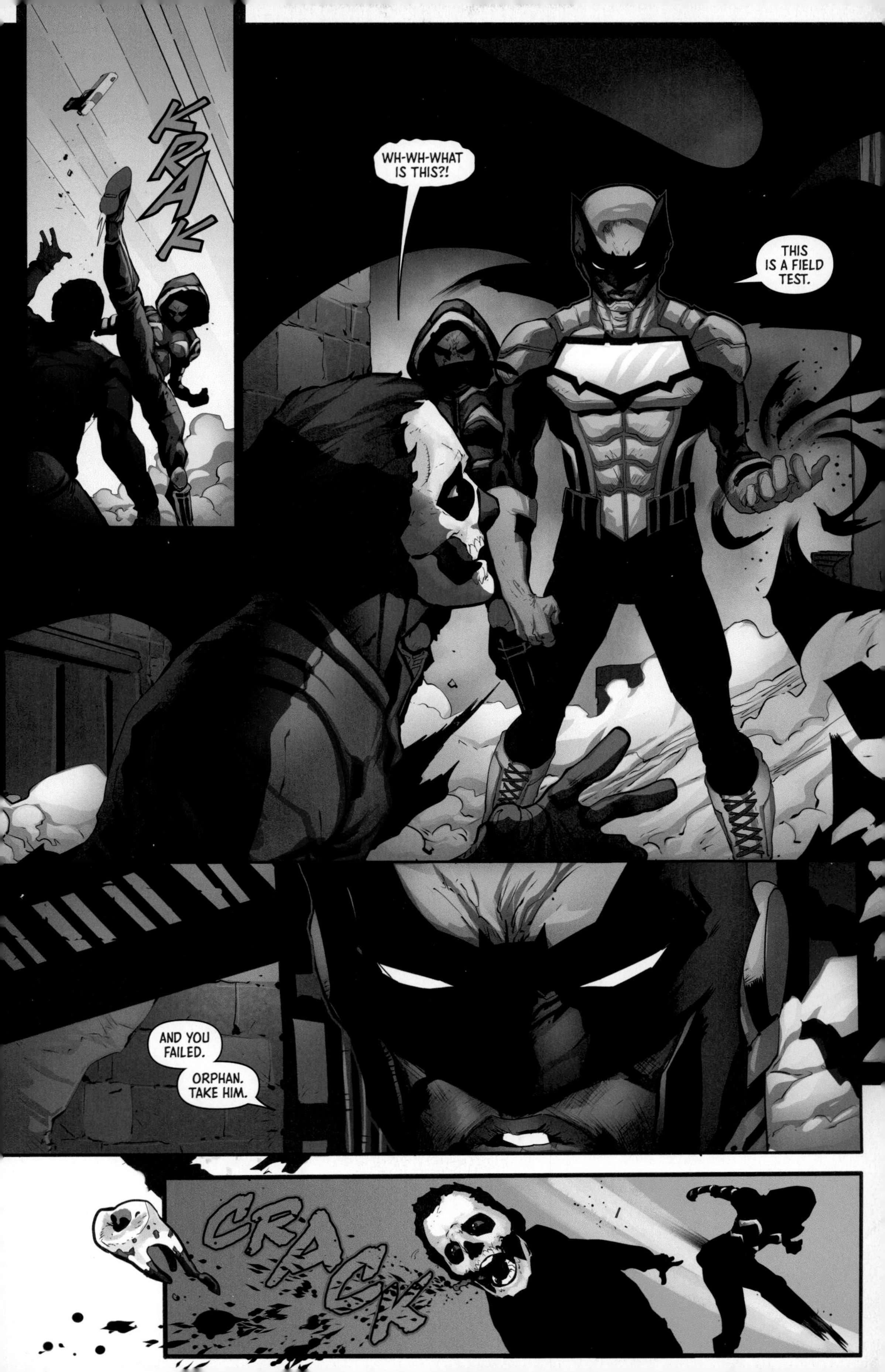

KRAK
WH-WH-WHAT IS THIS?!
THIS IS A FIELD TEST.
AND YOU FAILED.
ORPHAN. TAKE HIM.
CRACK

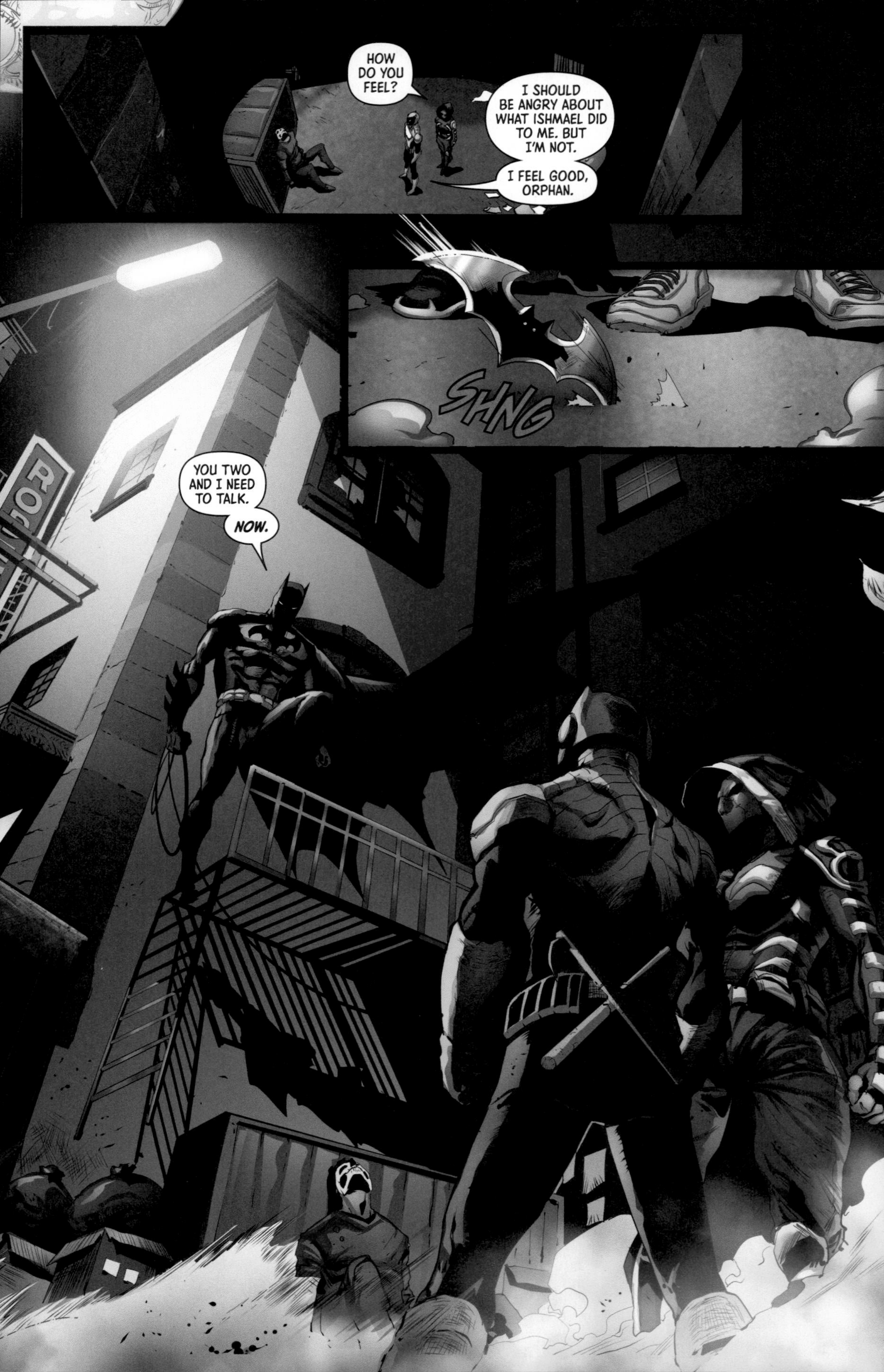
HOW DO YOU FEEL?
I SHOULD BE ANGRY ABOUT WHAT ISHMAEL DID TO ME. BUT I'M NOT.
I FEEL GOOD, ORPHAN.
SHNG
YOU TWO AND I NEED TO TALK.
NOW.

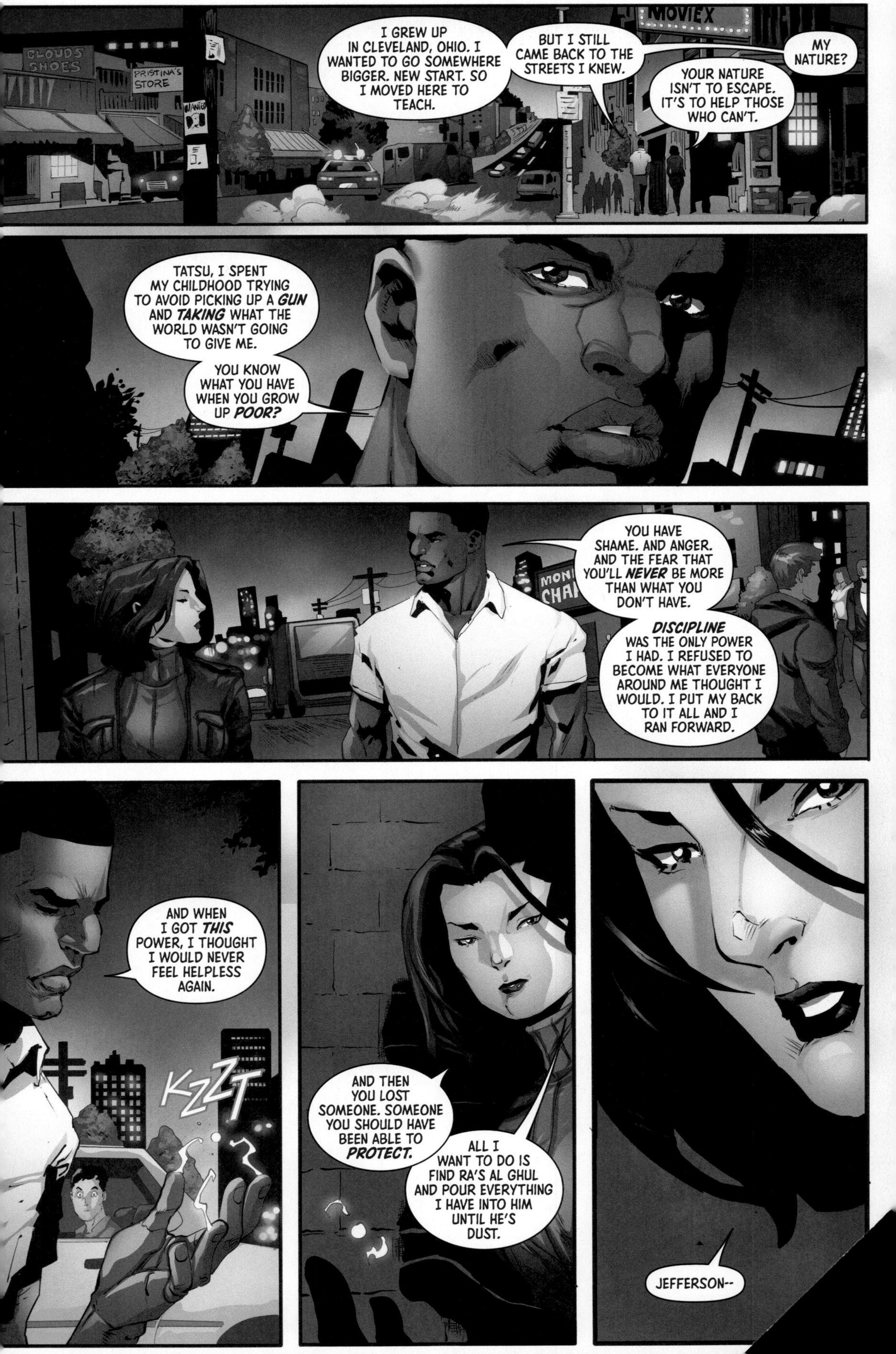
CLOUDS SHOES
PRISTINA'S STORE
MOVIEX
I GREW UP IN CLEVELAND, OHIO. I WANTED TO GO SOMEWHERE BIGGER. NEW START. SO I MOVED HERE TO TEACH.
BUT I STILL CAME BACK TO THE STREETS I KNEW.
YOUR NATURE ISN'T TO ESCAPE. IT'S TO HELP THOSE WHO CAN'T.
MY NATURE?
TATSU, I SPENT MY CHILDHOOD TRYING TO AVOID PICKING UP A *GUN* AND *TAKING* WHAT THE WORLD WASN'T GOING TO GIVE ME.
YOU KNOW WHAT YOU HAVE WHEN YOU GROW UP *POOR?*
YOU HAVE SHAME. AND ANGER. AND THE FEAR THAT YOU'LL *NEVER* BE MORE THAN WHAT YOU DON'T HAVE.
DISCIPLINE WAS THE ONLY POWER I HAD. I REFUSED TO BECOME WHAT EVERYONE AROUND ME THOUGHT I WOULD. I PUT MY BACK TO IT ALL AND I RAN FORWARD.
AND WHEN I GOT *THIS* POWER, I THOUGHT I WOULD NEVER FEEL HELPLESS AGAIN.
KZZT
AND THEN YOU LOST SOMEONE. SOMEONE YOU SHOULD HAVE BEEN ABLE TO *PROTECT.*
ALL I WANT TO DO IS FIND RA'S AL GHUL AND POUR EVERYTHING I HAVE INTO HIM UNTIL HE'S DUST.
JEFFERSON--

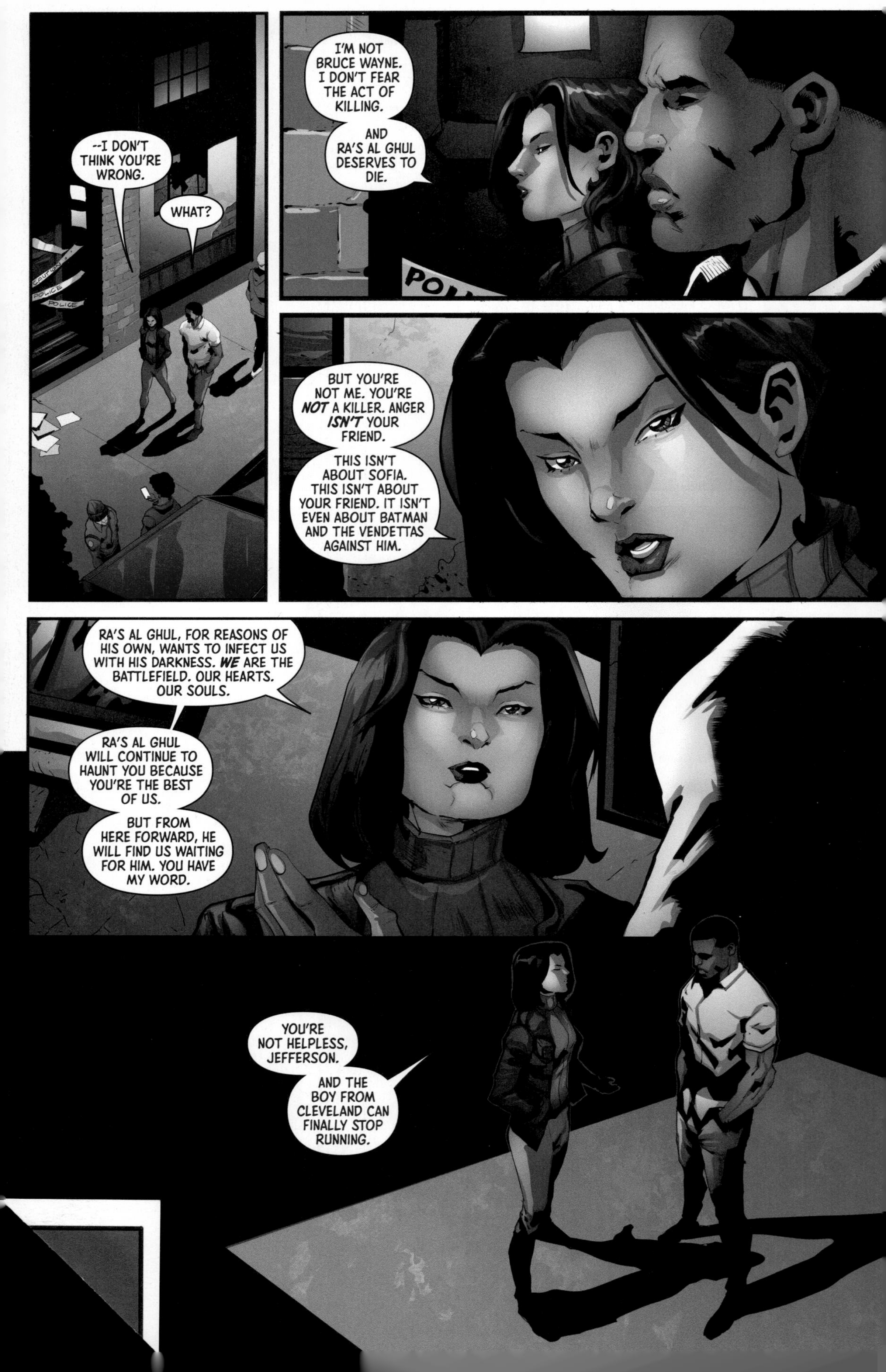
--I DON'T THINK YOU'RE WRONG.
WHAT?
I'M NOT BRUCE WAYNE. I DON'T FEAR THE ACT OF KILLING.
AND RA'S AL GHUL DESERVES TO DIE.
BUT YOU'RE NOT ME. YOU'RE *NOT* A KILLER. ANGER *ISN'T* YOUR FRIEND.
THIS ISN'T ABOUT SOFIA. THIS ISN'T ABOUT YOUR FRIEND. IT ISN'T EVEN ABOUT BATMAN AND THE VENDETTAS AGAINST HIM.
RA'S AL GHUL, FOR REASONS OF HIS OWN, WANTS TO INFECT US WITH HIS DARKNESS. *WE* ARE THE BATTLEFIELD. OUR HEARTS. OUR SOULS.
RA'S AL GHUL WILL CONTINUE TO HAUNT YOU BECAUSE YOU'RE THE BEST OF US.
BUT FROM HERE FORWARD, HE WILL FIND US WAITING FOR HIM. YOU HAVE MY WORD.
YOU'RE NOT HELPLESS, JEFFERSON.
AND THE BOY FROM CLEVELAND CAN FINALLY STOP RUNNING.

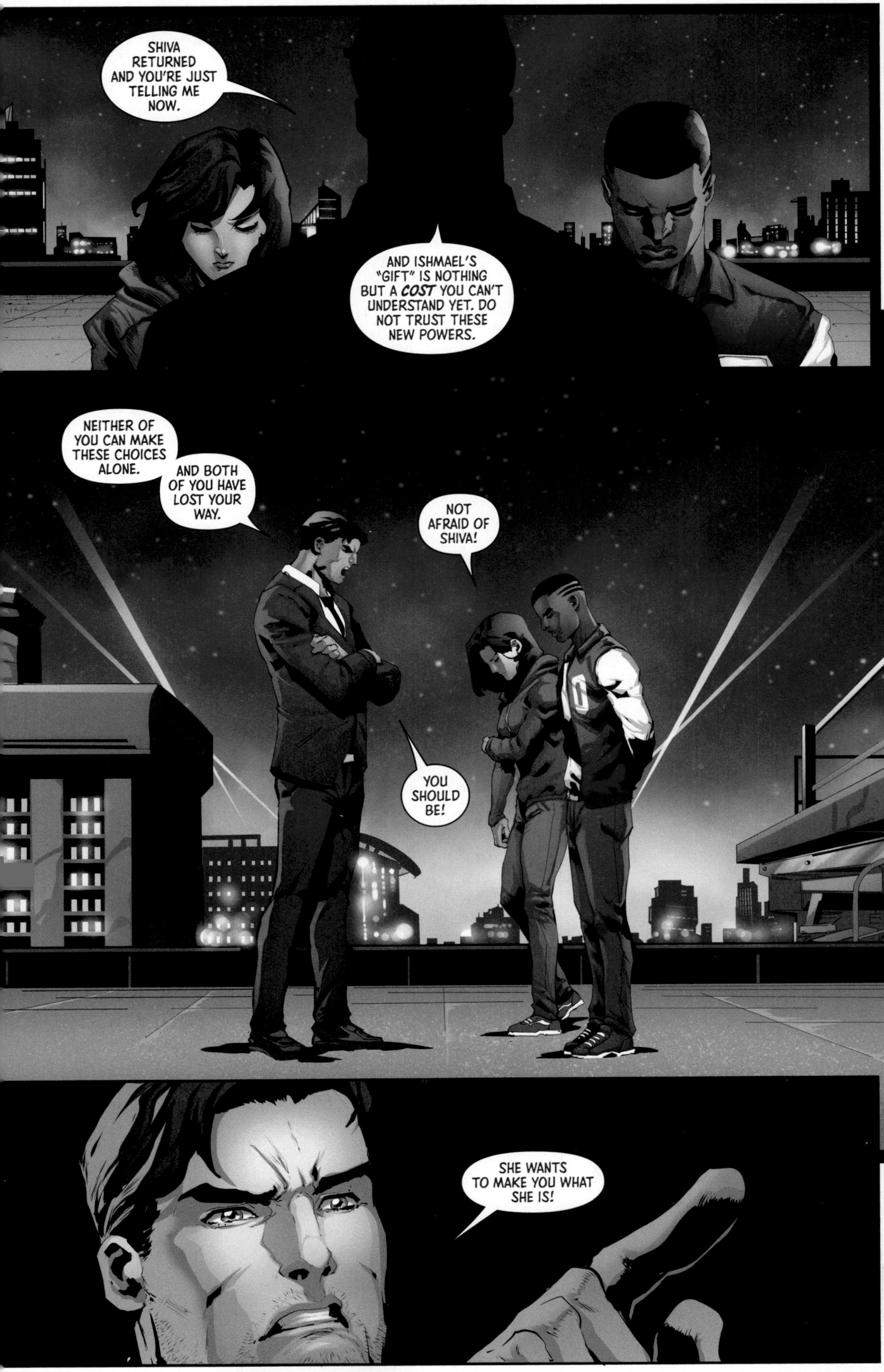
SHIVA RETURNED AND YOU'RE JUST TELLING ME NOW.
AND ISHMAEL'S "GIFT" IS NOTHING BUT A *COST* YOU CAN'T UNDERSTAND YET. DO NOT TRUST THESE NEW POWERS.
NEITHER OF YOU CAN MAKE THESE CHOICES ALONE.
AND BOTH OF YOU HAVE LOST YOUR WAY.
NOT AFRAID OF SHIVA!
YOU SHOULD BE!
SHE WANTS TO MAKE YOU WHAT SHE IS!

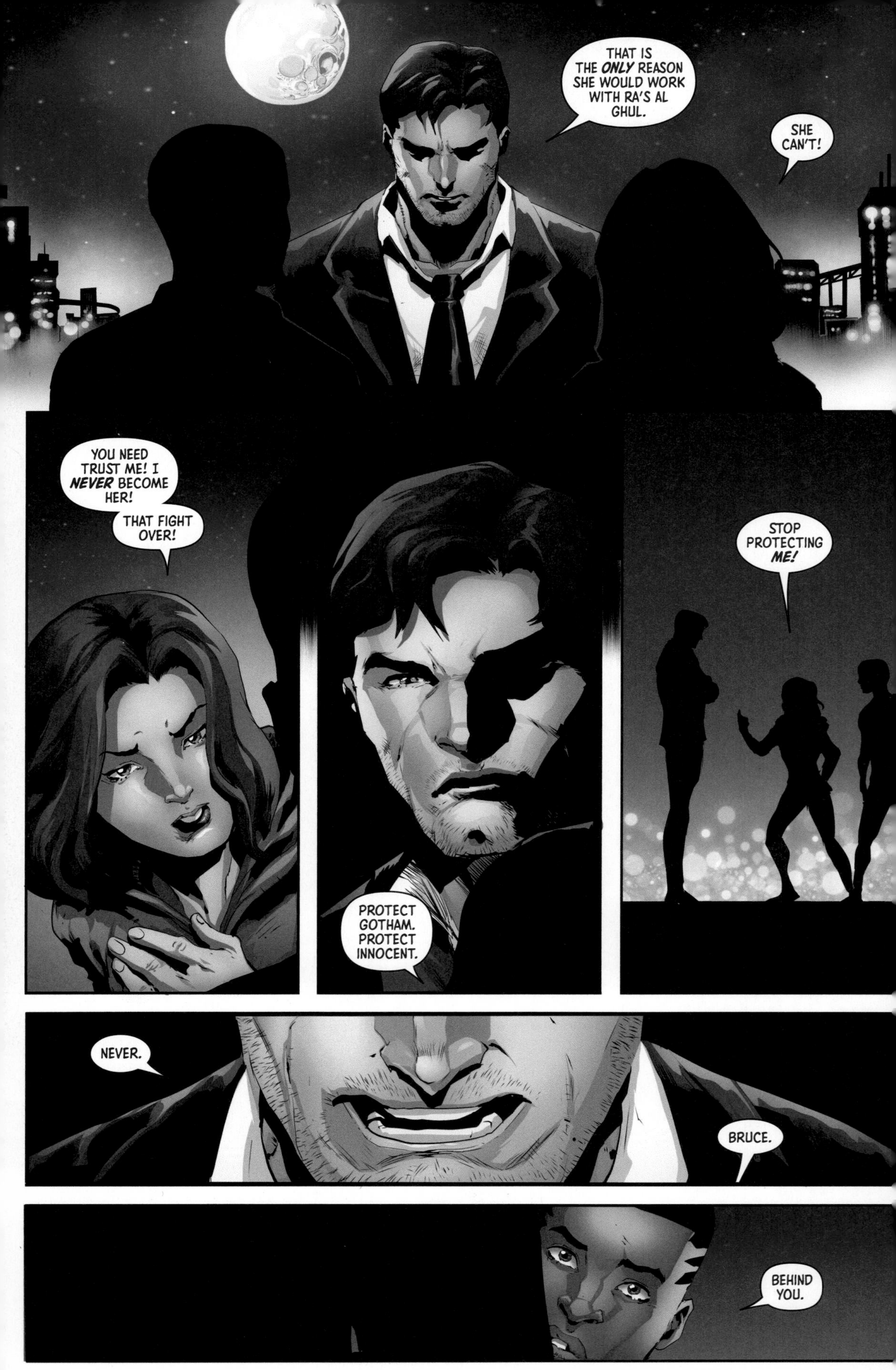
THAT IS THE *ONLY* REASON SHE WOULD WORK WITH RA'S AL GHUL.
SHE CAN'T!
YOU NEED TRUST ME! I *NEVER* BECOME HER!
THAT FIGHT OVER!
PROTECT GOTHAM. PROTECT INNOCENT.
STOP PROTECTING *ME!*
NEVER.
BRUCE.
BEHIND YOU.

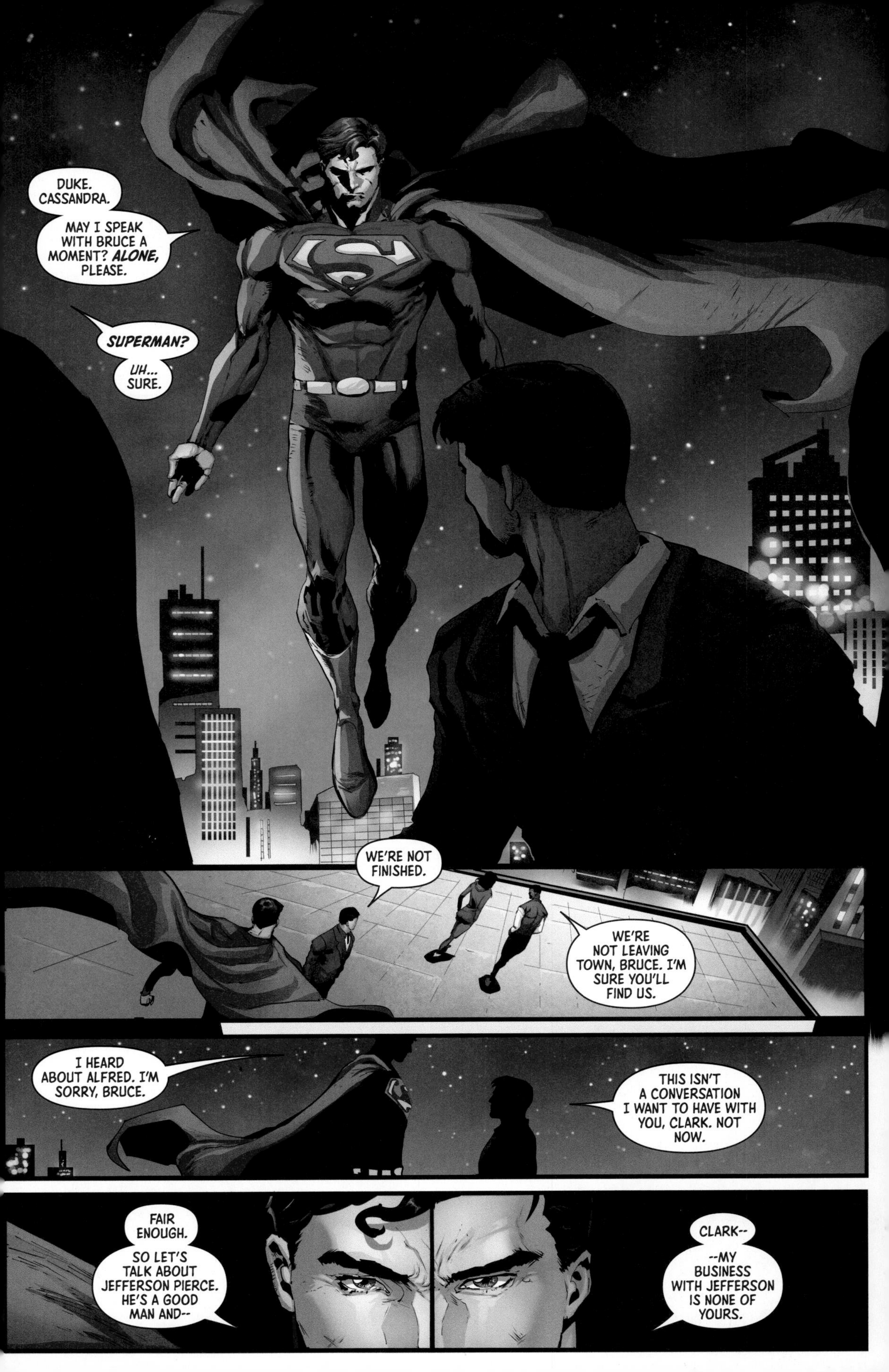
DUKE. CASSANDRA.
MAY I SPEAK WITH BRUCE A MOMENT? *ALONE,* PLEASE.
SUPERMAN?
UH... SURE.
WE'RE NOT FINISHED.
WE'RE NOT LEAVING TOWN, BRUCE. I'M SURE YOU'LL FIND US.
I HEARD ABOUT ALFRED. I'M SORRY, BRUCE.
THIS ISN'T A CONVERSATION I WANT TO HAVE WITH YOU, CLARK. NOT NOW.
FAIR ENOUGH.
SO LET'S TALK ABOUT JEFFERSON PIERCE. HE'S A GOOD MAN AND--
CLARK--
--MY BUSINESS WITH JEFFERSON IS NONE OF YOURS.

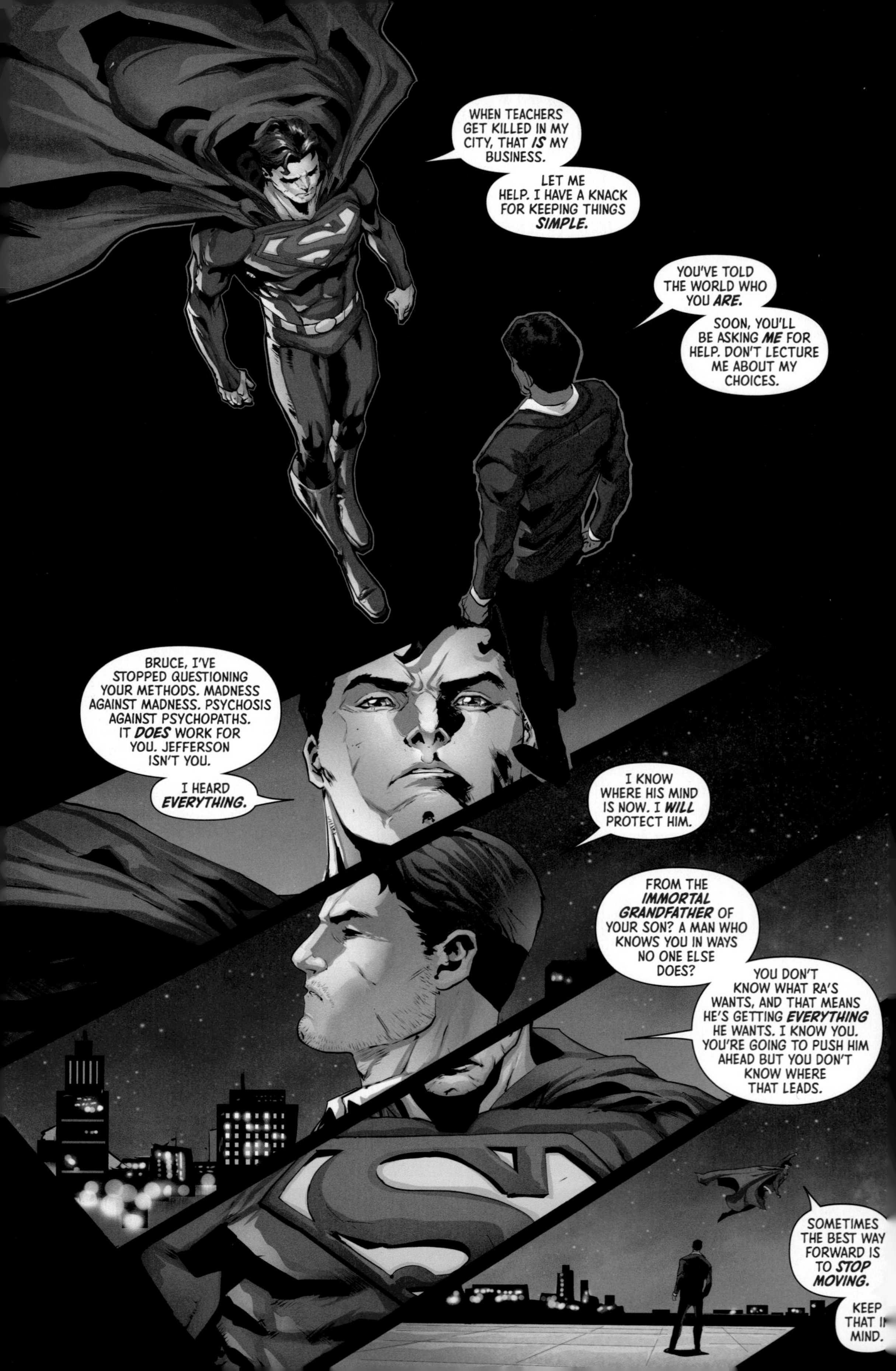
WHEN TEACHERS GET KILLED IN MY CITY, THAT *IS* MY BUSINESS.
LET ME HELP. I HAVE A KNACK FOR KEEPING THINGS *SIMPLE.*
YOU'VE TOLD THE WORLD WHO YOU *ARE.*
SOON, YOU'LL BE ASKING *ME* FOR HELP. DON'T LECTURE ME ABOUT MY CHOICES.
BRUCE, I'VE STOPPED QUESTIONING YOUR METHODS. MADNESS AGAINST MADNESS. PSYCHOSIS AGAINST PSYCHOPATHS. IT *DOES* WORK FOR YOU. JEFFERSON ISN'T YOU.
I HEARD *EVERYTHING.*
I KNOW WHERE HIS MIND IS NOW. I *WILL* PROTECT HIM.
FROM THE *IMMORTAL GRANDFATHER* OF YOUR SON? A MAN WHO KNOWS YOU IN WAYS NO ONE ELSE DOES?
YOU DON'T KNOW WHAT RA'S WANTS, AND THAT MEANS HE'S GETTING *EVERYTHING* HE WANTS. I KNOW YOU. YOU'RE GOING TO PUSH HIM AHEAD BUT YOU DON'T KNOW WHERE THAT LEADS.
SOMETIMES THE BEST WAY FORWARD IS TO *STOP MOVING.*
KEEP THAT IN MIND.

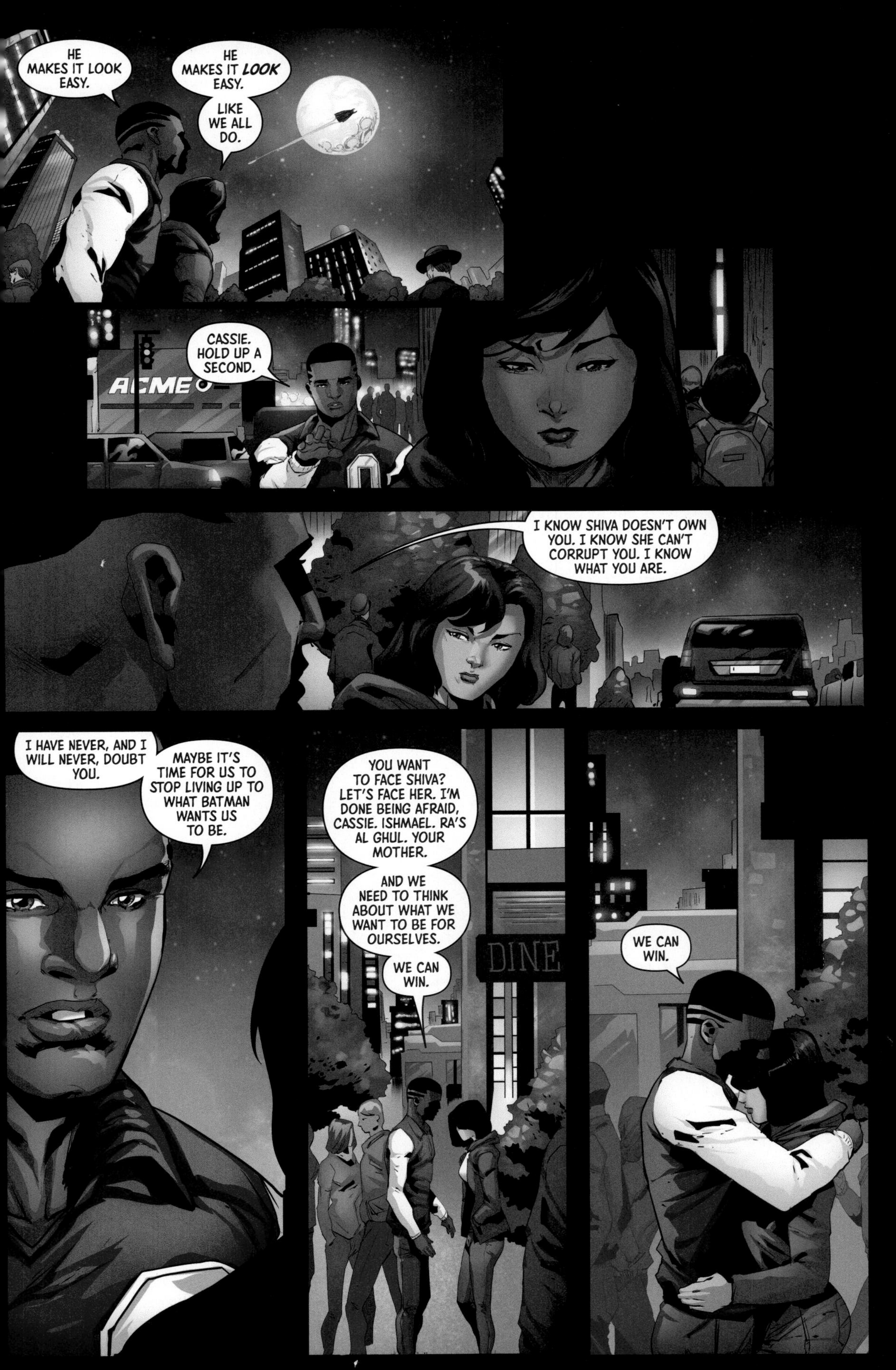
HE MAKES IT LOOK EASY.
HE MAKES IT *LOOK* EASY.
LIKE WE ALL DO.
CASSIE. HOLD UP A SECOND.
ACME
I KNOW SHIVA DOESN'T OWN YOU. I KNOW SHE CAN'T CORRUPT YOU. I KNOW WHAT YOU ARE.
I HAVE NEVER, AND I WILL NEVER, DOUBT YOU.
MAYBE IT'S TIME FOR US TO STOP LIVING UP TO WHAT BATMAN WANTS US TO BE.
YOU WANT TO FACE SHIVA? LET'S FACE HER. I'M DONE BEING AFRAID, CASSIE. ISHMAEL. RA'S AL GHUL. YOUR MOTHER.
AND WE NEED TO THINK ABOUT WHAT WE WANT TO BE FOR OURSELVES.
WE CAN WIN.
DINE
WE CAN WIN.

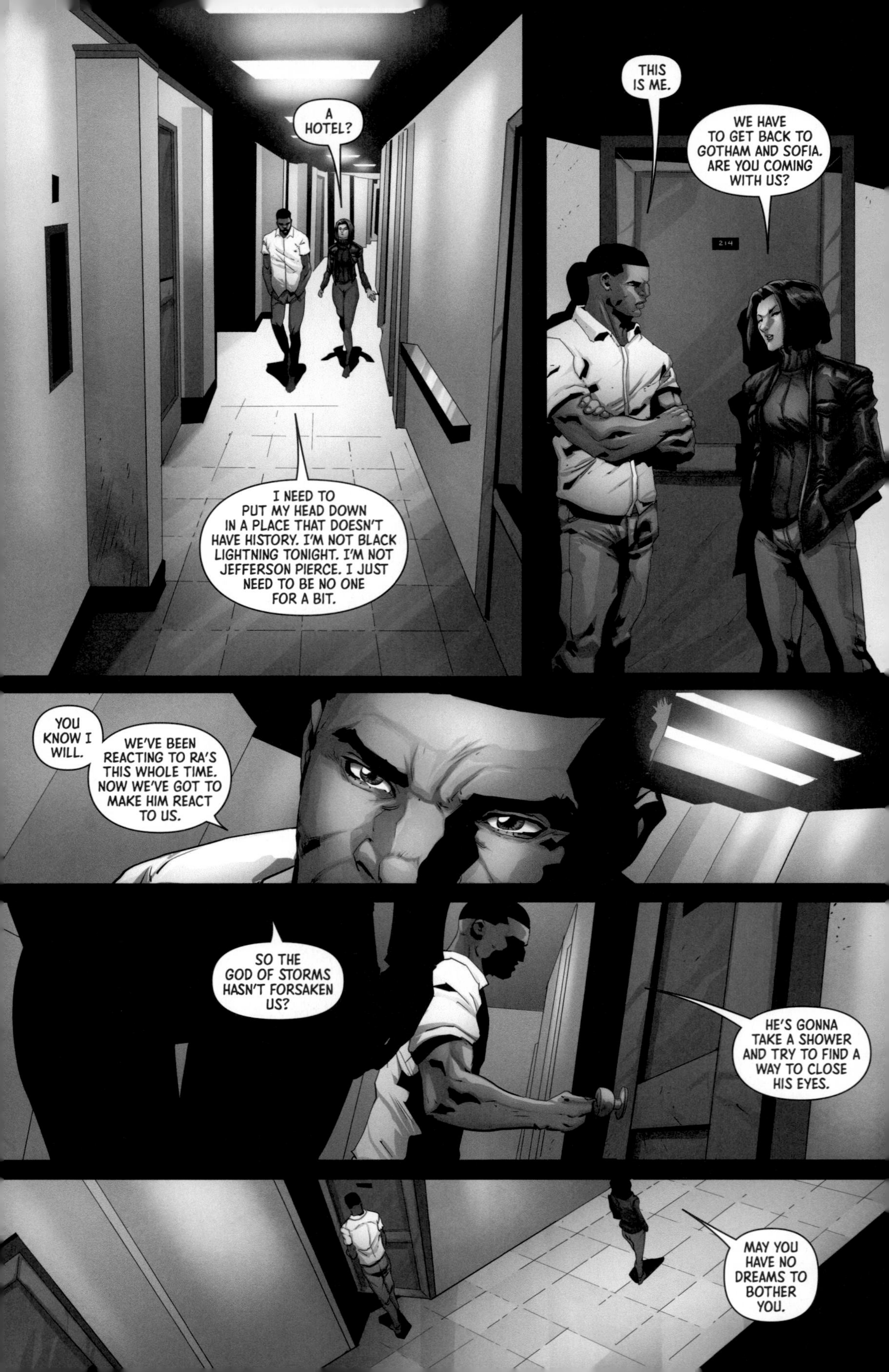
A HOTEL?
I NEED TO PUT MY HEAD DOWN IN A PLACE THAT DOESN'T HAVE HISTORY. I'M NOT BLACK LIGHTNING TONIGHT. I'M NOT JEFFERSON PIERCE. I JUST NEED TO BE NO ONE FOR A BIT.
THIS IS ME.
WE HAVE TO GET BACK TO GOTHAM AND SOFIA. ARE YOU COMING WITH US?
YOU KNOW I WILL.
WE'VE BEEN REACTING TO RA'S THIS WHOLE TIME. NOW WE'VE GOT TO MAKE HIM REACT TO US.
SO THE GOD OF STORMS HASN'T FORSAKEN US?
HE'S GONNA TAKE A SHOWER AND TRY TO FIND A WAY TO CLOSE HIS EYES.
MAY YOU HAVE NO DREAMS TO BOTHER YOU.

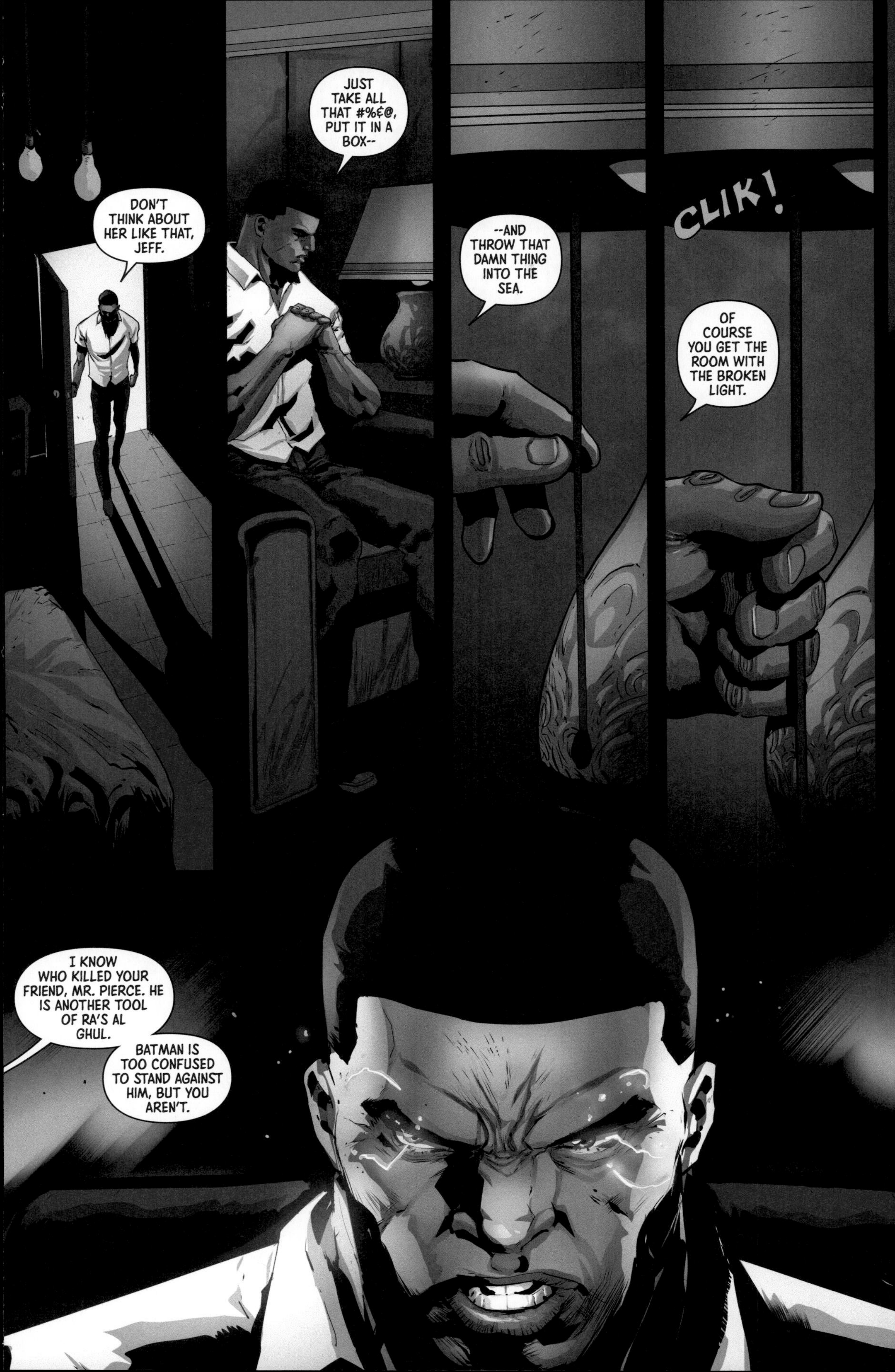
DON'T THINK ABOUT HER LIKE THAT, JEFF.
JUST TAKE ALL THAT #%€@, PUT IT IN A BOX--
--AND THROW THAT DAMN THING INTO THE SEA.
CLIK!
OF COURSE YOU GET THE ROOM WITH THE BROKEN LIGHT.
I KNOW WHO KILLED YOUR FRIEND, MR. PIERCE. HE IS ANOTHER TOOL OF RA'S AL GHUL.
BATMAN IS TOO CONFUSED TO STAND AGAINST HIM, BUT YOU AREN'T.

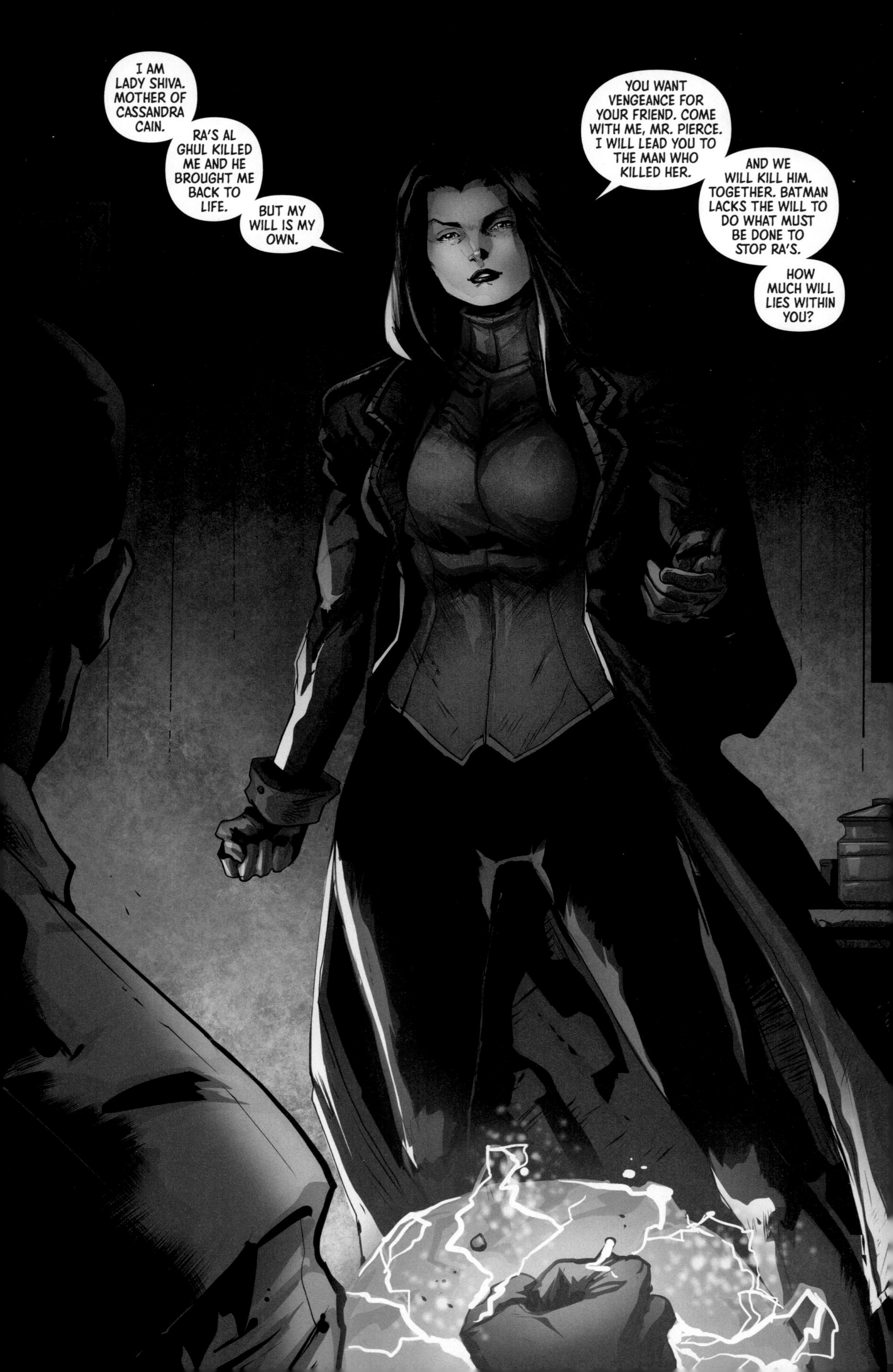
I AM LADY SHIVA. MOTHER OF CASSANDRA CAIN.
RA'S AL GHUL KILLED ME AND HE BROUGHT ME BACK TO LIFE.
BUT MY WILL IS MY OWN.
YOU WANT VENGEANCE FOR YOUR FRIEND. COME WITH ME, MR. PIERCE. I WILL LEAD YOU TO THE MAN WHO KILLED HER.
AND WE WILL KILL HIM. TOGETHER. BATMAN LACKS THE WILL TO DO WHAT MUST BE DONE TO STOP RA'S.
HOW MUCH WILL LIES WITHIN YOU?

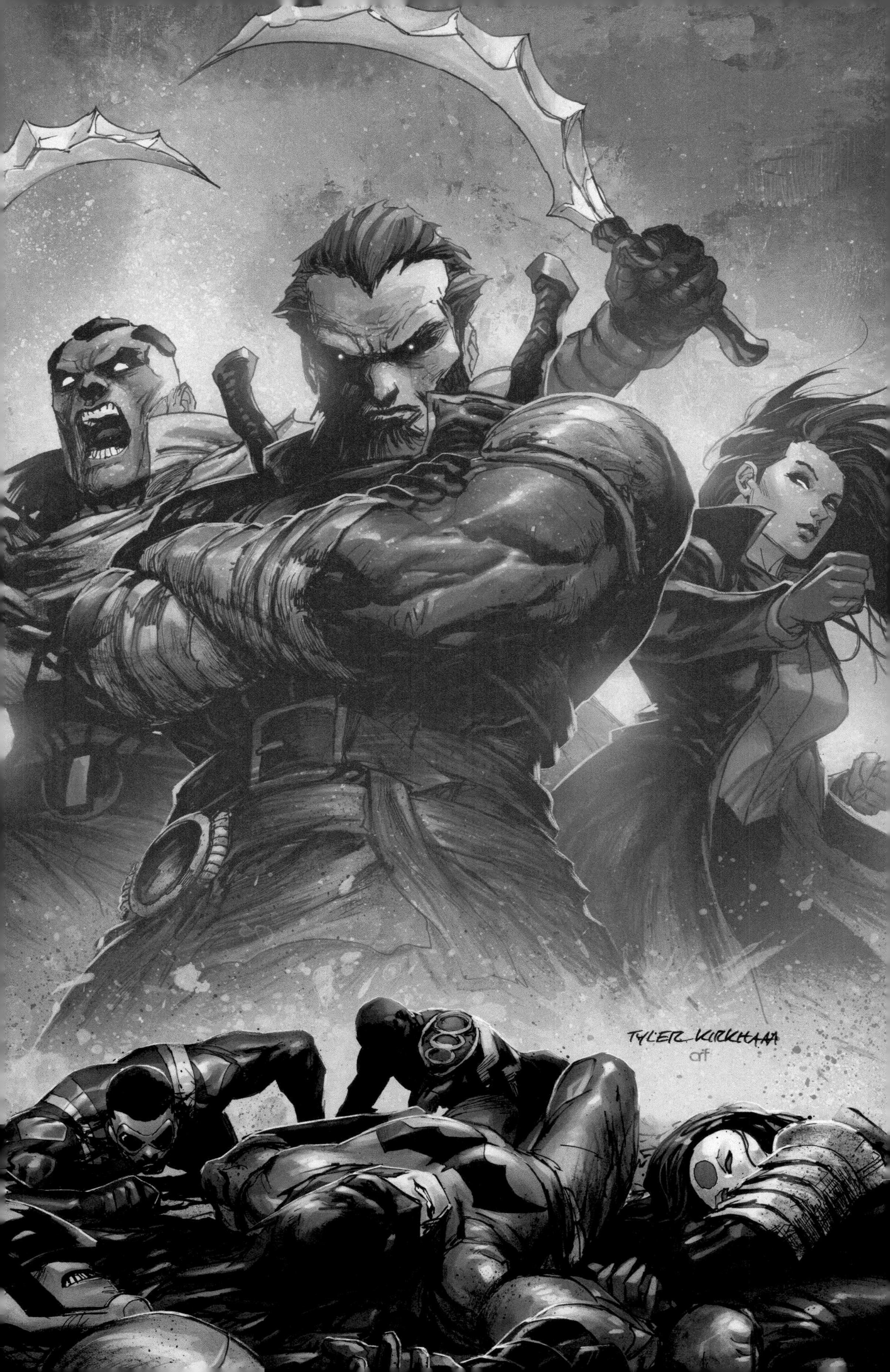
TYLER KIRKHAM
art

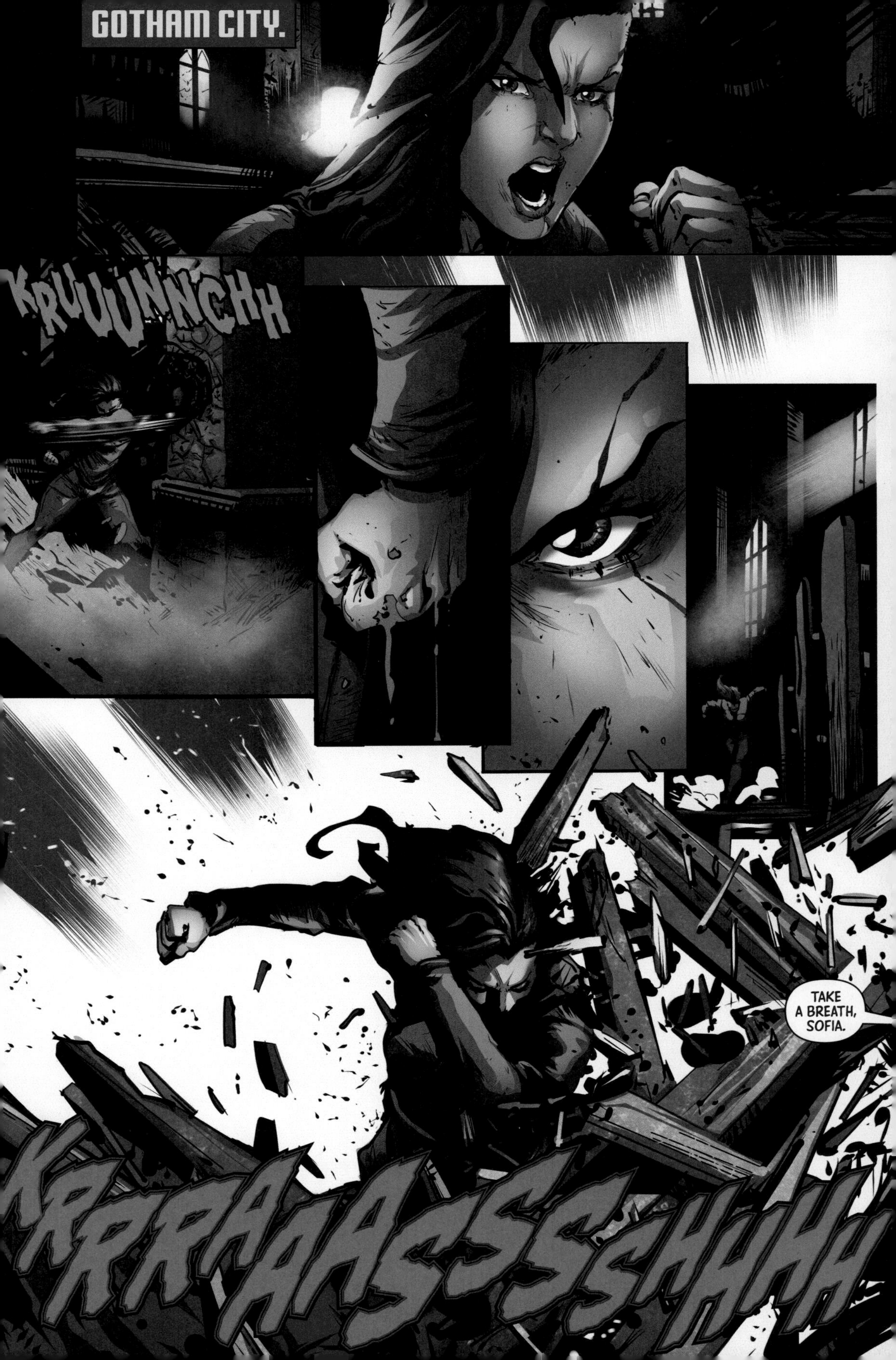
GOTHAM CITY.
KRUUUNNCHH
TAKE A BREATH, SOFIA.
KRRRAAASSSHHH

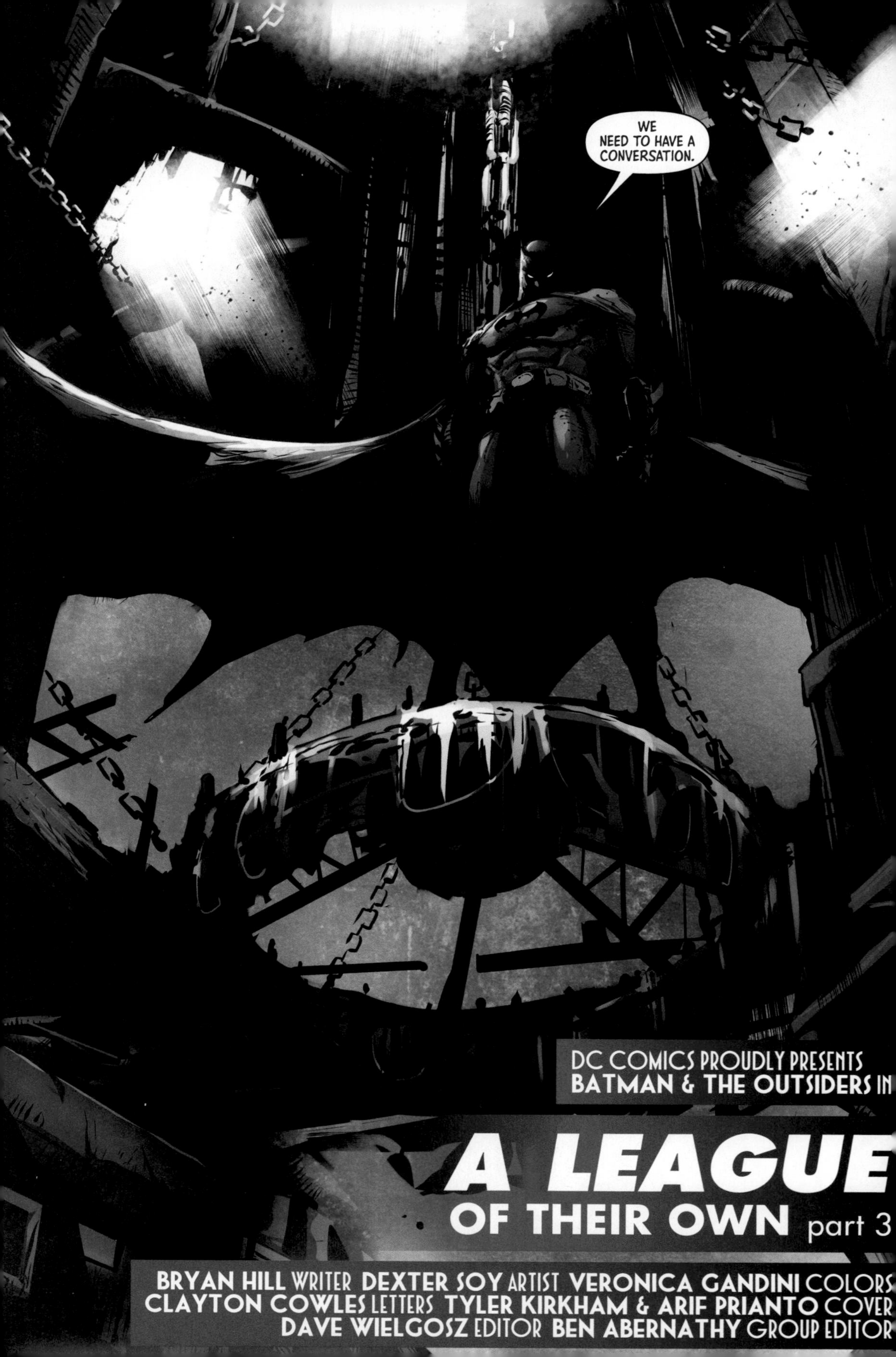
WE NEED TO HAVE A CONVERSATION.
DC COMICS PROUDLY PRESENTS
BATMAN & THE OUTSIDERS IN
A LEAGUE OF THEIR OWN part 3
BRYAN HILL WRITER DEXTER SOY ARTIST VERONICA GANDINI COLORS
CLAYTON COWLES LETTERS TYLER KIRKHAM & ARIF PRIANTO COVER
DAVE WIELGOSZ EDITOR BEN ABERNATHY GROUP EDITOR

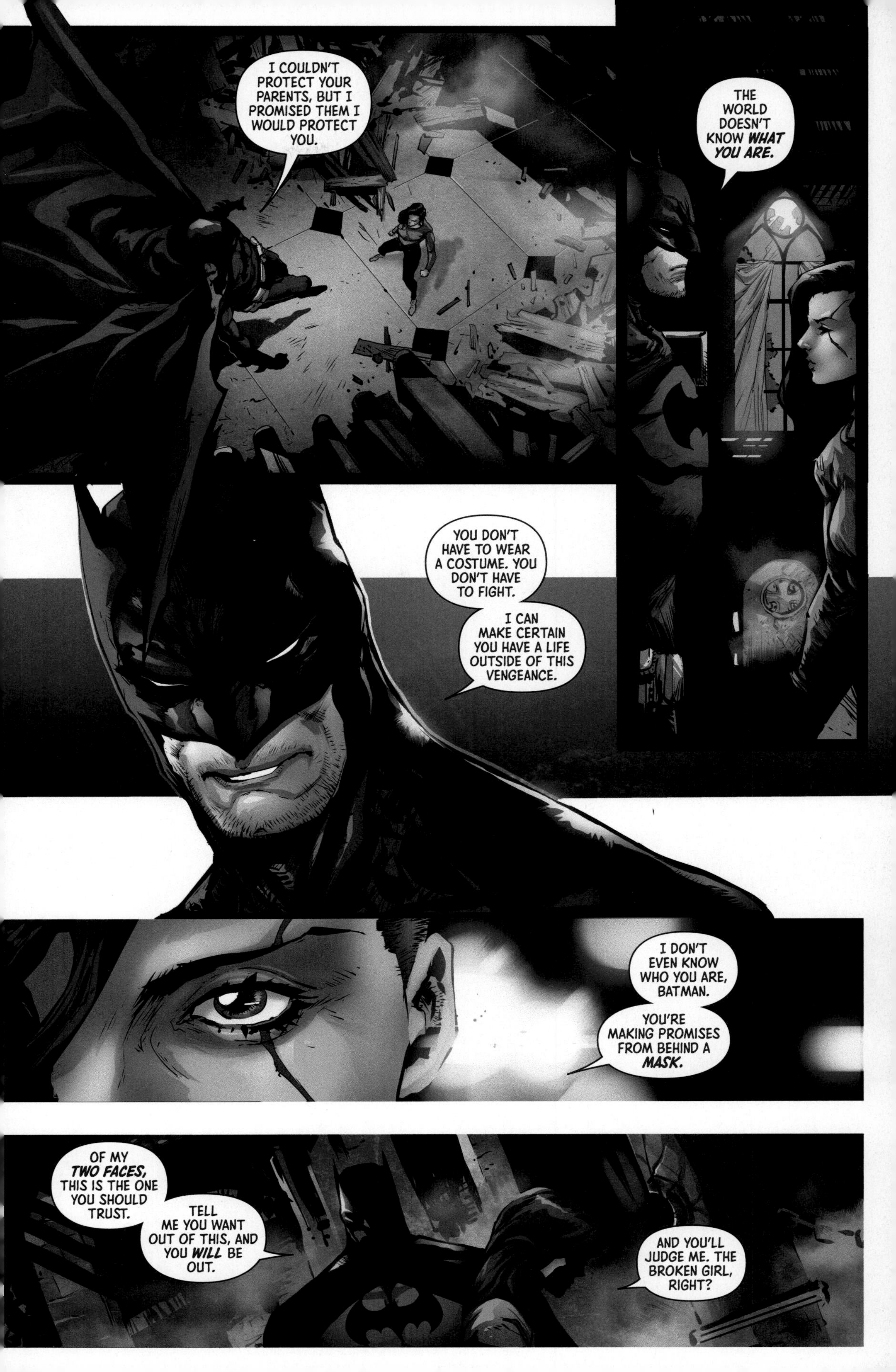
I COULDN'T PROTECT YOUR PARENTS, BUT I PROMISED THEM I WOULD PROTECT YOU.
THE WORLD DOESN'T KNOW *WHAT YOU ARE.*
YOU DON'T HAVE TO WEAR A COSTUME. YOU DON'T HAVE TO FIGHT.
I CAN MAKE CERTAIN YOU HAVE A LIFE OUTSIDE OF THIS VENGEANCE.
I DON'T EVEN KNOW WHO YOU ARE, BATMAN.
YOU'RE MAKING PROMISES FROM BEHIND A *MASK.*
OF MY *TWO FACES,* THIS IS THE ONE YOU SHOULD TRUST.
TELL ME YOU WANT OUT OF THIS, AND YOU *WILL* BE OUT.
AND YOU'LL JUDGE ME. THE BROKEN GIRL, RIGHT?

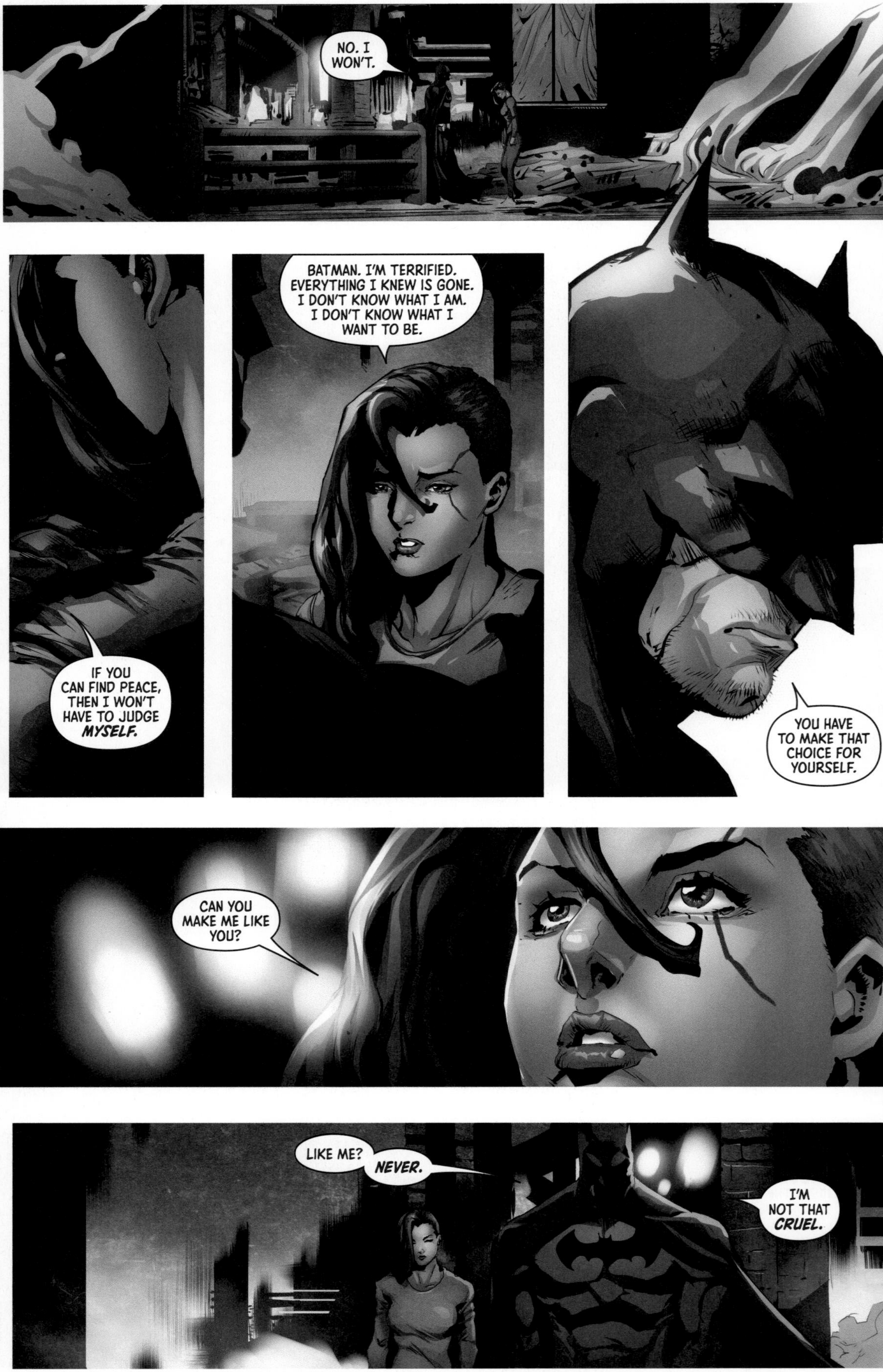
NO. I WON'T.
BATMAN. I'M TERRIFIED. EVERYTHING I KNEW IS GONE. I DON'T KNOW WHAT I AM. I DON'T KNOW WHAT I WANT TO BE.
IF YOU CAN FIND PEACE, THEN I WON'T HAVE TO JUDGE *MYSELF.*
YOU HAVE TO MAKE THAT CHOICE FOR YOURSELF.
CAN YOU MAKE ME LIKE YOU?
LIKE ME? *NEVER.*
I'M NOT THAT *CRUEL.*

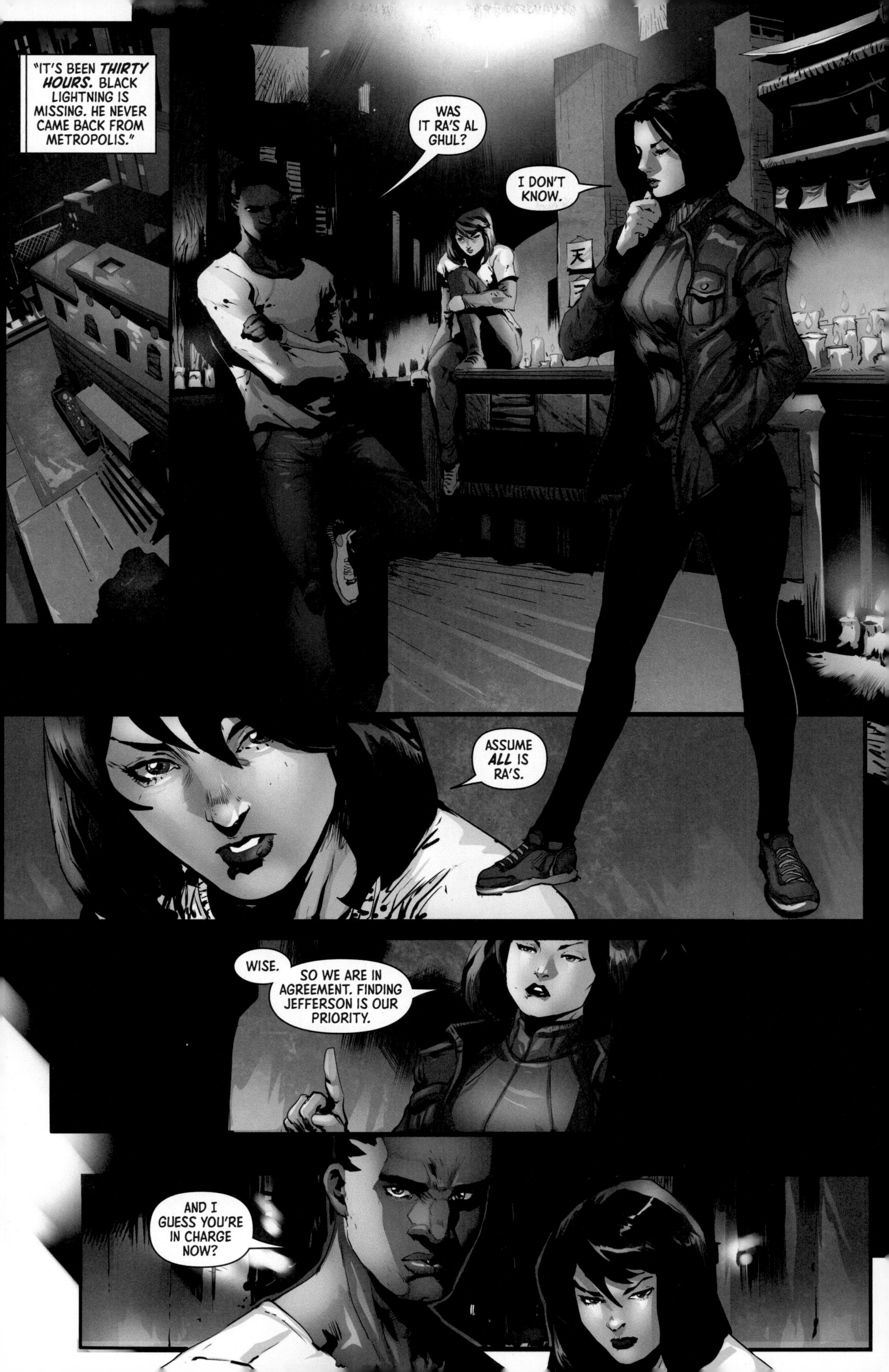
"IT'S BEEN THIRTY HOURS. BLACK LIGHTNING IS MISSING. HE NEVER CAME BACK FROM METROPOLIS."
WAS IT RA'S AL GHUL?
I DON'T KNOW.
ASSUME ALL IS RA'S.
WISE.
SO WE ARE IN AGREEMENT. FINDING JEFFERSON IS OUR PRIORITY.
AND I GUESS YOU'RE IN CHARGE NOW?

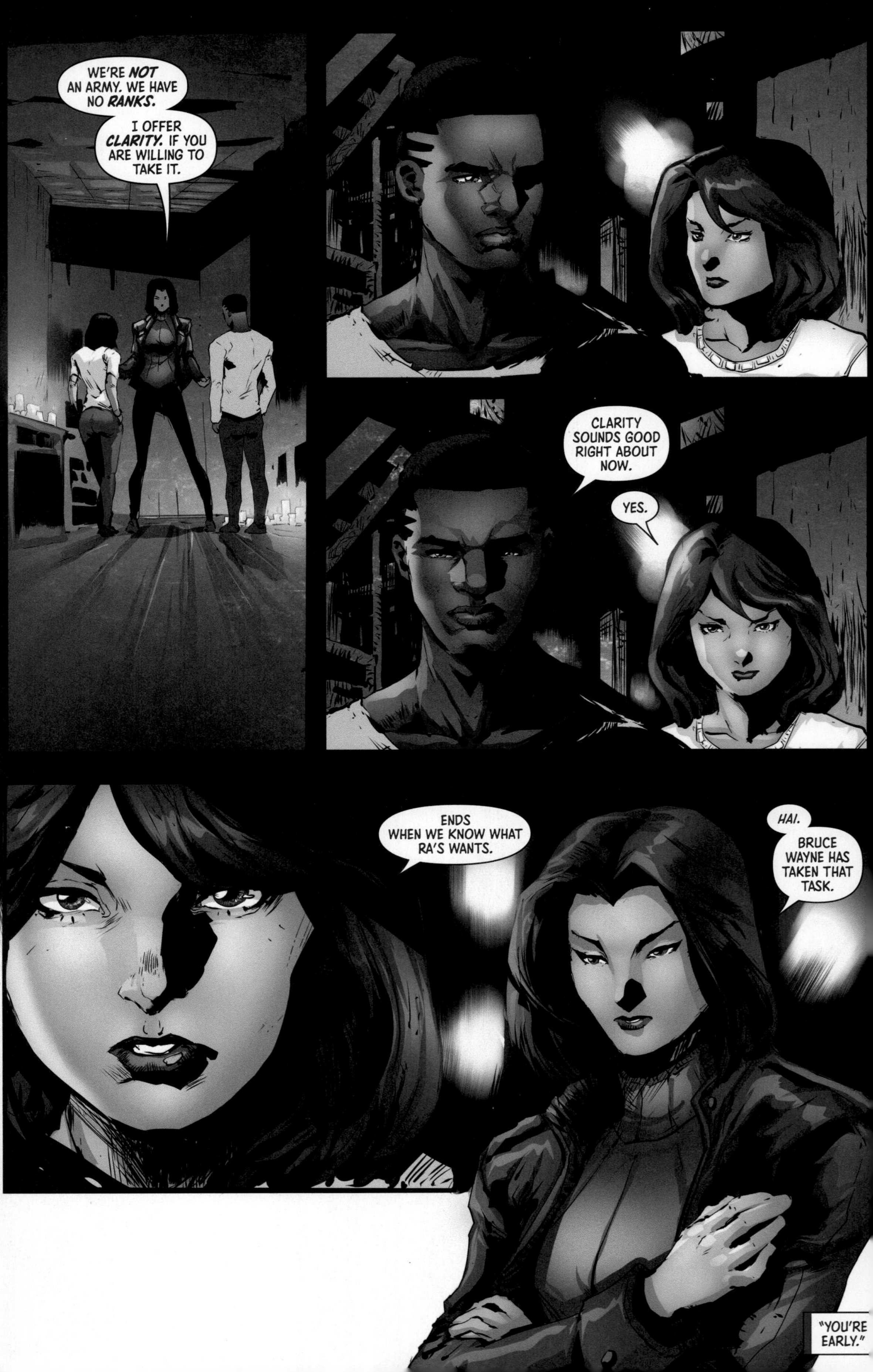

WE'RE **NOT** AN ARMY. WE HAVE NO **RANKS.**
I OFFER **CLARITY.** IF YOU ARE WILLING TO TAKE IT.
CLARITY SOUNDS GOOD RIGHT ABOUT NOW.
YES.
ENDS WHEN WE KNOW WHAT RA'S WANTS.
HAI.
BRUCE WAYNE HAS TAKEN THAT TASK.
"YOU'RE EARLY."

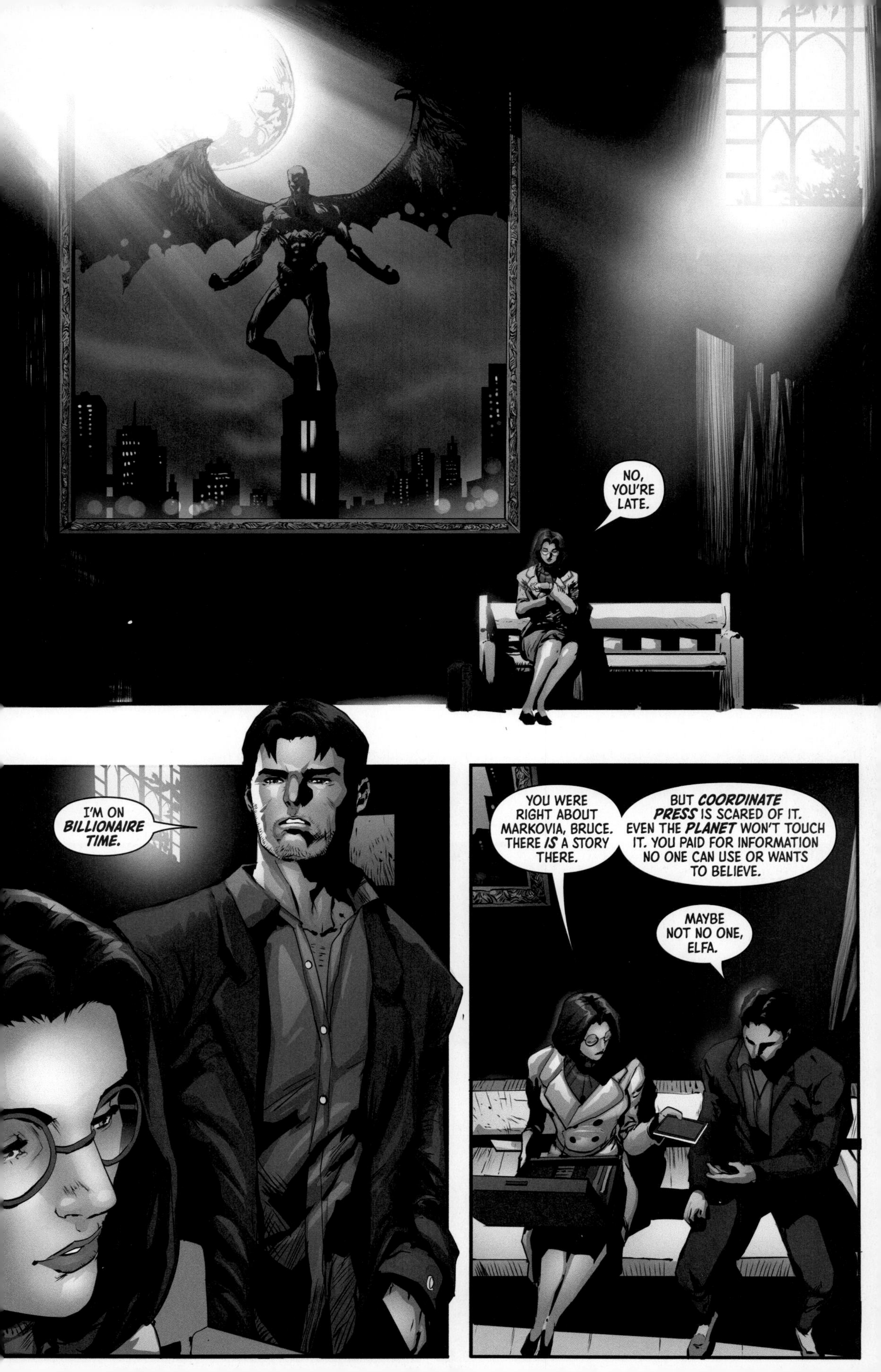
NO, YOU'RE LATE.
I'M ON *BILLIONAIRE TIME.*
YOU WERE RIGHT ABOUT MARKOVIA, BRUCE. THERE *IS* A STORY THERE.
BUT *COORDINATE PRESS* IS SCARED OF IT. EVEN THE *PLANET* WON'T TOUCH IT. YOU PAID FOR INFORMATION NO ONE CAN USE OR WANTS TO BELIEVE.
MAYBE NOT NO ONE, ELFA.

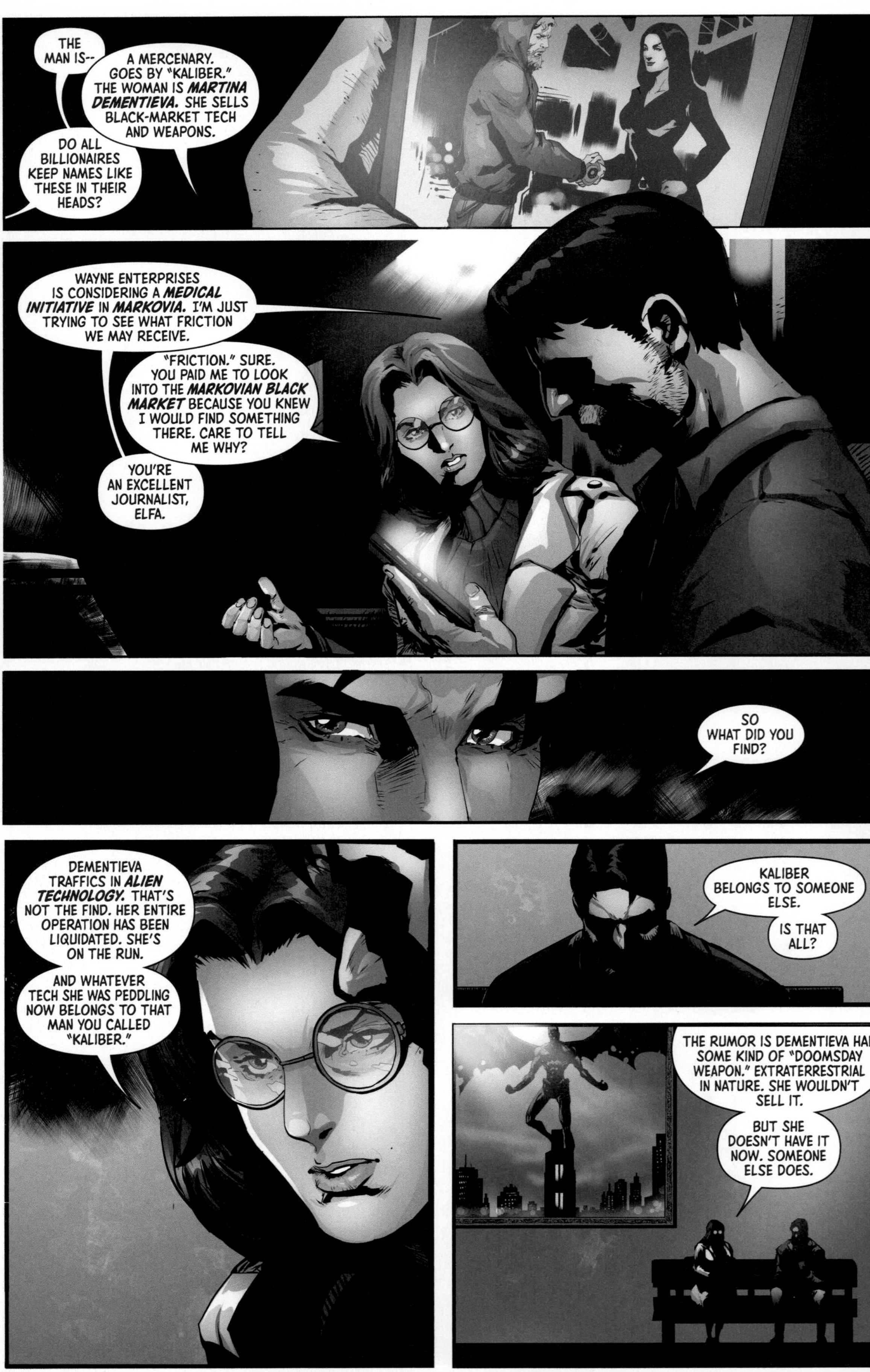
THE MAN IS--
A MERCENARY. GOES BY "KALIBER." THE WOMAN IS *MARTINA DEMENTIEVA.* SHE SELLS BLACK-MARKET TECH AND WEAPONS.
DO ALL BILLIONAIRES KEEP NAMES LIKE THESE IN THEIR HEADS?
WAYNE ENTERPRISES IS CONSIDERING A *MEDICAL INITIATIVE* IN *MARKOVIA.* I'M JUST TRYING TO SEE WHAT FRICTION WE MAY RECEIVE.
"FRICTION." SURE. YOU PAID ME TO LOOK INTO THE *MARKOVIAN BLACK MARKET* BECAUSE YOU KNEW I WOULD FIND SOMETHING THERE. CARE TO TELL ME WHY?
YOU'RE AN EXCELLENT JOURNALIST, ELFA.
SO WHAT DID YOU FIND?
DEMENTIEVA TRAFFICS IN *ALIEN TECHNOLOGY.* THAT'S NOT THE FIND. HER ENTIRE OPERATION HAS BEEN LIQUIDATED. SHE'S ON THE RUN.
AND WHATEVER TECH SHE WAS PEDDLING NOW BELONGS TO THAT MAN YOU CALLED "KALIBER."
KALIBER BELONGS TO SOMEONE ELSE.
IS THAT ALL?
THE RUMOR IS DEMENTIEVA HAD SOME KIND OF "DOOMSDAY WEAPON." EXTRATERRESTRIAL IN NATURE. SHE WOULDN'T SELL IT.
BUT SHE DOESN'T HAVE IT NOW. SOMEONE ELSE DOES.

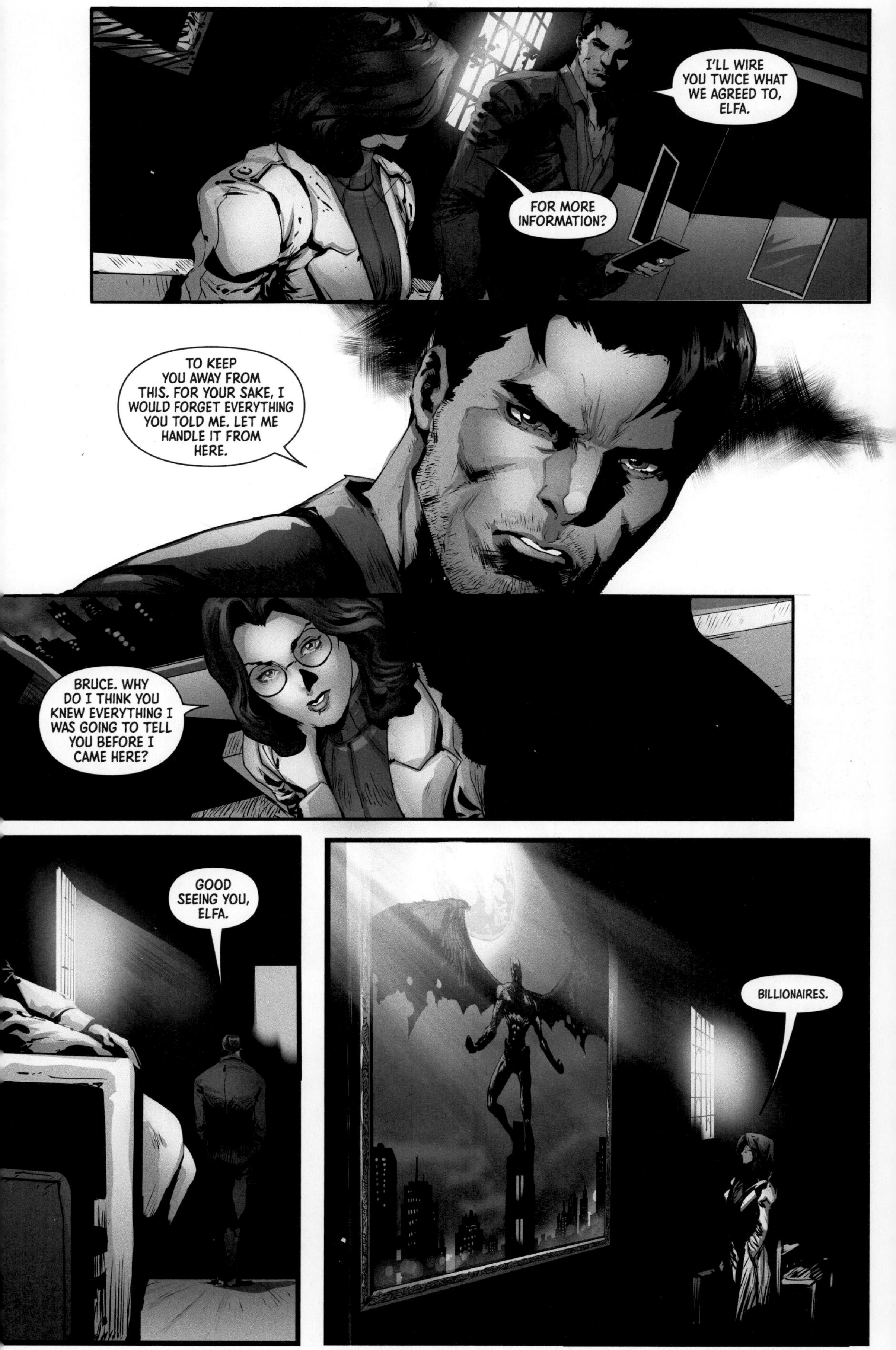
I'LL WIRE YOU TWICE WHAT WE AGREED TO, ELFA.
FOR MORE INFORMATION?
TO KEEP YOU AWAY FROM THIS. FOR YOUR SAKE, I WOULD FORGET EVERYTHING YOU TOLD ME. LET ME HANDLE IT FROM HERE.
BRUCE. WHY DO I THINK YOU KNEW EVERYTHING I WAS GOING TO TELL YOU BEFORE I CAME HERE?
GOOD SEEING YOU, ELFA.
BILLIONAIRES.

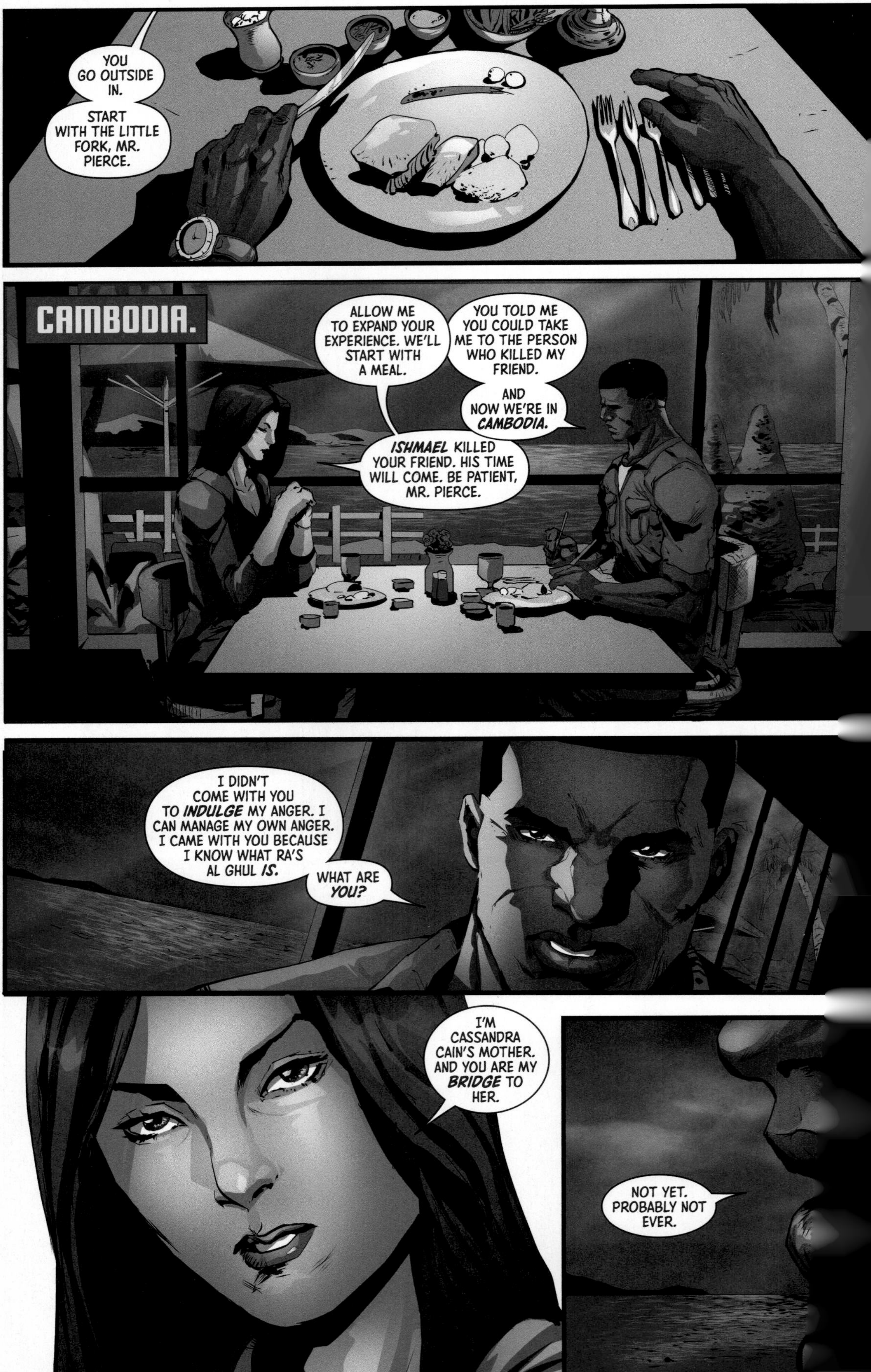
YOU GO OUTSIDE IN.
START WITH THE LITTLE FORK, MR. PIERCE.
CAMBODIA.
ALLOW ME TO EXPAND YOUR EXPERIENCE. WE'LL START WITH A MEAL.
YOU TOLD ME YOU COULD TAKE ME TO THE PERSON WHO KILLED MY FRIEND.
AND NOW WE'RE IN *CAMBODIA*.
ISHMAEL KILLED YOUR FRIEND. HIS TIME WILL COME. BE PATIENT, MR. PIERCE.
I DIDN'T COME WITH YOU TO *INDULGE* MY ANGER. I CAN MANAGE MY OWN ANGER. I CAME WITH YOU BECAUSE I KNOW WHAT RA'S AL GHUL *IS*.
WHAT ARE *YOU*?
I'M CASSANDRA CAIN'S MOTHER. AND YOU ARE MY *BRIDGE* TO HER.
NOT YET. PROBABLY NOT EVER.

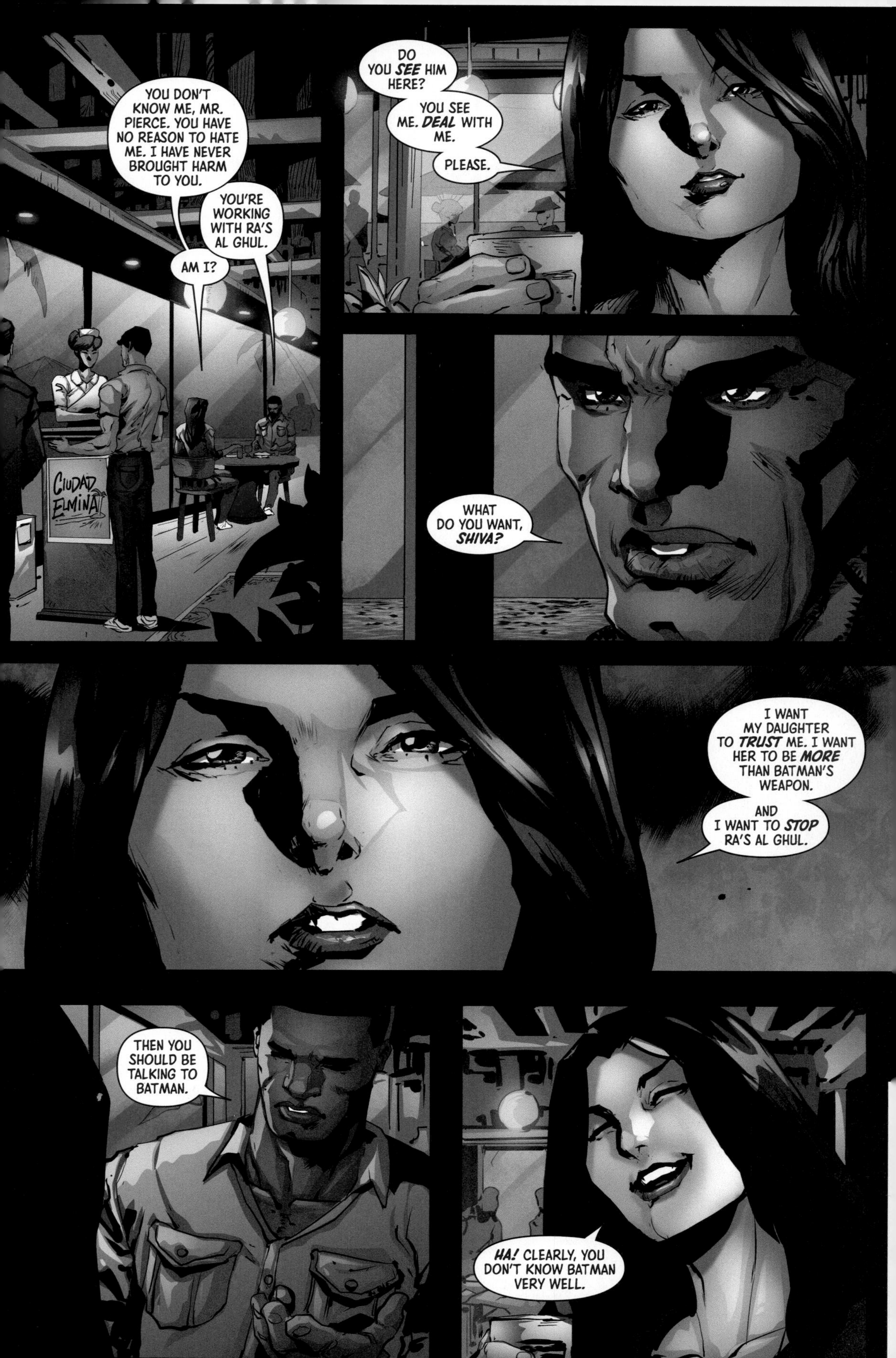

YOU DON'T KNOW ME, MR. PIERCE. YOU HAVE NO REASON TO HATE ME. I HAVE NEVER BROUGHT HARM TO YOU.
YOU'RE WORKING WITH RA'S AL GHUL.
AM I?
CIUDAD ELMINA
DO YOU *SEE* HIM HERE?
YOU SEE ME. *DEAL* WITH ME.
PLEASE.
WHAT DO YOU WANT, *SHIVA?*
I WANT MY DAUGHTER TO *TRUST* ME. I WANT HER TO BE *MORE* THAN BATMAN'S WEAPON.
AND I WANT TO *STOP* RA'S AL GHUL.
THEN YOU SHOULD BE TALKING TO BATMAN.
HA! CLEARLY, YOU DON'T KNOW BATMAN VERY WELL.

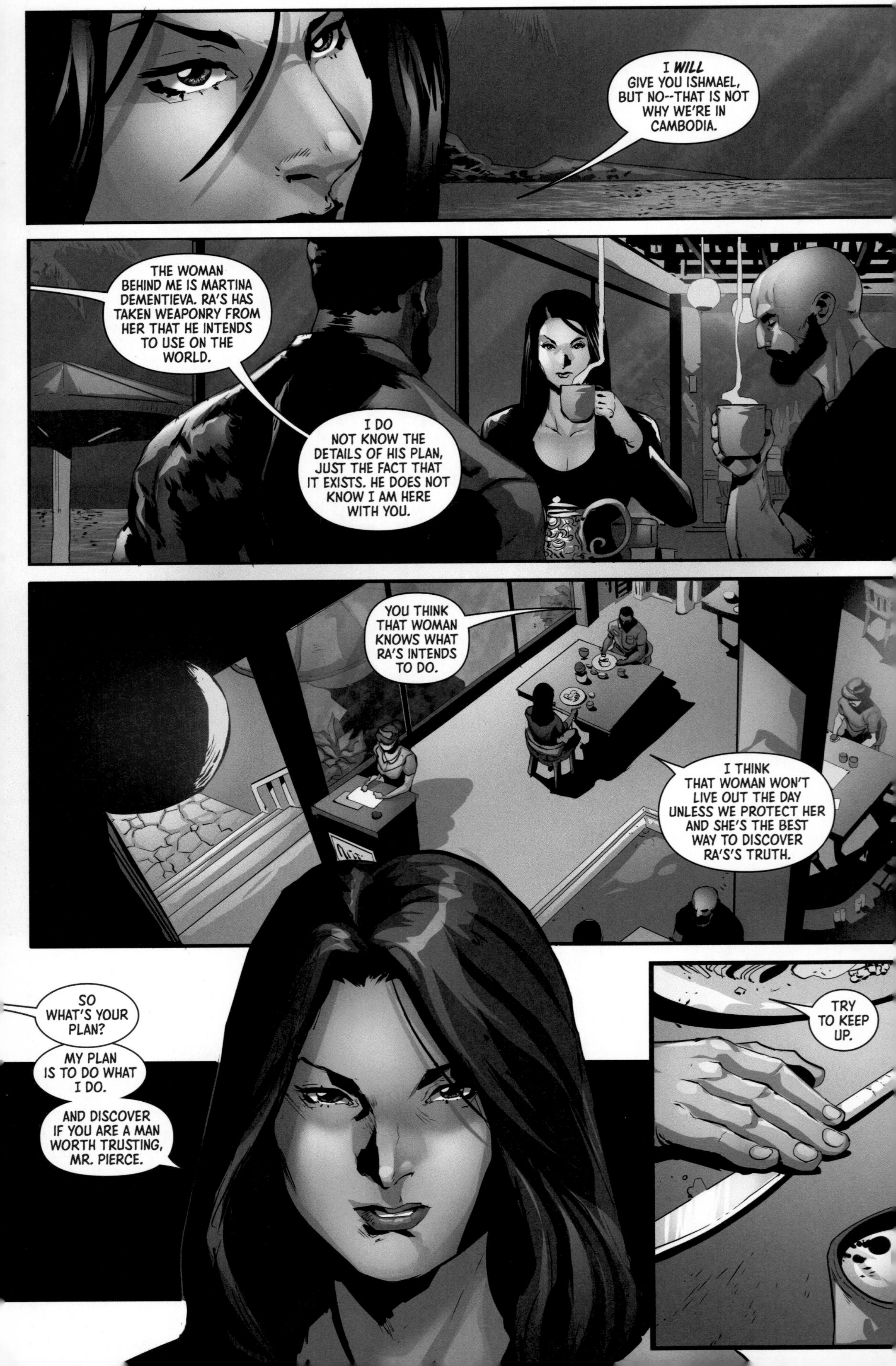
I WILL GIVE YOU ISHMAEL, BUT NO--THAT IS NOT WHY WE'RE IN CAMBODIA.
THE WOMAN BEHIND ME IS MARTINA DEMENTIEVA. RA'S HAS TAKEN WEAPONRY FROM HER THAT HE INTENDS TO USE ON THE WORLD.
I DO NOT KNOW THE DETAILS OF HIS PLAN, JUST THE FACT THAT IT EXISTS. HE DOES NOT KNOW I AM HERE WITH YOU.
YOU THINK THAT WOMAN KNOWS WHAT RA'S INTENDS TO DO.
I THINK THAT WOMAN WON'T LIVE OUT THE DAY UNLESS WE PROTECT HER AND SHE'S THE BEST WAY TO DISCOVER RA'S'S TRUTH.
SO WHAT'S YOUR PLAN?
MY PLAN IS TO DO WHAT I DO.
AND DISCOVER IF YOU ARE A MAN WORTH TRUSTING, MR. PIERCE.
TRY TO KEEP UP.

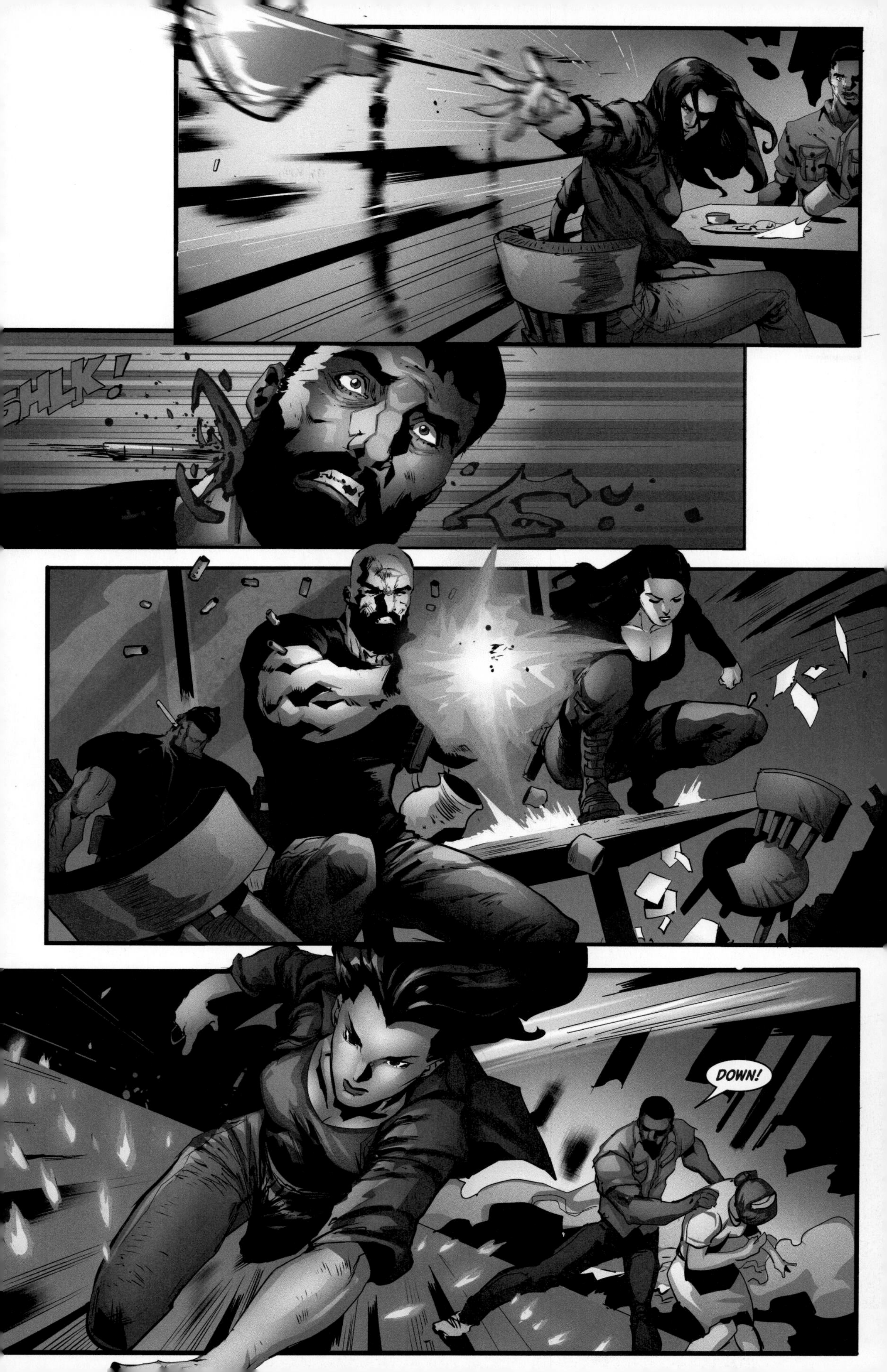
SHLK!
DOWN!

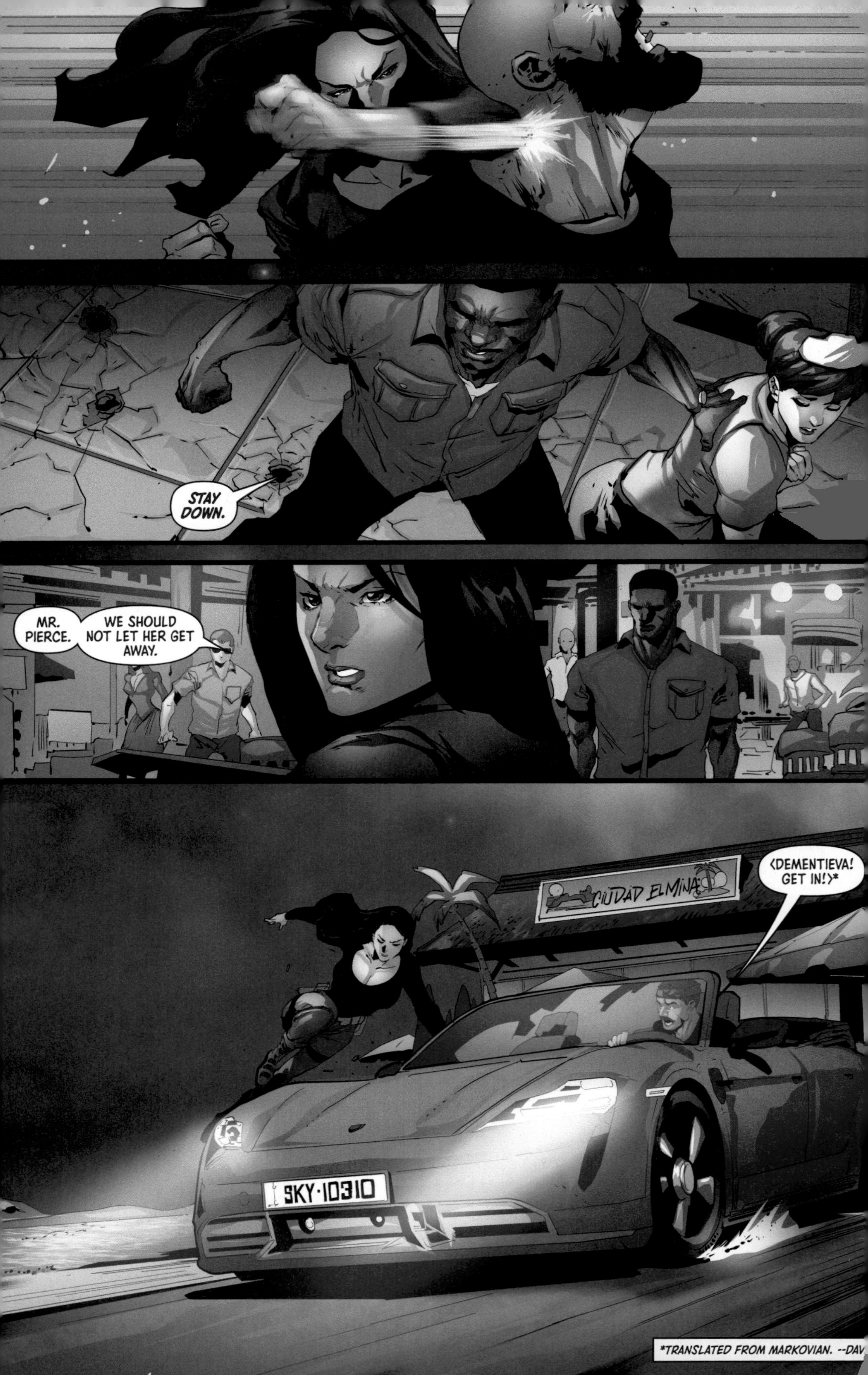
STAY DOWN.
MR. PIERCE.
WE SHOULD NOT LET HER GET AWAY.
CIUDAD ELMINA
‹DEMENTIEVA! GET IN!›*
SKY·10310
*TRANSLATED FROM MARKOVIAN. --DAV

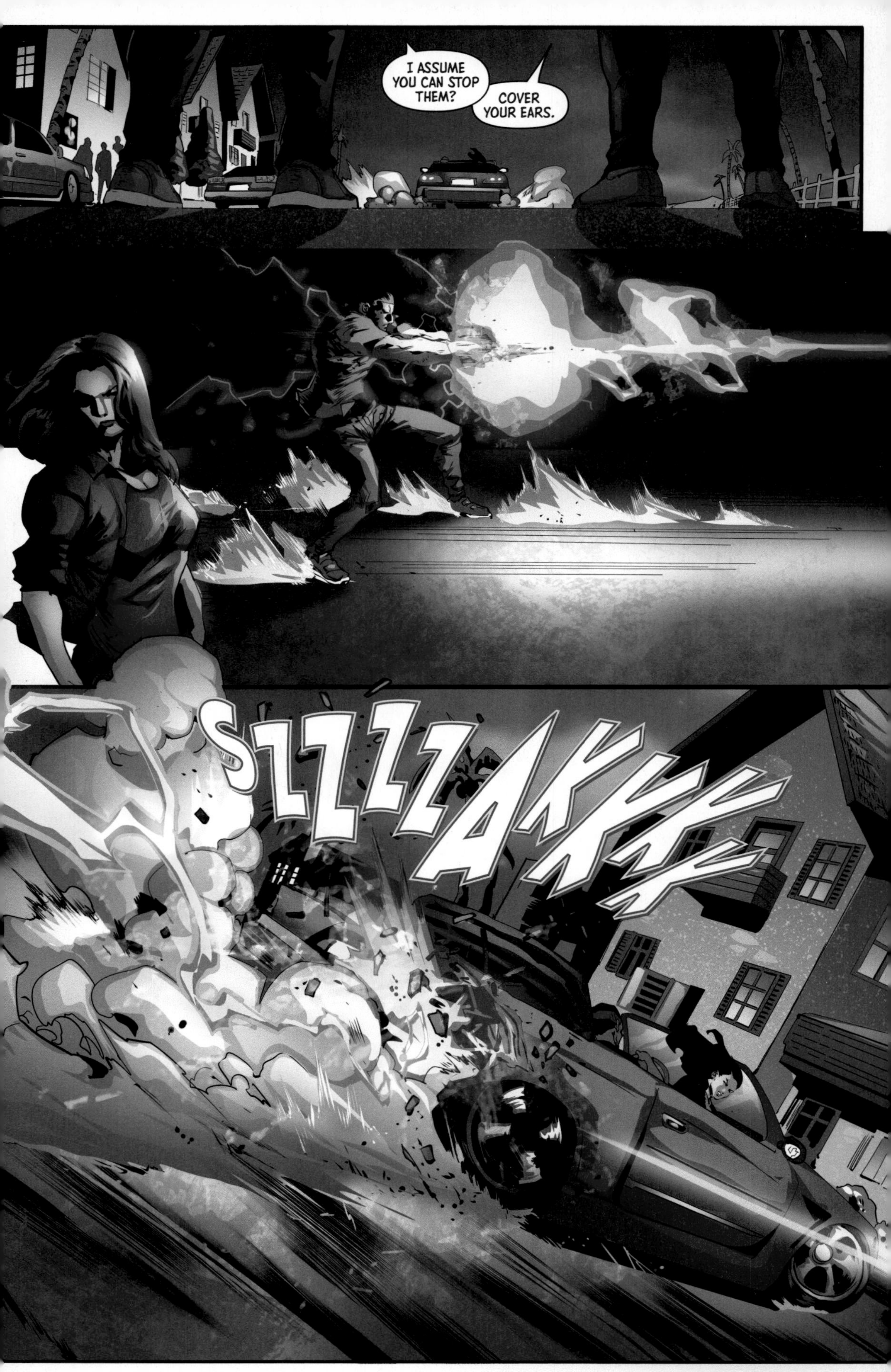
I ASSUME YOU CAN STOP THEM?
COVER YOUR EARS.
SZZZZAKKKK

<MARTINA...
HELP...NEED...
HELP...>

BANG!

<AND I
NEED BETTER
BODYGUARDS>

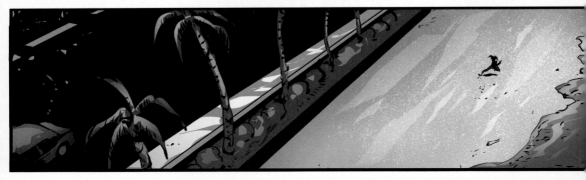

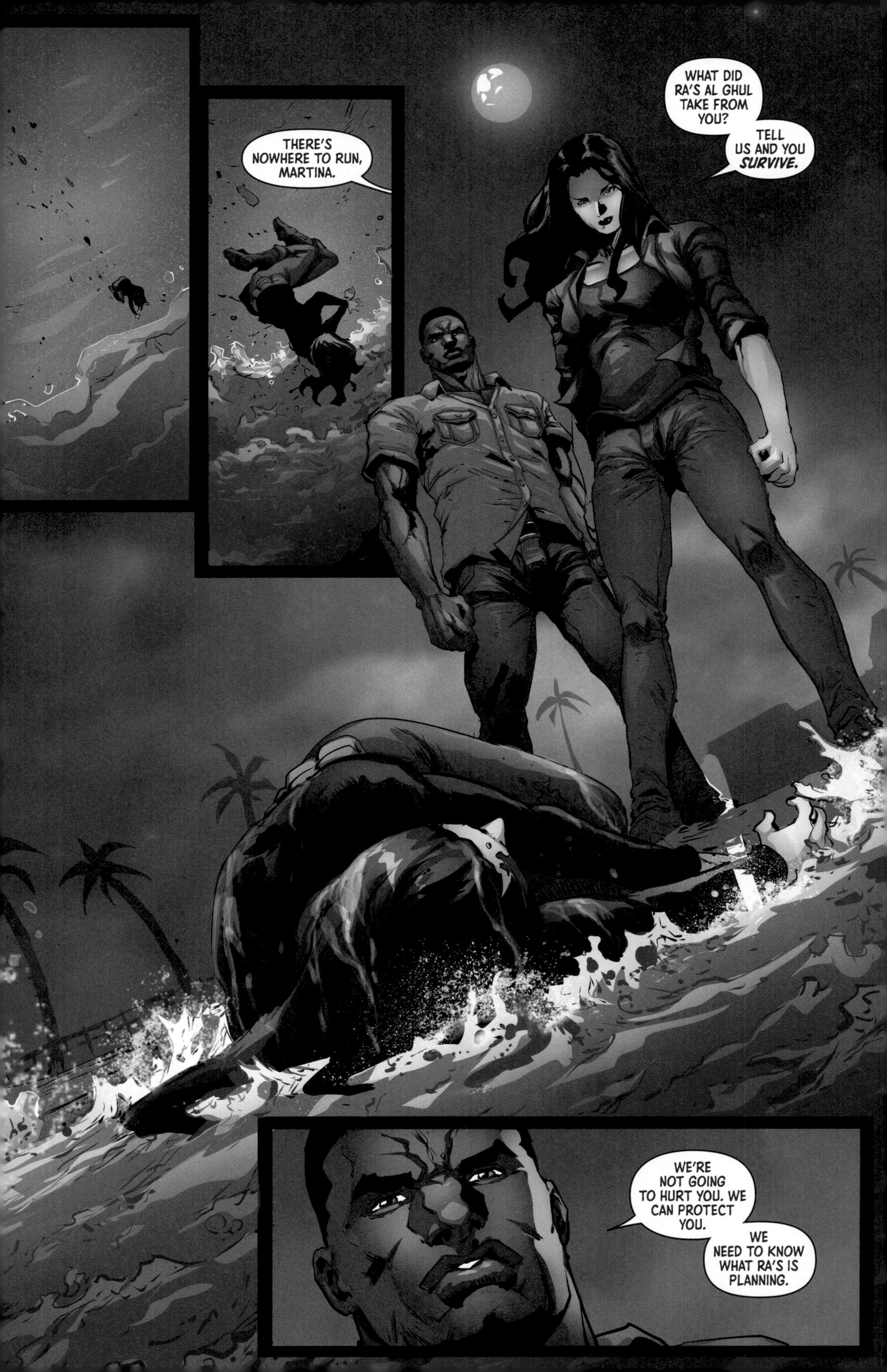
THERE'S NOWHERE TO RUN, MARTINA.
WHAT DID RA'S AL GHUL TAKE FROM YOU?
TELL US AND YOU SURVIVE.
WE'RE NOT GOING TO HURT YOU. WE CAN PROTECT YOU.
WE NEED TO KNOW WHAT RA'S IS PLANNING.

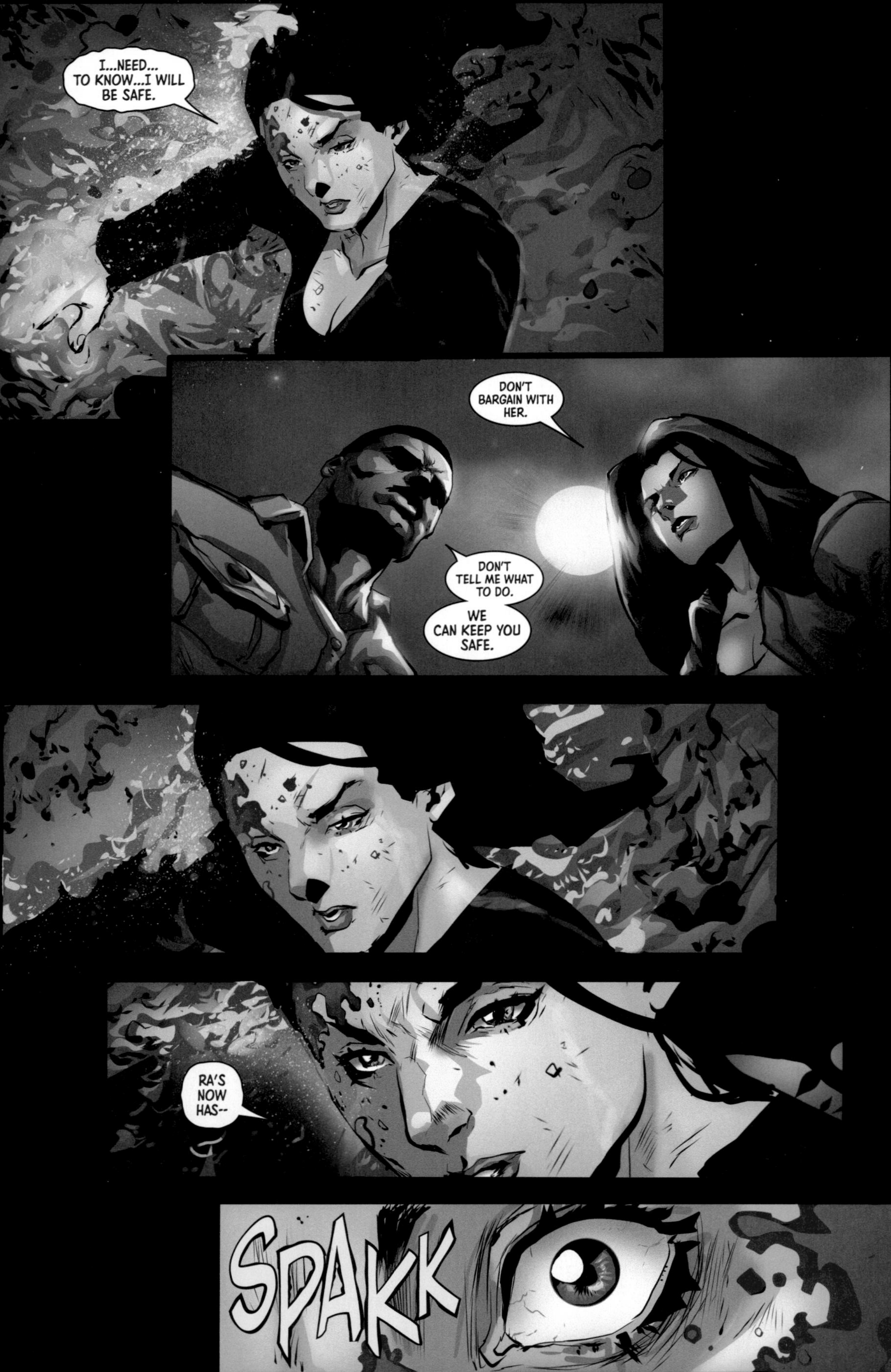
I...NEED... TO KNOW...I WILL BE SAFE.
DON'T BARGAIN WITH HER.
DON'T TELL ME WHAT TO DO.
WE CAN KEEP YOU SAFE.
RA'S NOW HAS--
SPAKK

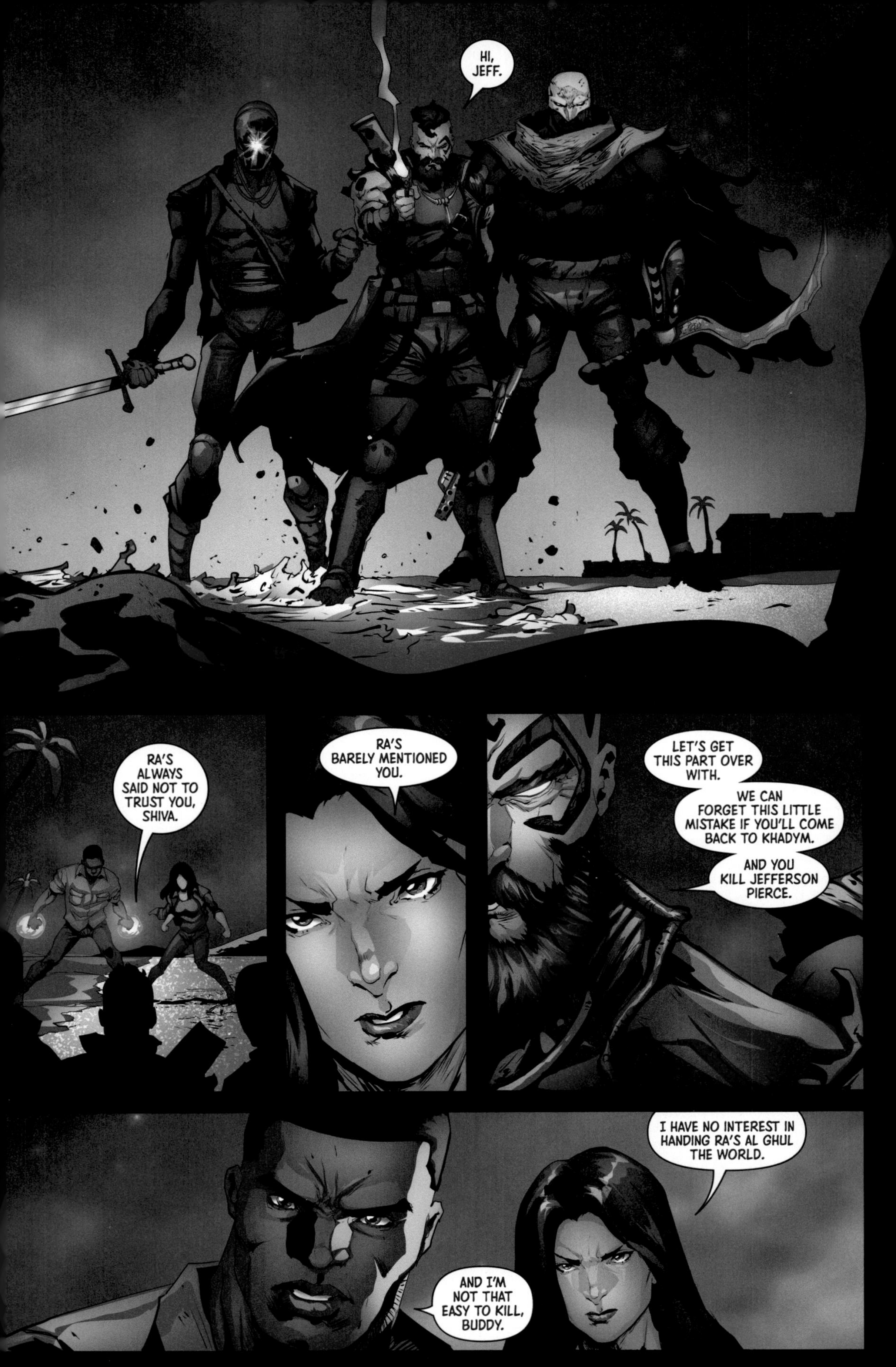
HI, JEFF.
RA'S ALWAYS SAID NOT TO TRUST YOU, SHIVA.
RA'S BARELY MENTIONED YOU.
LET'S GET THIS PART OVER WITH.
WE CAN FORGET THIS LITTLE MISTAKE IF YOU'LL COME BACK TO KHADYM.
AND YOU KILL JEFFERSON PIERCE.
I HAVE NO INTEREST IN HANDING RA'S AL GHUL THE WORLD.
AND I'M NOT THAT EASY TO KILL, BUDDY.

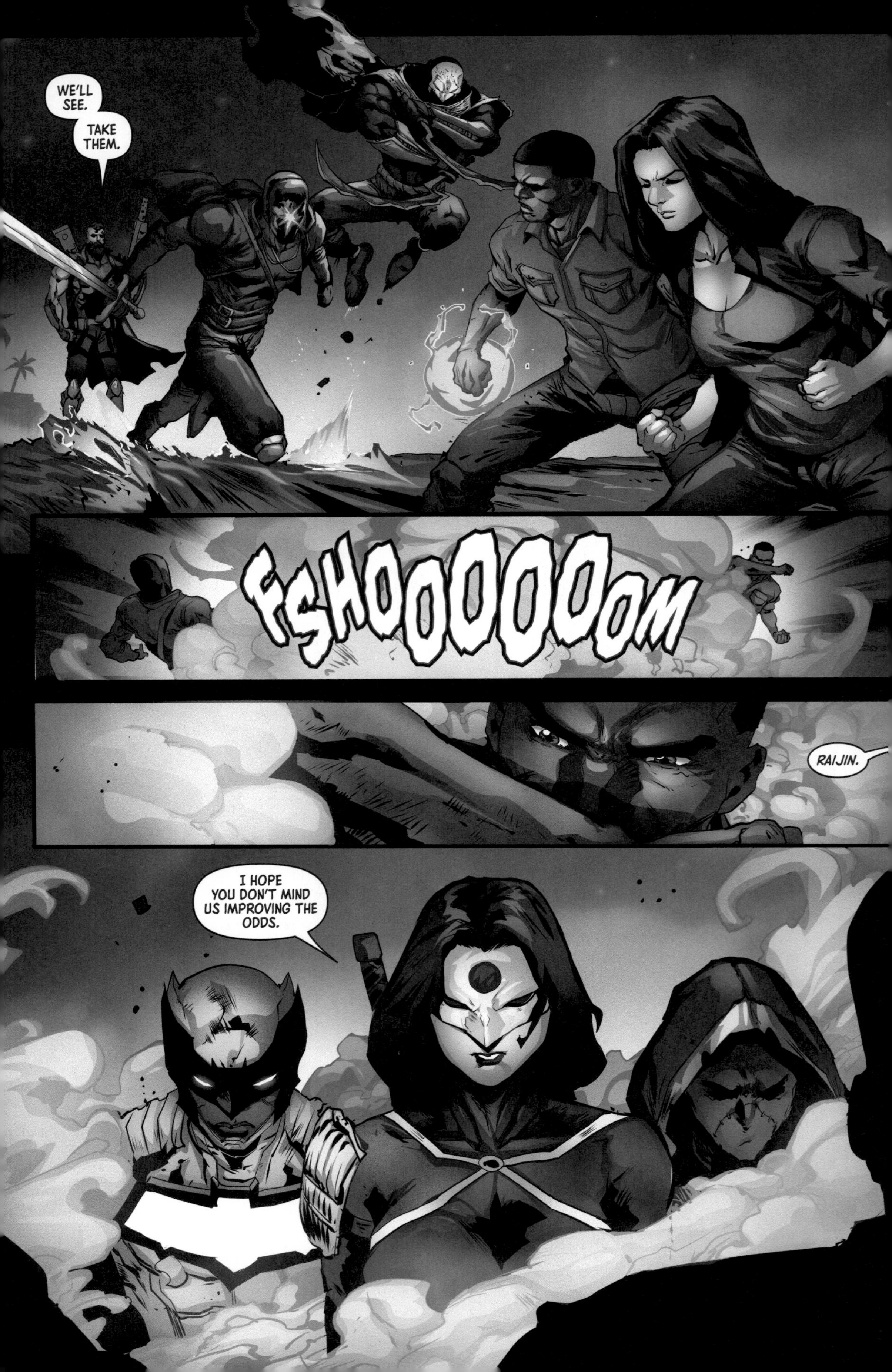
WE'LL SEE.
TAKE THEM.
FSHOOOOOOM
RAIJIN.
I HOPE YOU DON'T MIND US IMPROVING THE ODDS.

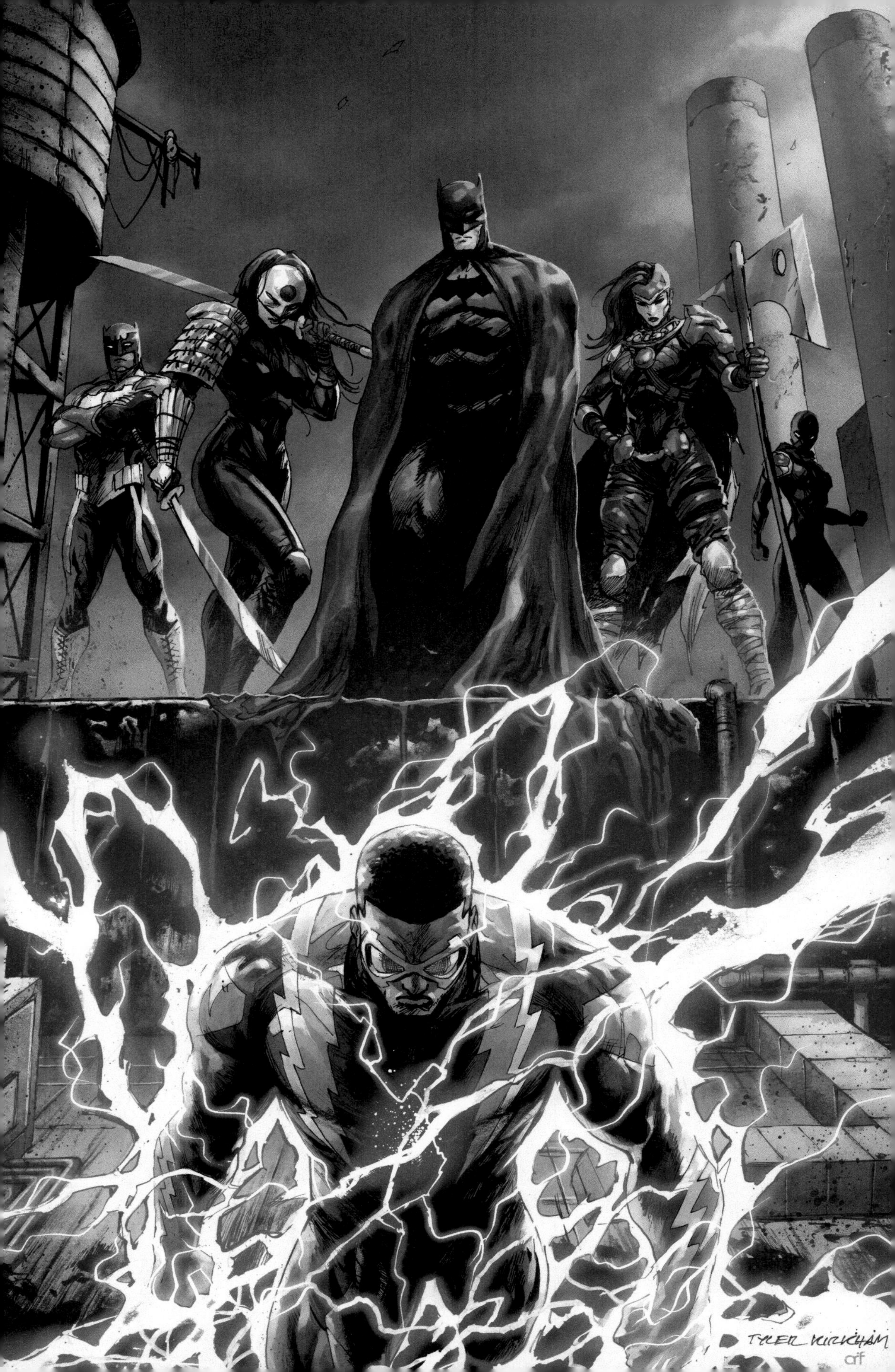
TYLER KIRKHAM
arf

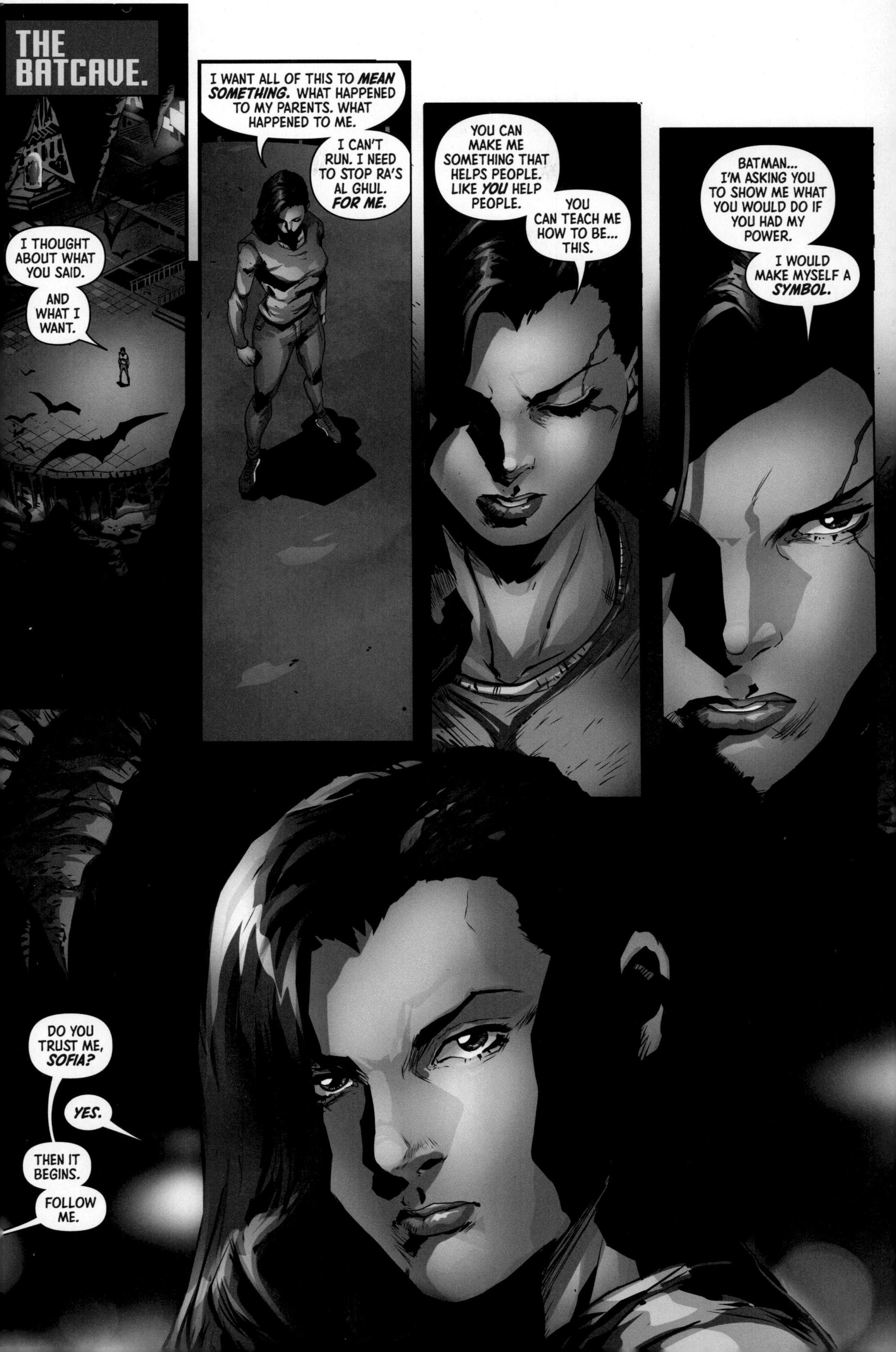
THE BATCAVE.
I THOUGHT ABOUT WHAT YOU SAID.
AND WHAT I WANT.
I WANT ALL OF THIS TO MEAN SOMETHING. WHAT HAPPENED TO MY PARENTS. WHAT HAPPENED TO ME.
I CAN'T RUN. I NEED TO STOP RA'S AL GHUL. FOR ME.
YOU CAN MAKE ME SOMETHING THAT HELPS PEOPLE. LIKE YOU HELP PEOPLE.
YOU CAN TEACH ME HOW TO BE... THIS.
BATMAN... I'M ASKING YOU TO SHOW ME WHAT YOU WOULD DO IF YOU HAD MY POWER.
I WOULD MAKE MYSELF A SYMBOL.
DO YOU TRUST ME, SOFIA?
YES.
THEN IT BEGINS.
FOLLOW ME.

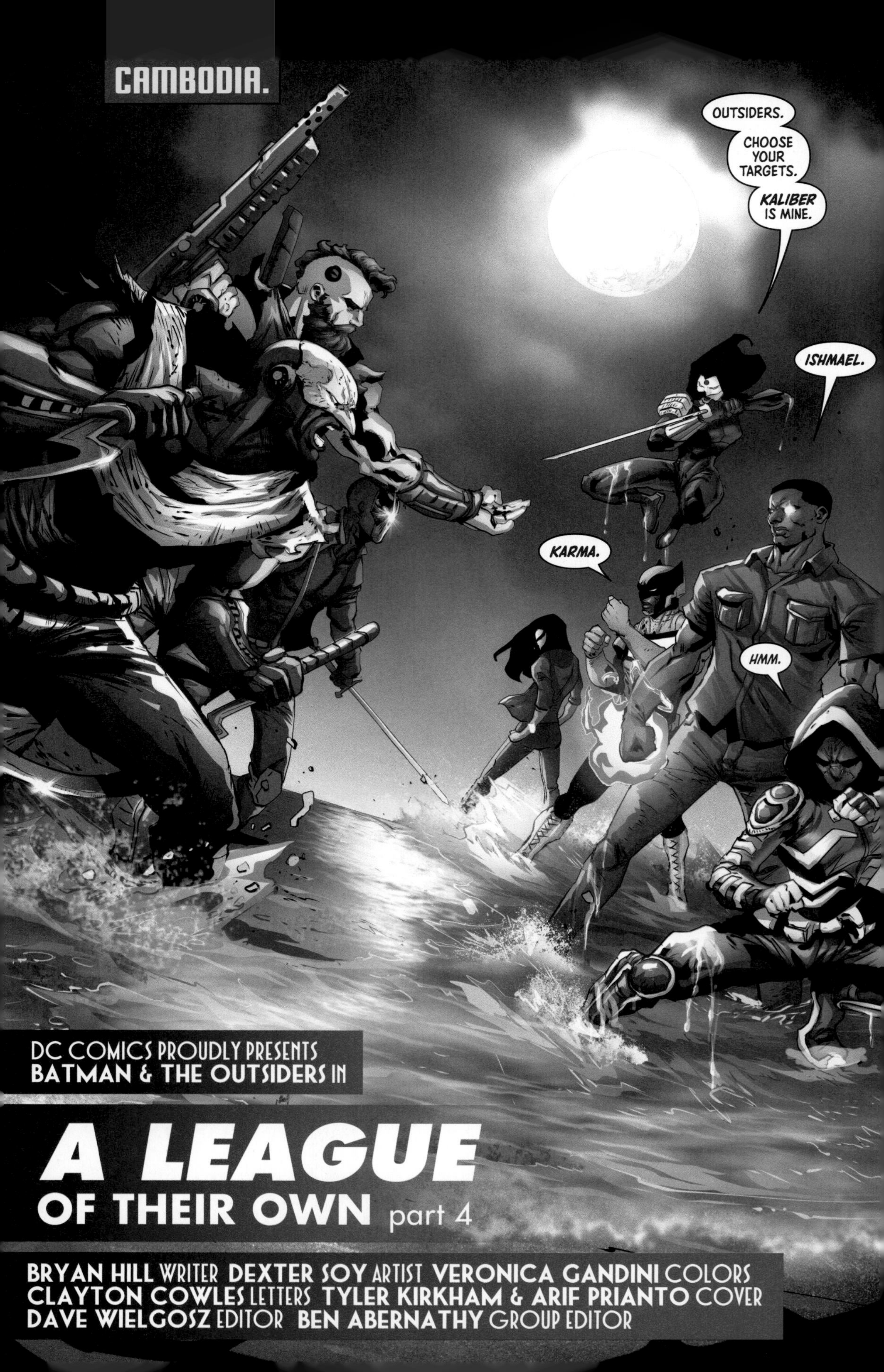
CAMBODIA.
OUTSIDERS.
CHOOSE YOUR TARGETS.
KALIBER IS MINE.
ISHMAEL.
KARMA.
HMM.
DC COMICS PROUDLY PRESENTS
BATMAN & THE OUTSIDERS IN
A LEAGUE OF THEIR OWN part 4
BRYAN HILL WRITER DEXTER SOY ARTIST VERONICA GANDINI COLORS
CLAYTON COWLES LETTERS TYLER KIRKHAM & ARIF PRIANTO COVER
DAVE WIELGOSZ EDITOR BEN ABERNATHY GROUP EDITOR

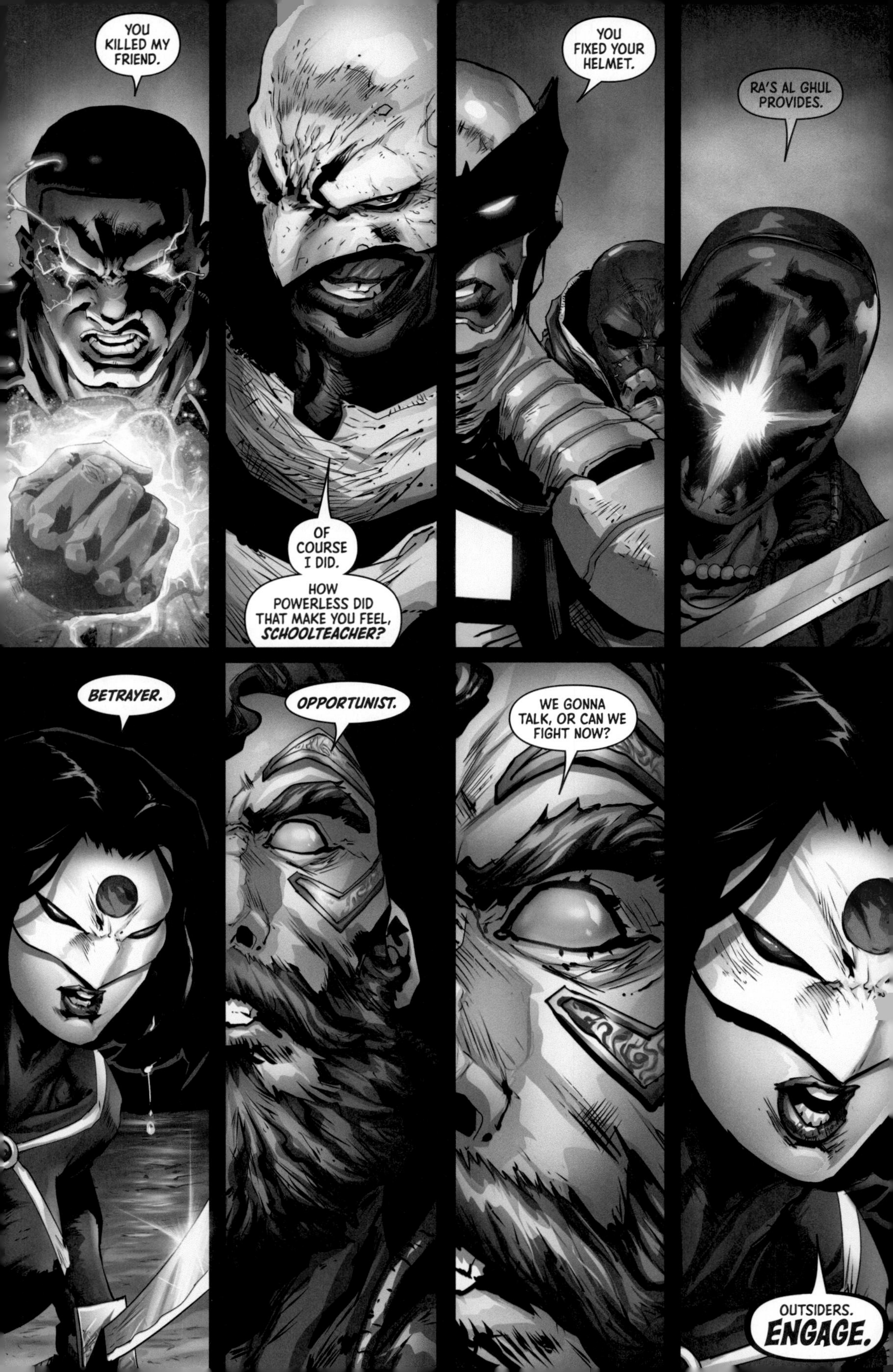
YOU KILLED MY FRIEND.
OF COURSE I DID.
HOW POWERLESS DID THAT MAKE YOU FEEL, *SCHOOLTEACHER?*
YOU FIXED YOUR HELMET.
RA'S AL GHUL PROVIDES.
BETRAYER.
OPPORTUNIST.
WE GONNA TALK, OR CAN WE FIGHT NOW?
OUTSIDERS. **ENGAGE.**

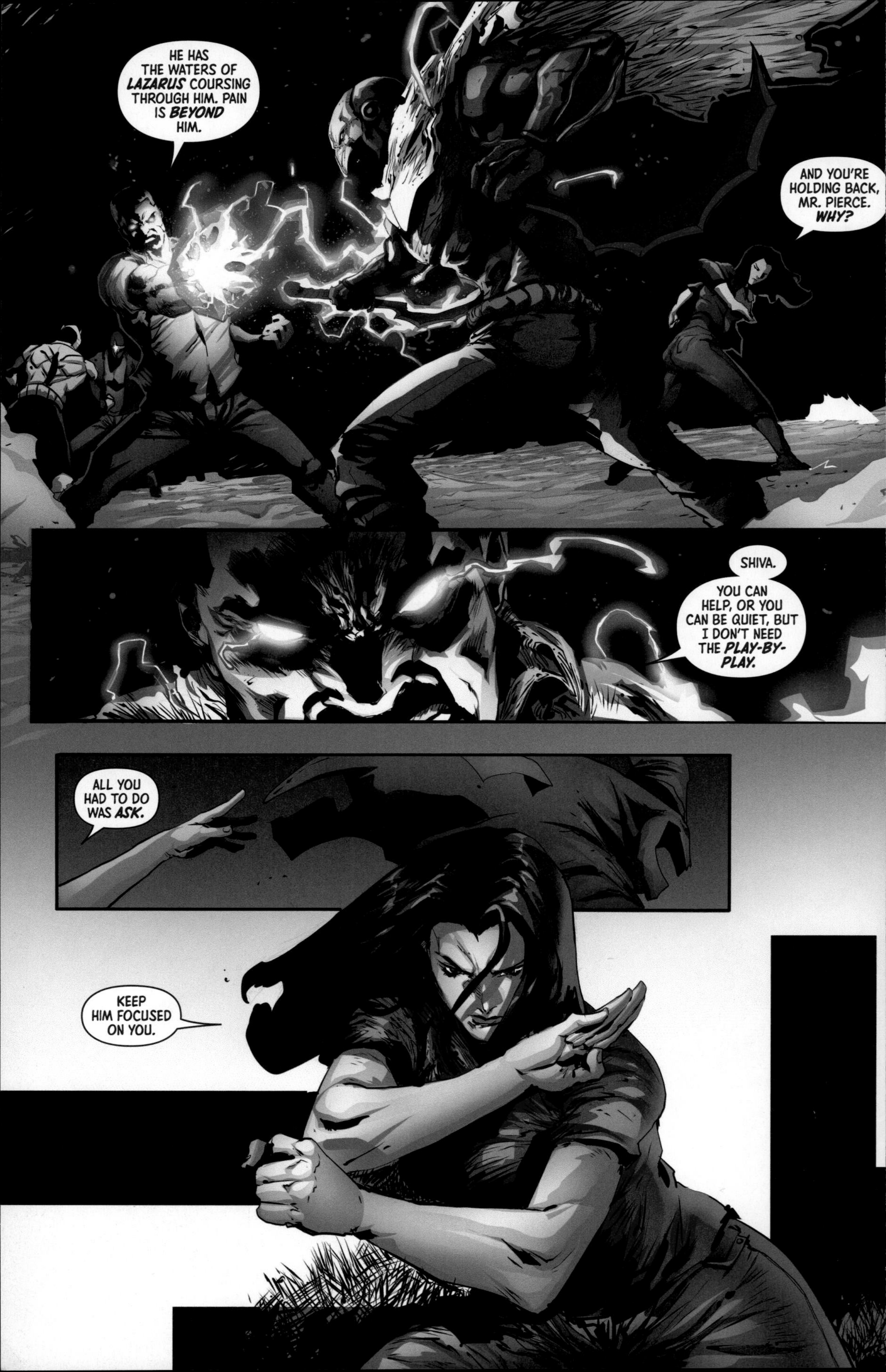
HE HAS THE WATERS OF *LAZARUS* COURSING THROUGH HIM. PAIN IS *BEYOND* HIM.
AND YOU'RE HOLDING BACK, MR. PIERCE. *WHY?*
SHIVA.
YOU CAN HELP, OR YOU CAN BE QUIET, BUT I DON'T NEED THE *PLAY-BY-PLAY.*
ALL YOU HAD TO DO WAS *ASK.*
KEEP HIM FOCUSED ON YOU.

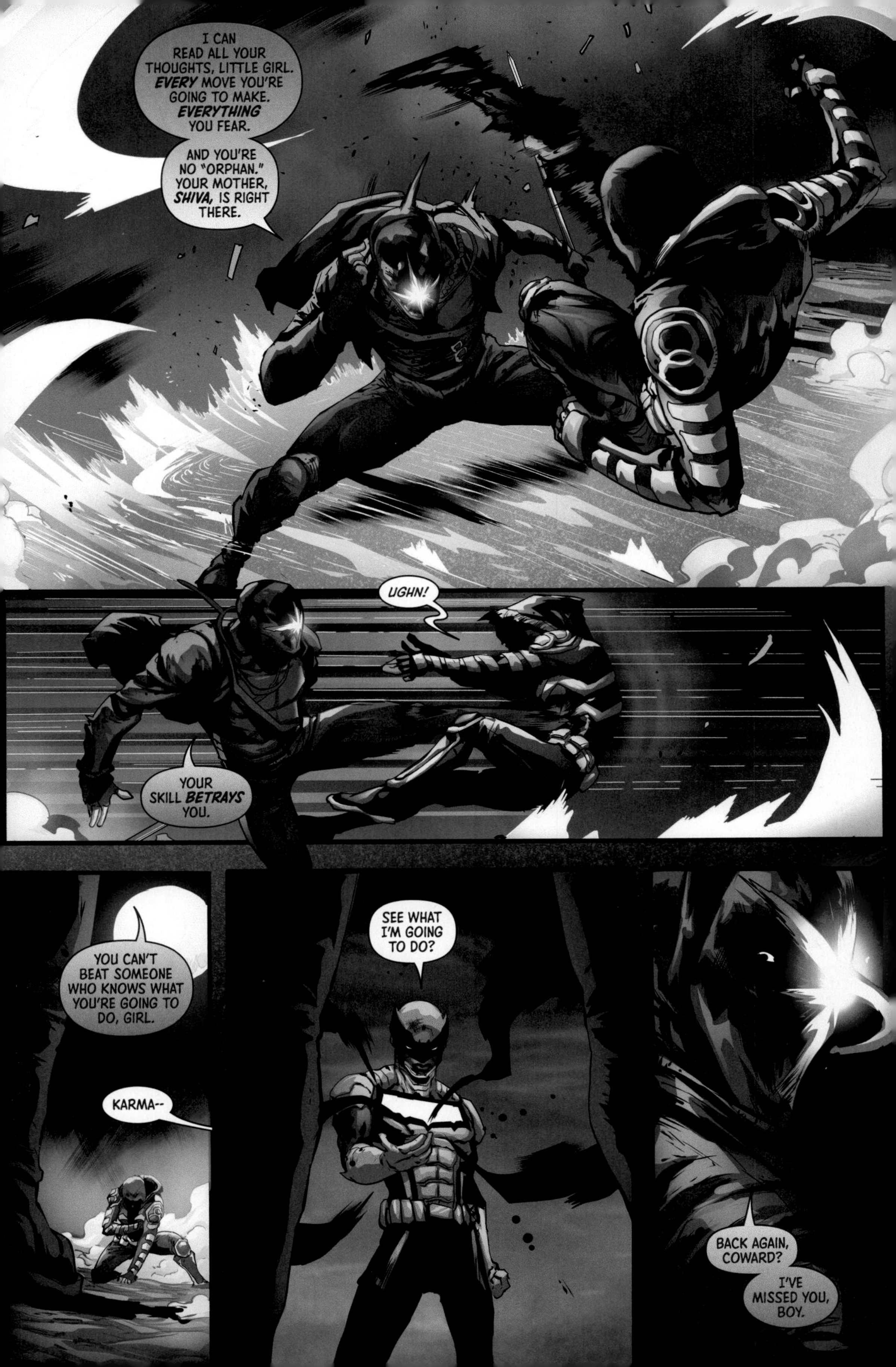
I CAN READ ALL YOUR THOUGHTS, LITTLE GIRL. EVERY MOVE YOU'RE GOING TO MAKE. EVERYTHING YOU FEAR.
AND YOU'RE NO "ORPHAN." YOUR MOTHER, SHIVA, IS RIGHT THERE.
UGHN!
YOUR SKILL BETRAYS YOU.
YOU CAN'T BEAT SOMEONE WHO KNOWS WHAT YOU'RE GOING TO DO, GIRL.
KARMA--
SEE WHAT I'M GOING TO DO?
BACK AGAIN, COWARD?
I'VE MISSED YOU, BOY.

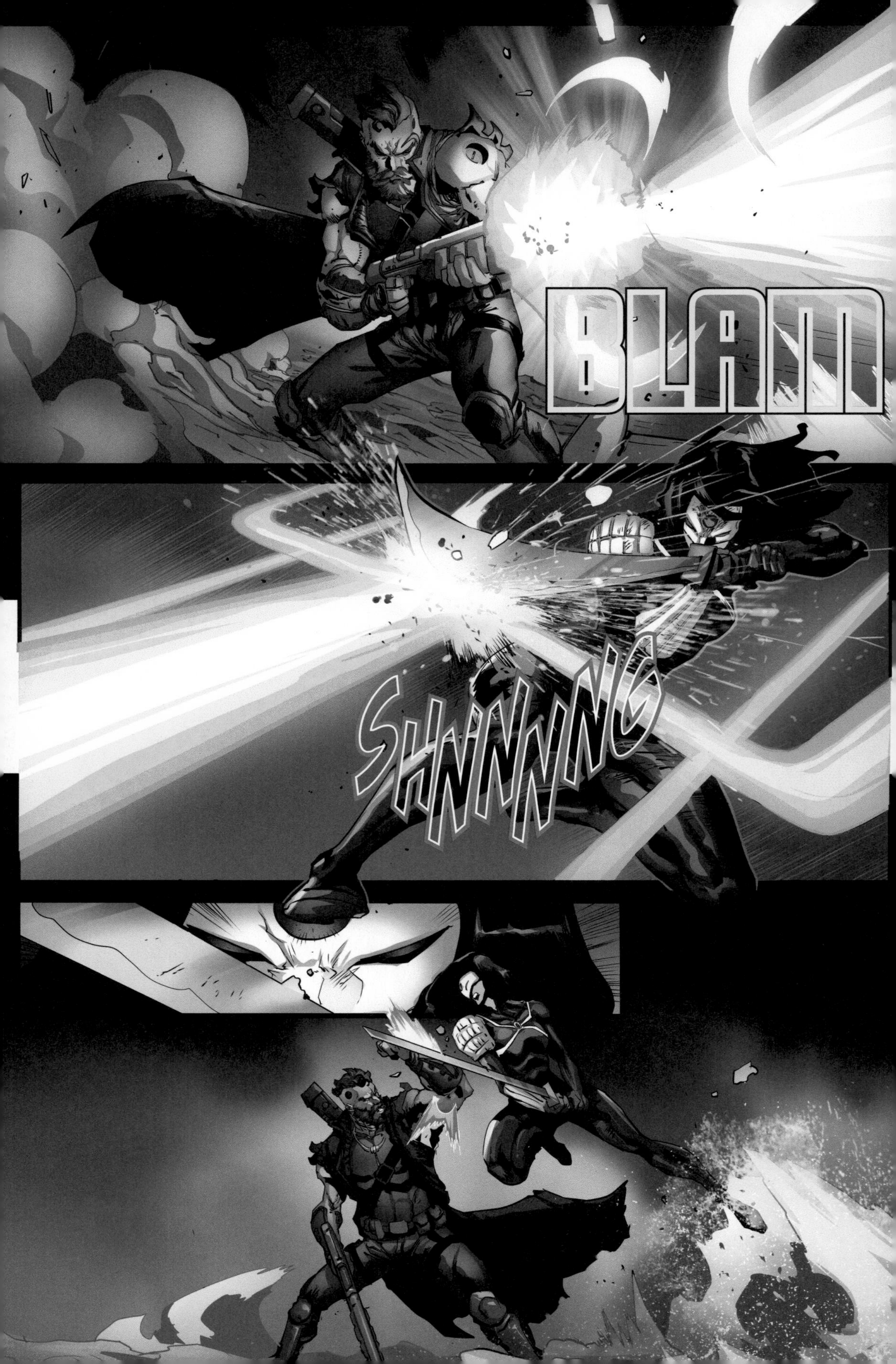
BLAM
SHNNNNG

MR.
PIERCE.

THREE--

TWO--

ONE--

NOW--WHILE HE'S
LOST FOCUS!

KRAK

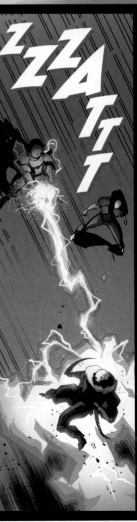

ZZZATT

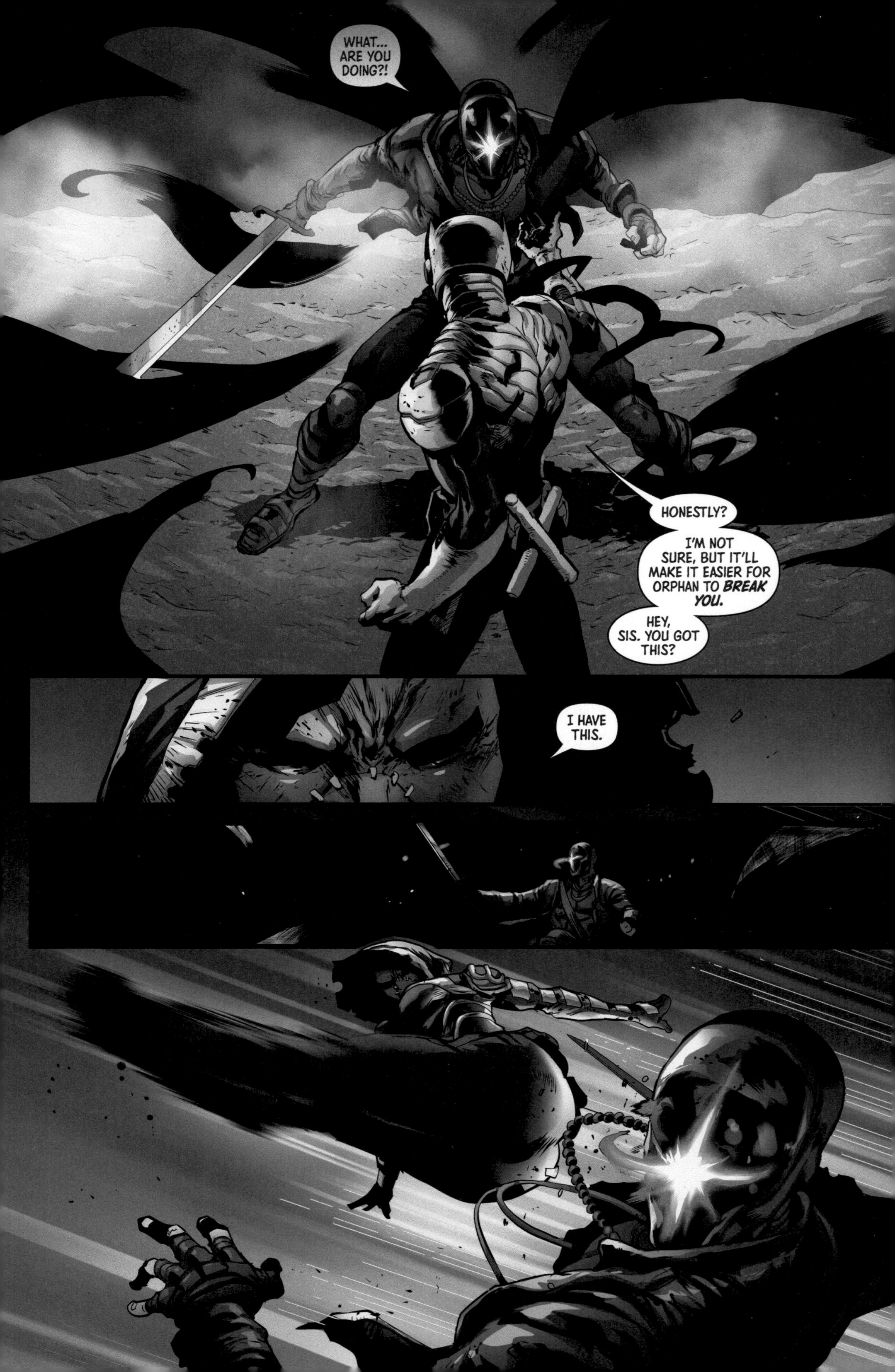
WHAT... ARE YOU DOING?!
HONESTLY?
I'M NOT SURE, BUT IT'LL MAKE IT EASIER FOR ORPHAN TO **BREAK YOU.**
HEY, SIS. YOU GOT THIS?
I HAVE THIS.

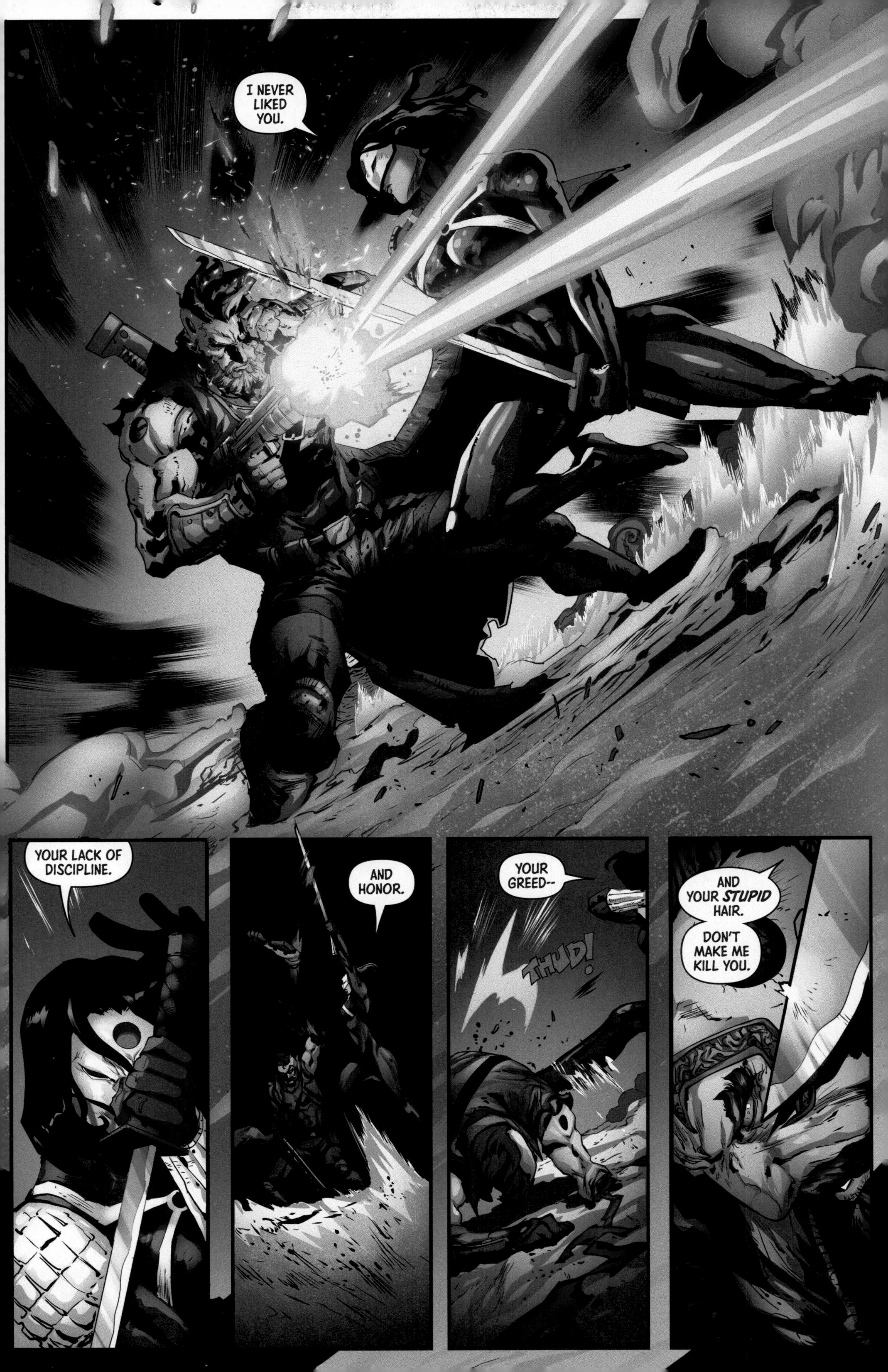
I NEVER LIKED YOU.
YOUR LACK OF DISCIPLINE.
AND HONOR.
YOUR GREED--
THUD!
AND YOUR STUPID HAIR.
DON'T MAKE ME KILL YOU.

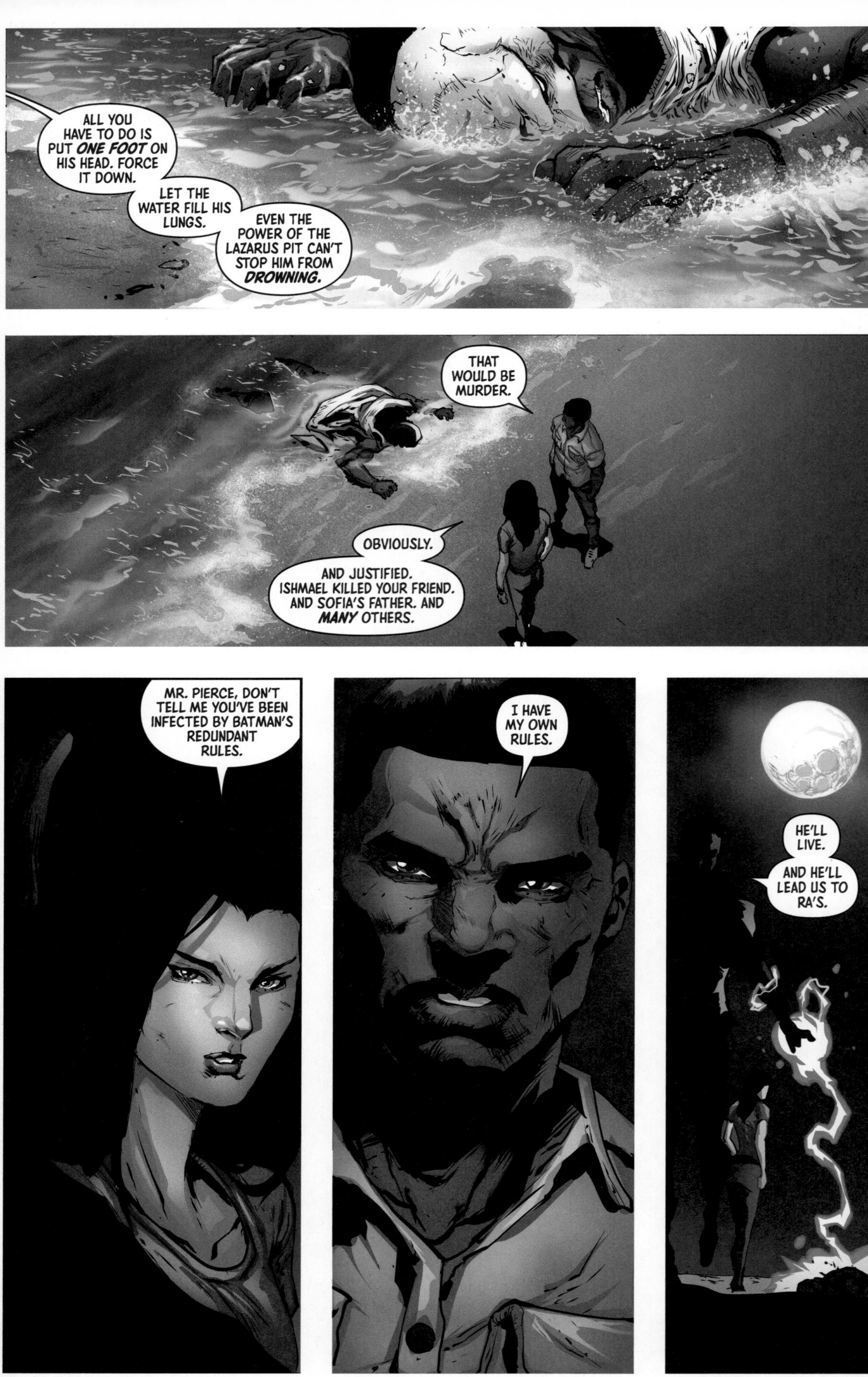
ALL YOU HAVE TO DO IS PUT *ONE FOOT* ON HIS HEAD. FORCE IT DOWN.
LET THE WATER FILL HIS LUNGS.
EVEN THE POWER OF THE LAZARUS PIT CAN'T STOP HIM FROM *DROWNING.*
THAT WOULD BE MURDER.
OBVIOUSLY.
AND JUSTIFIED. ISHMAEL KILLED YOUR FRIEND. AND SOFIA'S FATHER. AND *MANY* OTHERS.
MR. PIERCE, DON'T TELL ME YOU'VE BEEN INFECTED BY BATMAN'S REDUNDANT RULES.
I HAVE MY OWN RULES.
HE'LL LIVE.
AND HE'LL LEAD US TO RA'S.

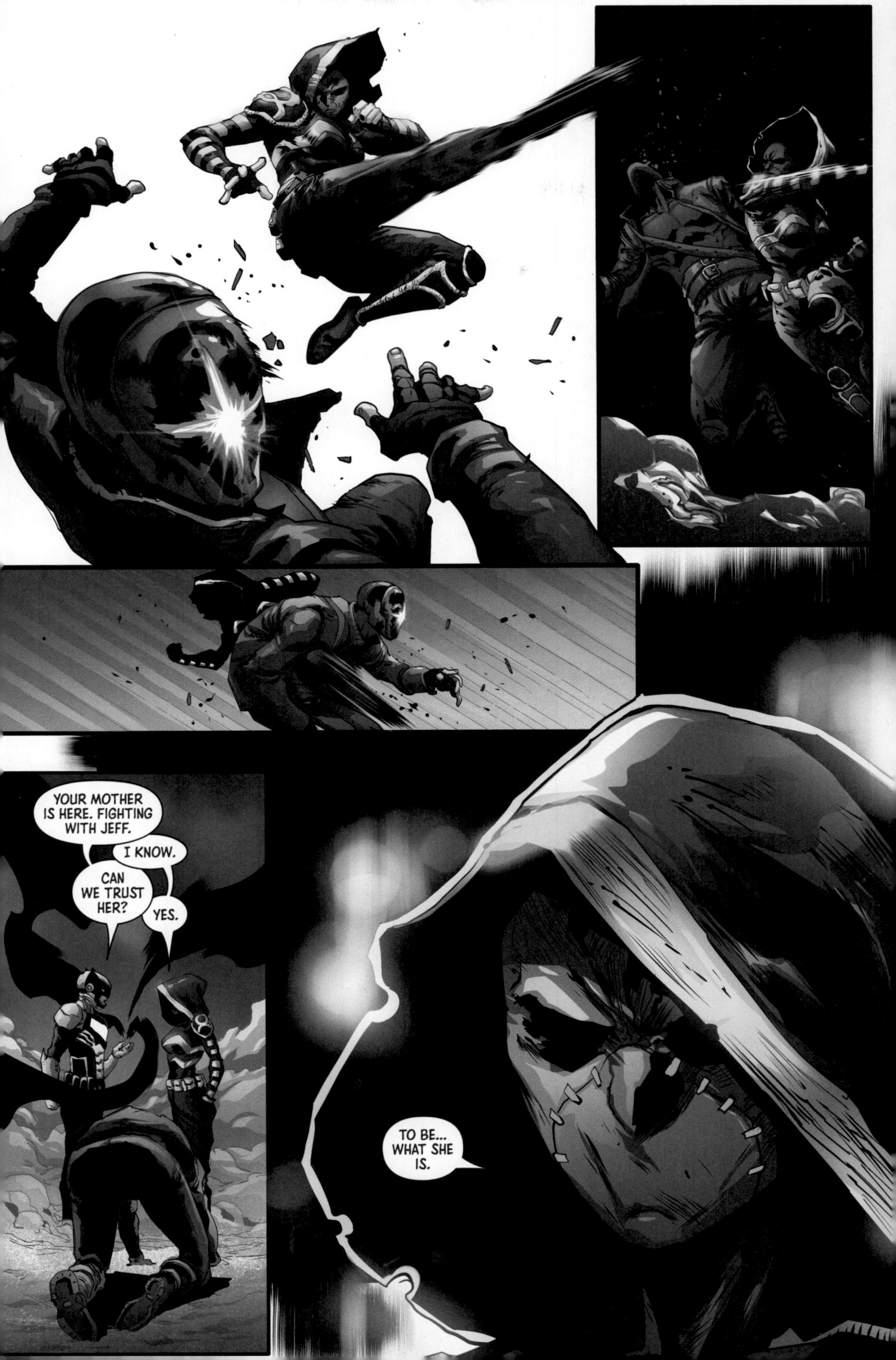

YOUR MOTHER IS HERE. FIGHTING WITH JEFF.
I KNOW.
CAN WE TRUST HER?
YES.
TO BE... WHAT SHE IS.

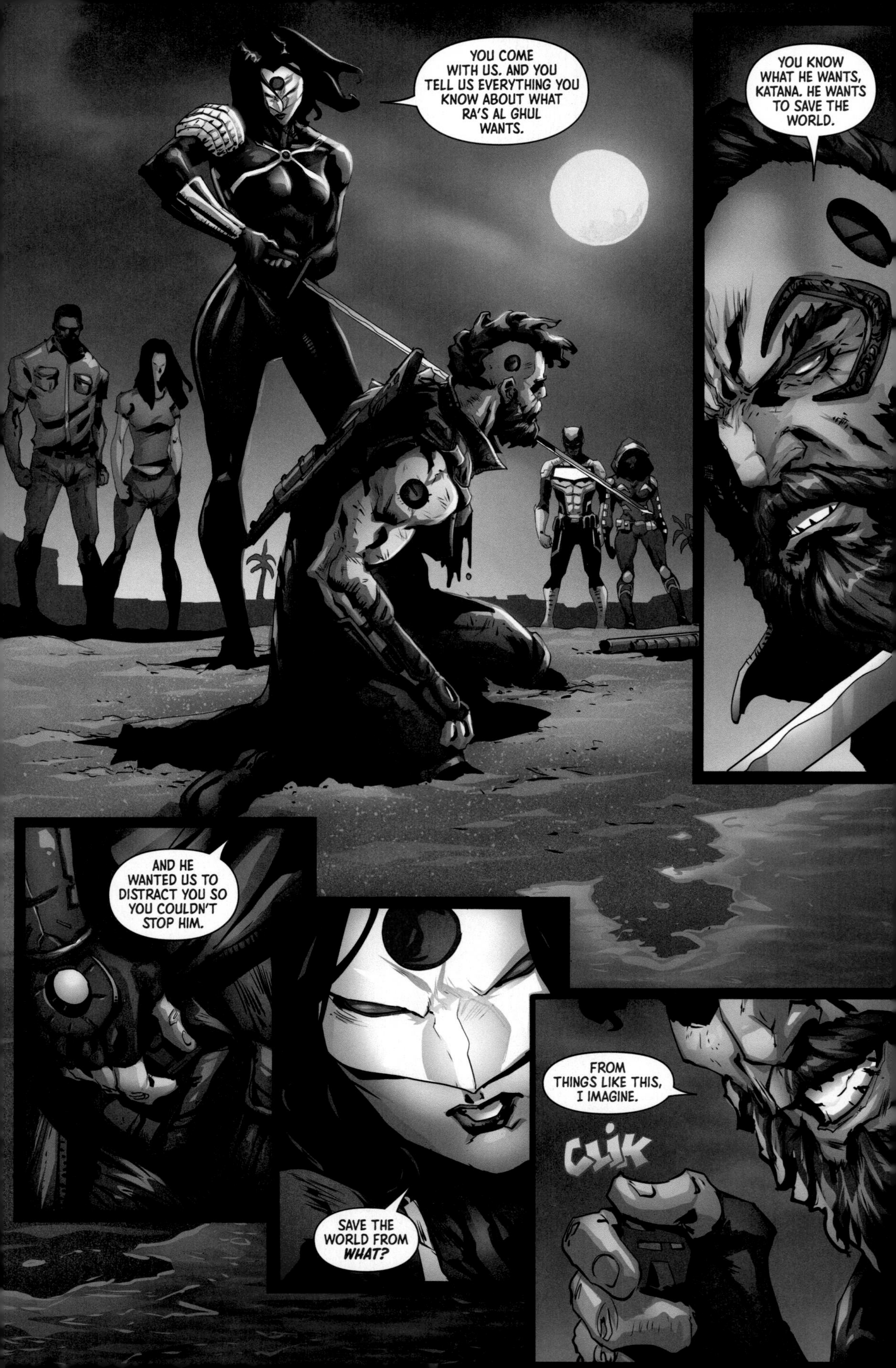
YOU COME WITH US. AND YOU TELL US EVERYTHING YOU KNOW ABOUT WHAT RA'S AL GHUL WANTS.
YOU KNOW WHAT HE WANTS, KATANA. HE WANTS TO SAVE THE WORLD.
AND HE WANTED US TO DISTRACT YOU SO YOU COULDN'T STOP HIM.
SAVE THE WORLD FROM *WHAT?*
FROM THINGS LIKE THIS, I IMAGINE.
CLIK

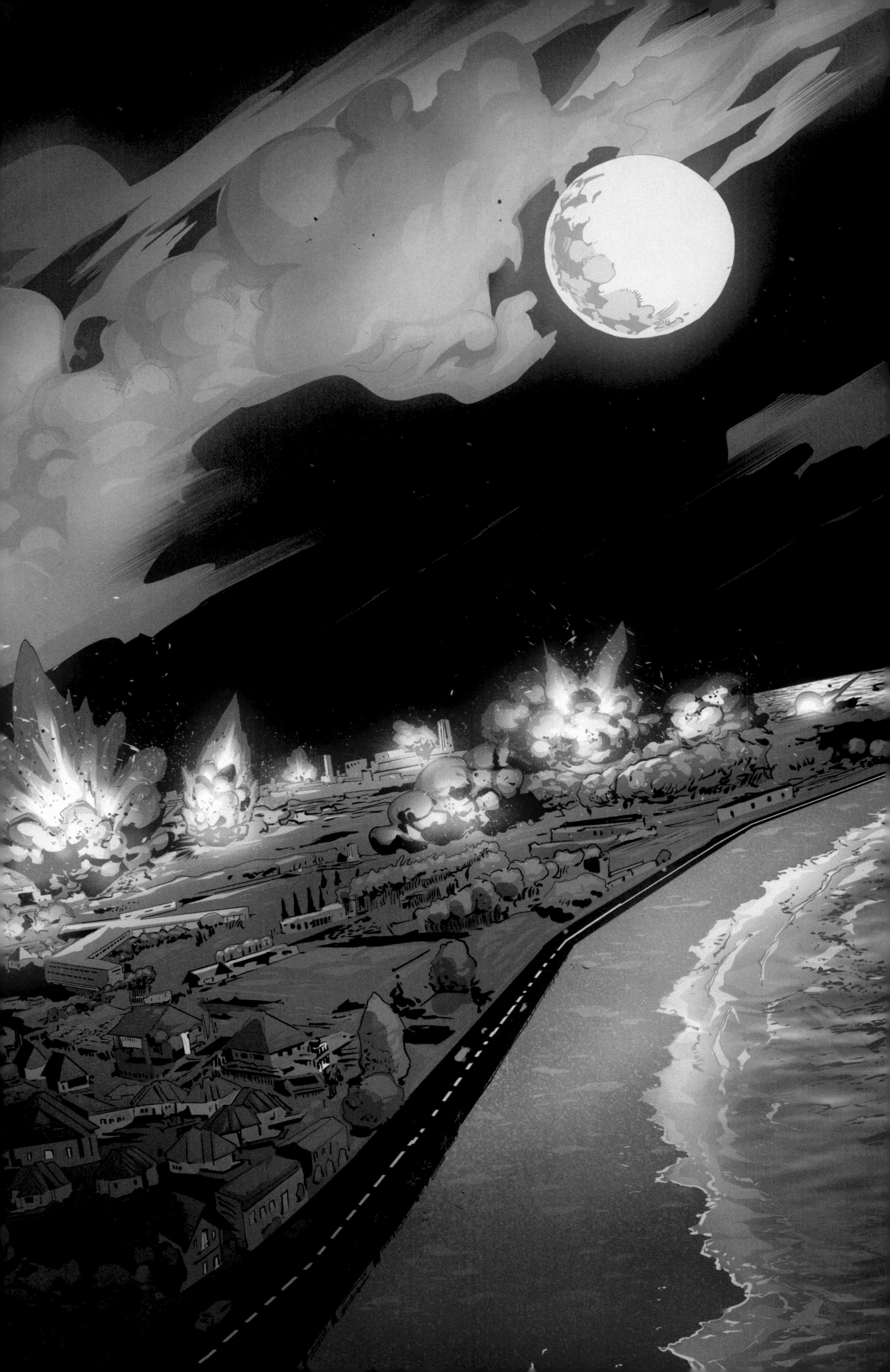

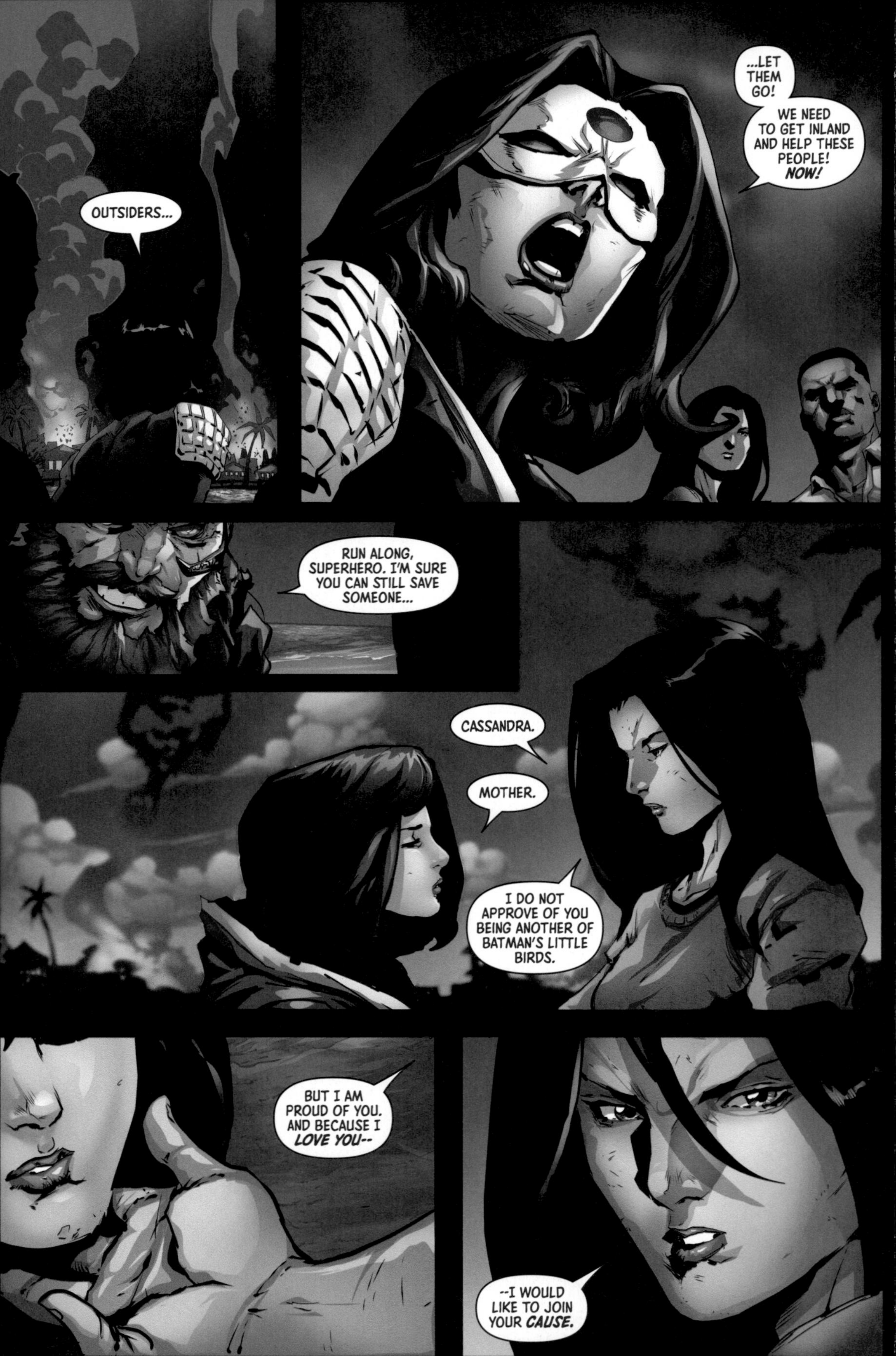
OUTSIDERS...
...LET THEM GO!
WE NEED TO GET INLAND AND HELP THESE PEOPLE! NOW!
RUN ALONG, SUPERHERO. I'M SURE YOU CAN STILL SAVE SOMEONE...
CASSANDRA.
MOTHER.
I DO NOT APPROVE OF YOU BEING ANOTHER OF BATMAN'S LITTLE BIRDS.
BUT I AM PROUD OF YOU. AND BECAUSE I LOVE YOU--
--I WOULD LIKE TO JOIN YOUR CAUSE.

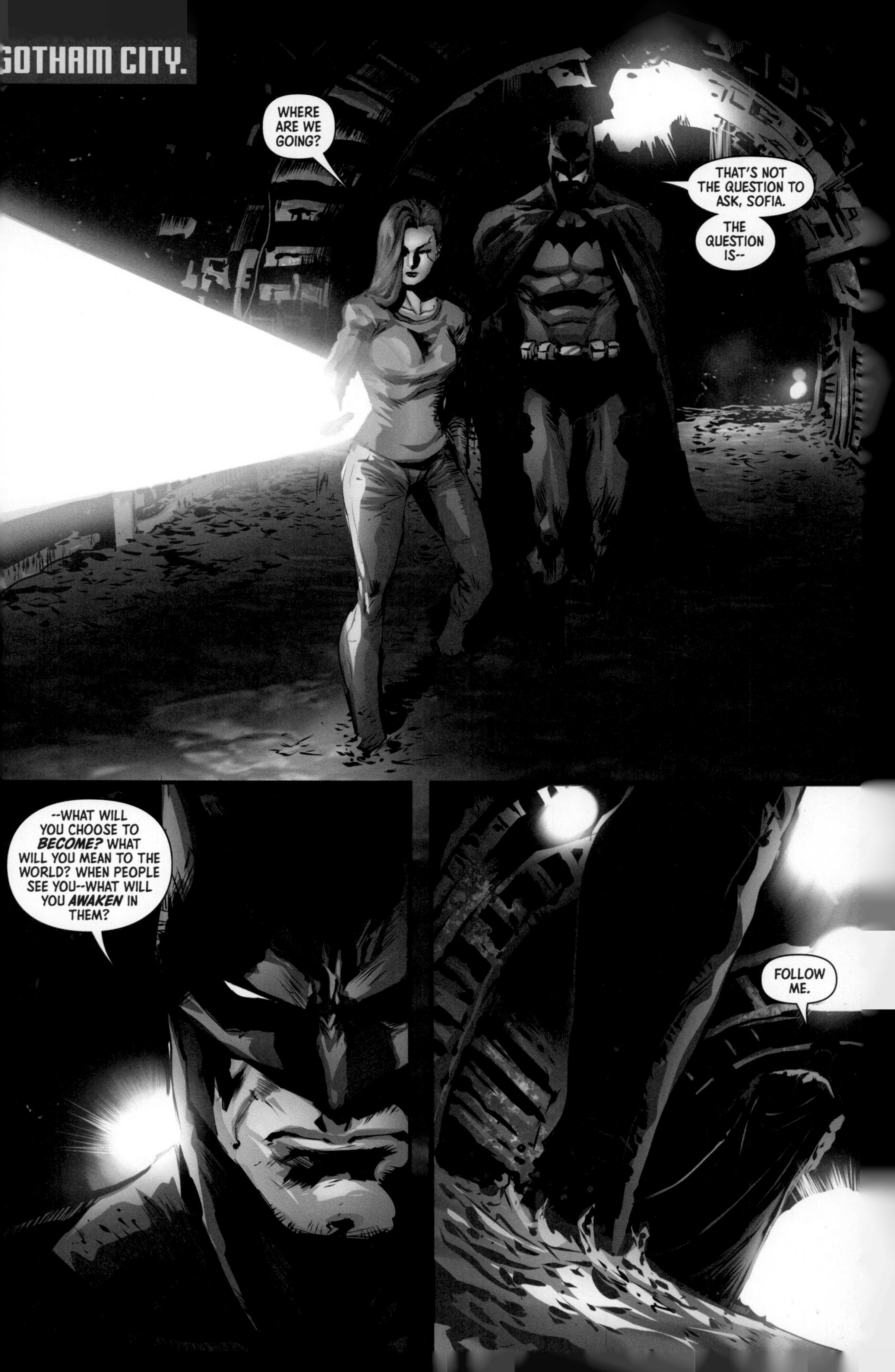
GOTHAM CITY.
WHERE ARE WE GOING?
THAT'S NOT THE QUESTION TO ASK, SOFIA.
THE QUESTION IS--
--WHAT WILL YOU CHOOSE TO *BECOME?* WHAT WILL YOU MEAN TO THE WORLD? WHEN PEOPLE SEE YOU--WHAT WILL YOU *AWAKEN* IN THEM?
FOLLOW ME.

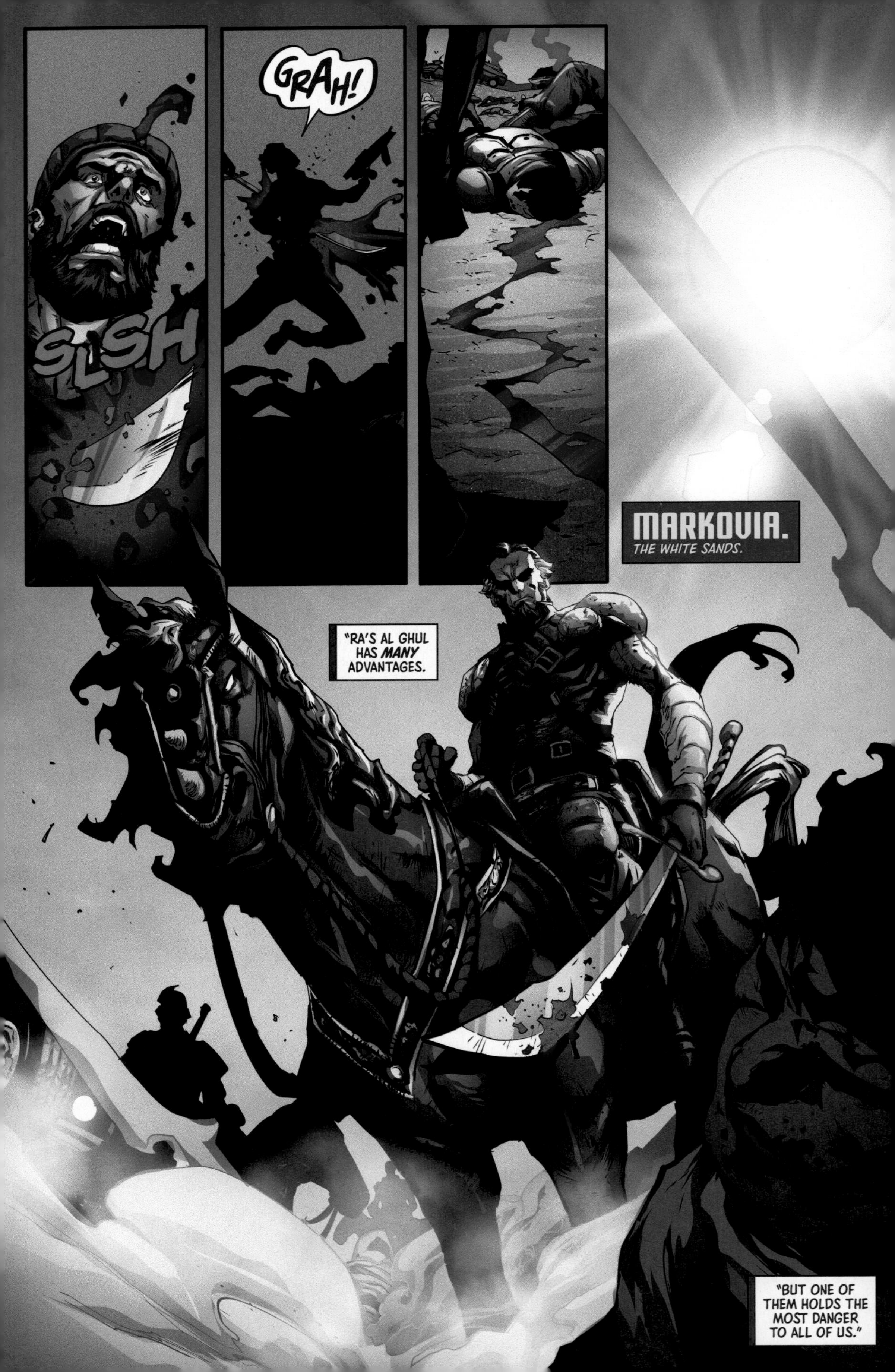
SLSH
GRAH!
MARKOVIA.
THE WHITE SANDS.
"RA'S AL GHUL HAS *MANY* ADVANTAGES.
"BUT ONE OF THEM HOLDS THE MOST DANGER TO ALL OF US."

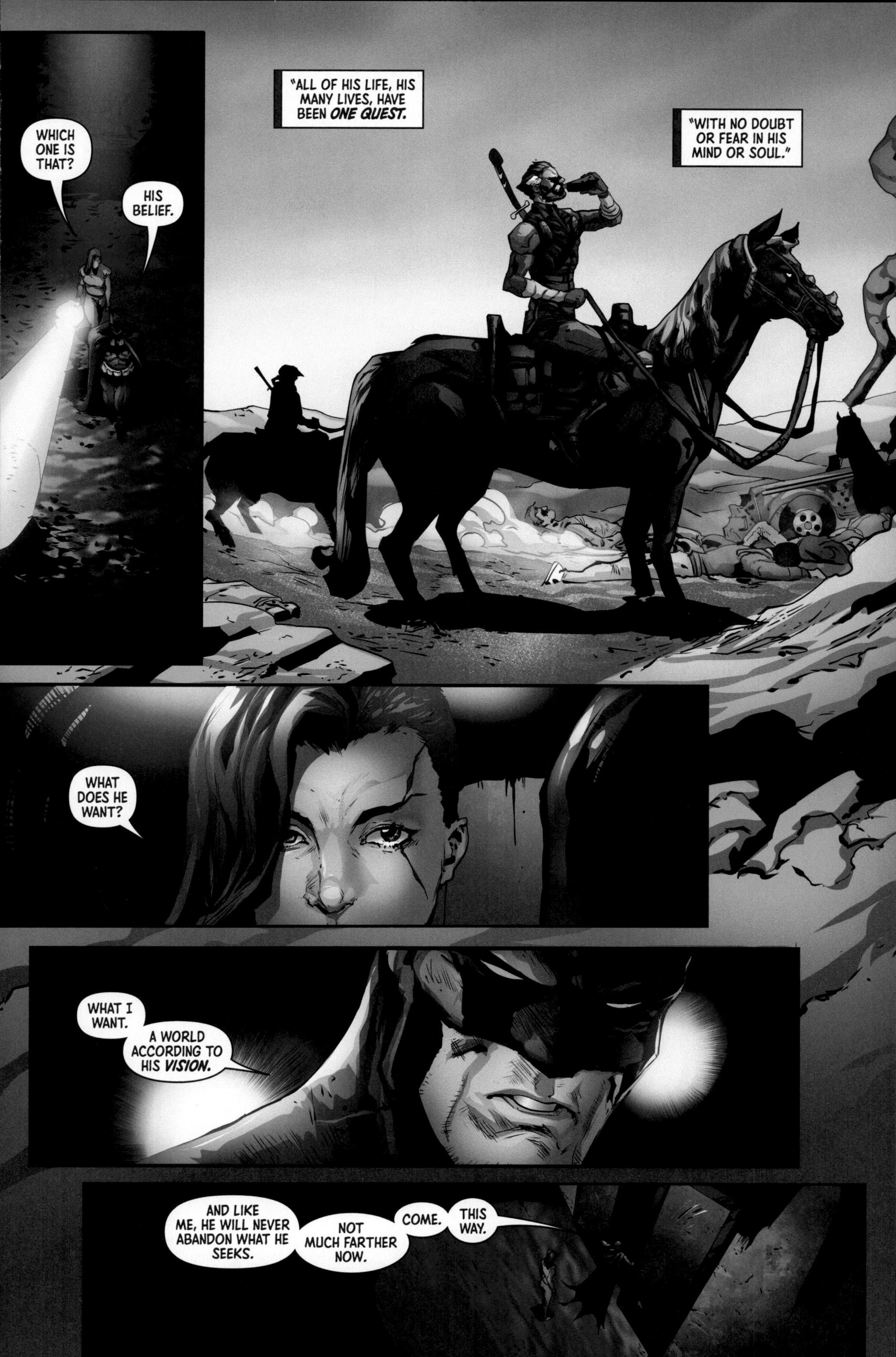
"ALL OF HIS LIFE, HIS MANY LIVES, HAVE BEEN ONE QUEST.
WHICH ONE IS THAT?
HIS BELIEF.
"WITH NO DOUBT OR FEAR IN HIS MIND OR SOUL."
WHAT DOES HE WANT?
WHAT I WANT.
A WORLD ACCORDING TO HIS VISION.
AND LIKE ME, HE WILL NEVER ABANDON WHAT HE SEEKS.
NOT MUCH FARTHER NOW.
COME.
THIS WAY.

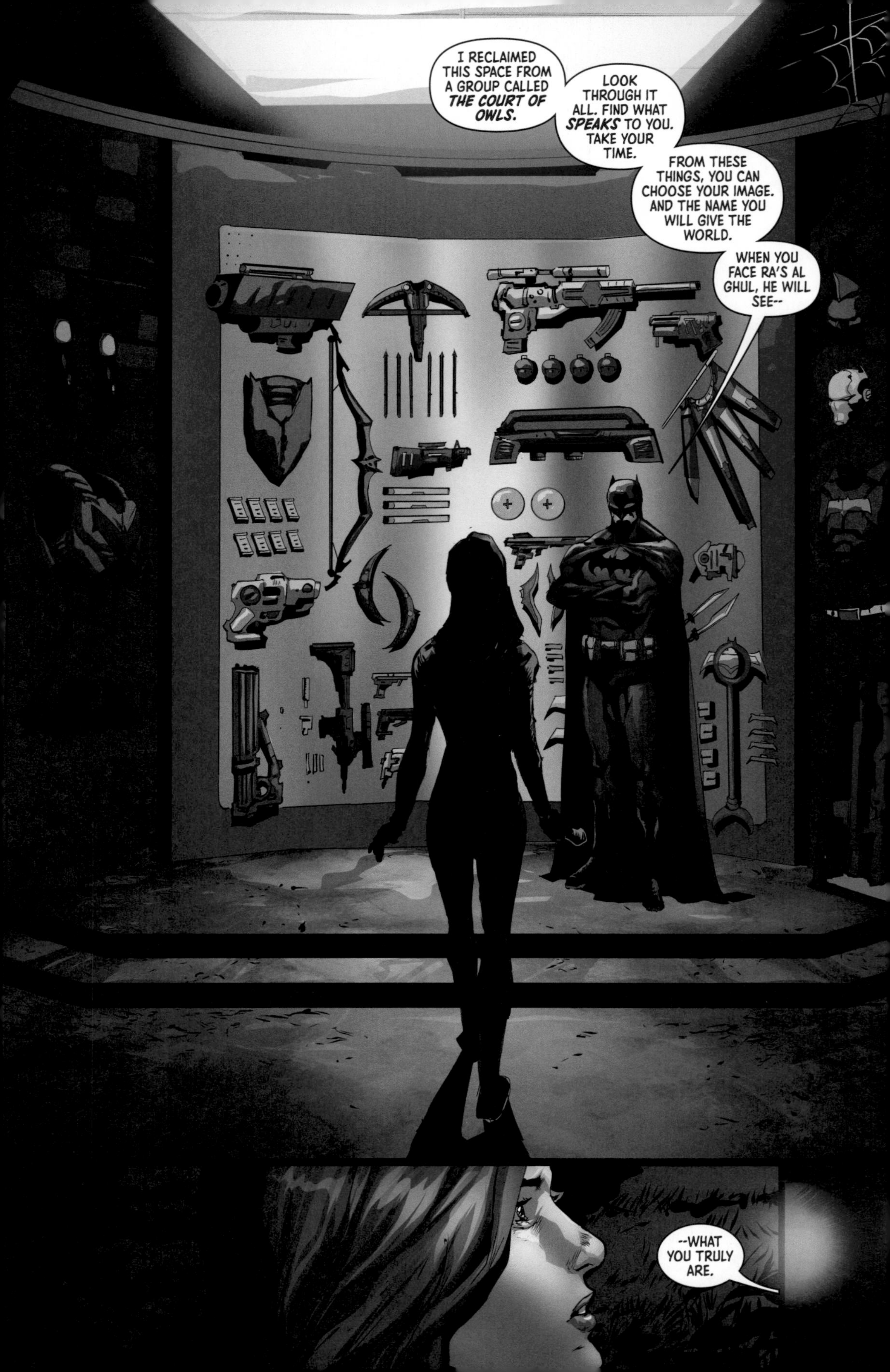
I RECLAIMED THIS SPACE FROM A GROUP CALLED ***THE COURT OF OWLS.***
LOOK THROUGH IT ALL. FIND WHAT ***SPEAKS*** TO YOU. TAKE YOUR TIME.
FROM THESE THINGS, YOU CAN CHOOSE YOUR IMAGE. AND THE NAME YOU WILL GIVE THE WORLD.
WHEN YOU FACE RA'S AL GHUL, HE WILL SEE--
--WHAT YOU TRULY ARE.

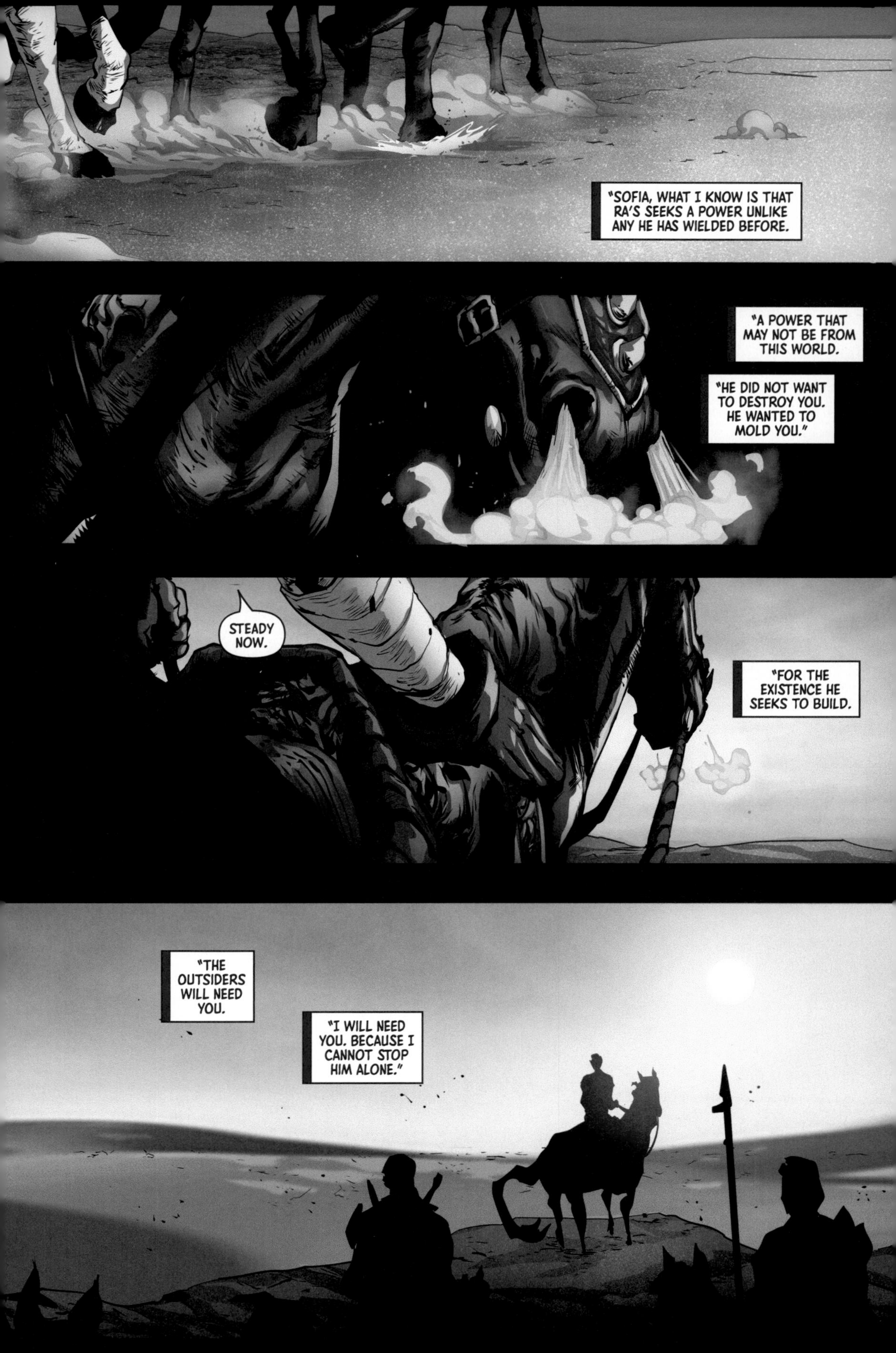
"SOFIA, WHAT I KNOW IS THAT RA'S SEEKS A POWER UNLIKE ANY HE HAS WIELDED BEFORE.
"A POWER THAT MAY NOT BE FROM THIS WORLD.
"HE DID NOT WANT TO DESTROY YOU. HE WANTED TO MOLD YOU."
STEADY NOW.
"FOR THE EXISTENCE HE SEEKS TO BUILD.
"THE OUTSIDERS WILL NEED YOU.
"I WILL NEED YOU. BECAUSE I CANNOT STOP HIM ALONE."

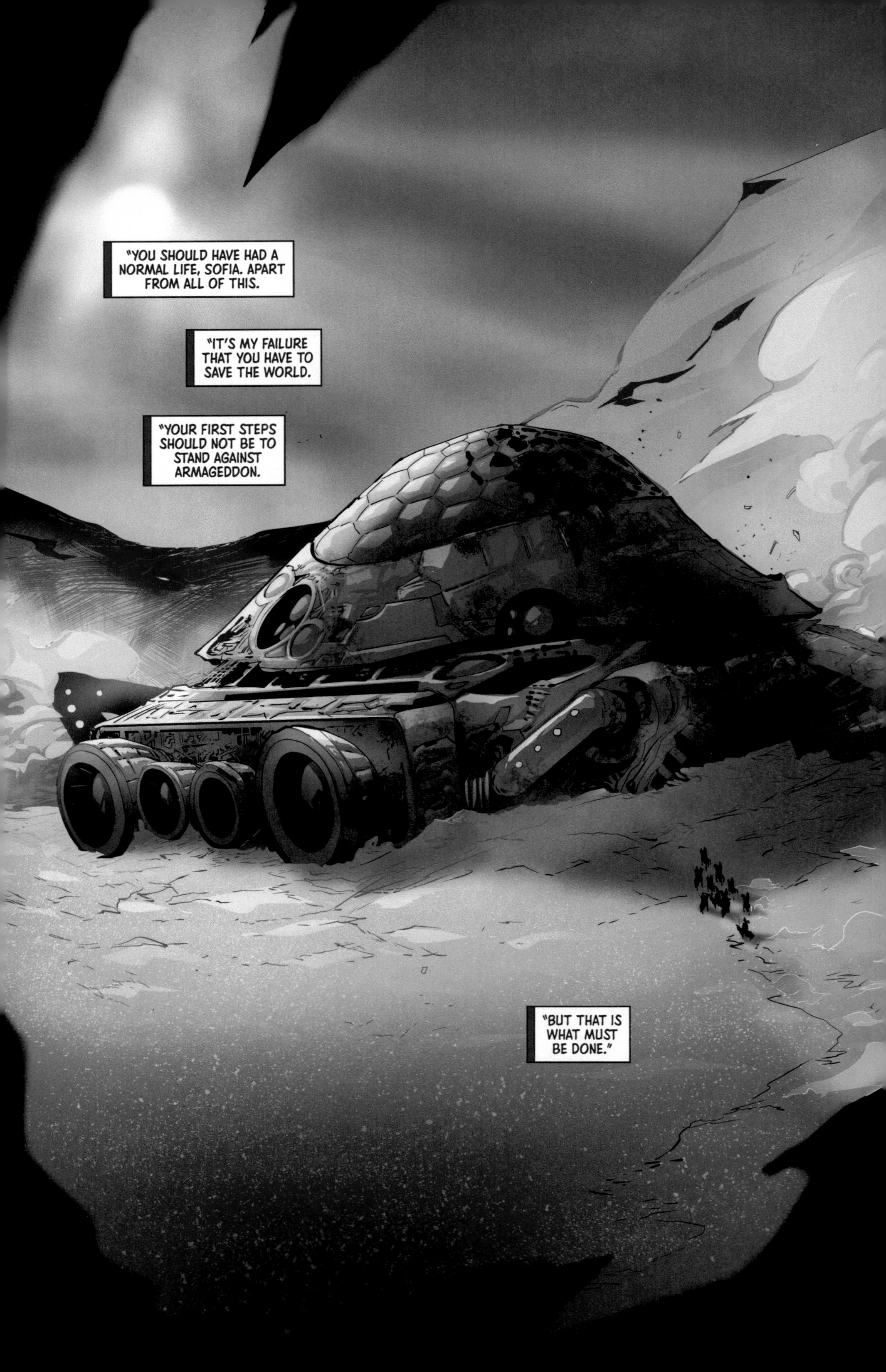
"YOU SHOULD HAVE HAD A NORMAL LIFE, SOFIA. APART FROM ALL OF THIS.
"IT'S MY FAILURE THAT YOU HAVE TO SAVE THE WORLD.
"YOUR FIRST STEPS SHOULD NOT BE TO STAND AGAINST ARMAGEDDON.
"BUT THAT IS WHAT MUST BE DONE."

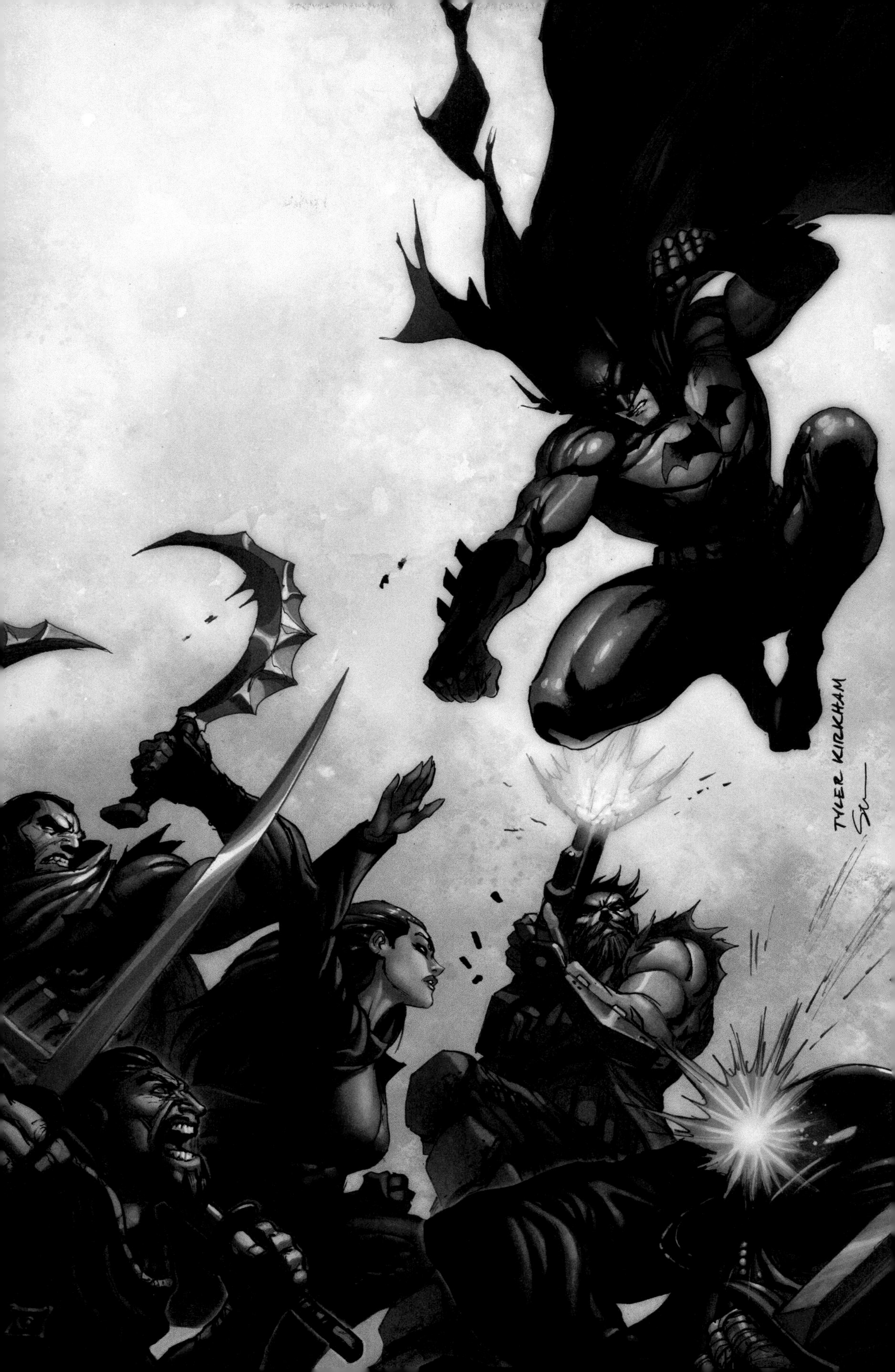
TYLER KIRKHAM

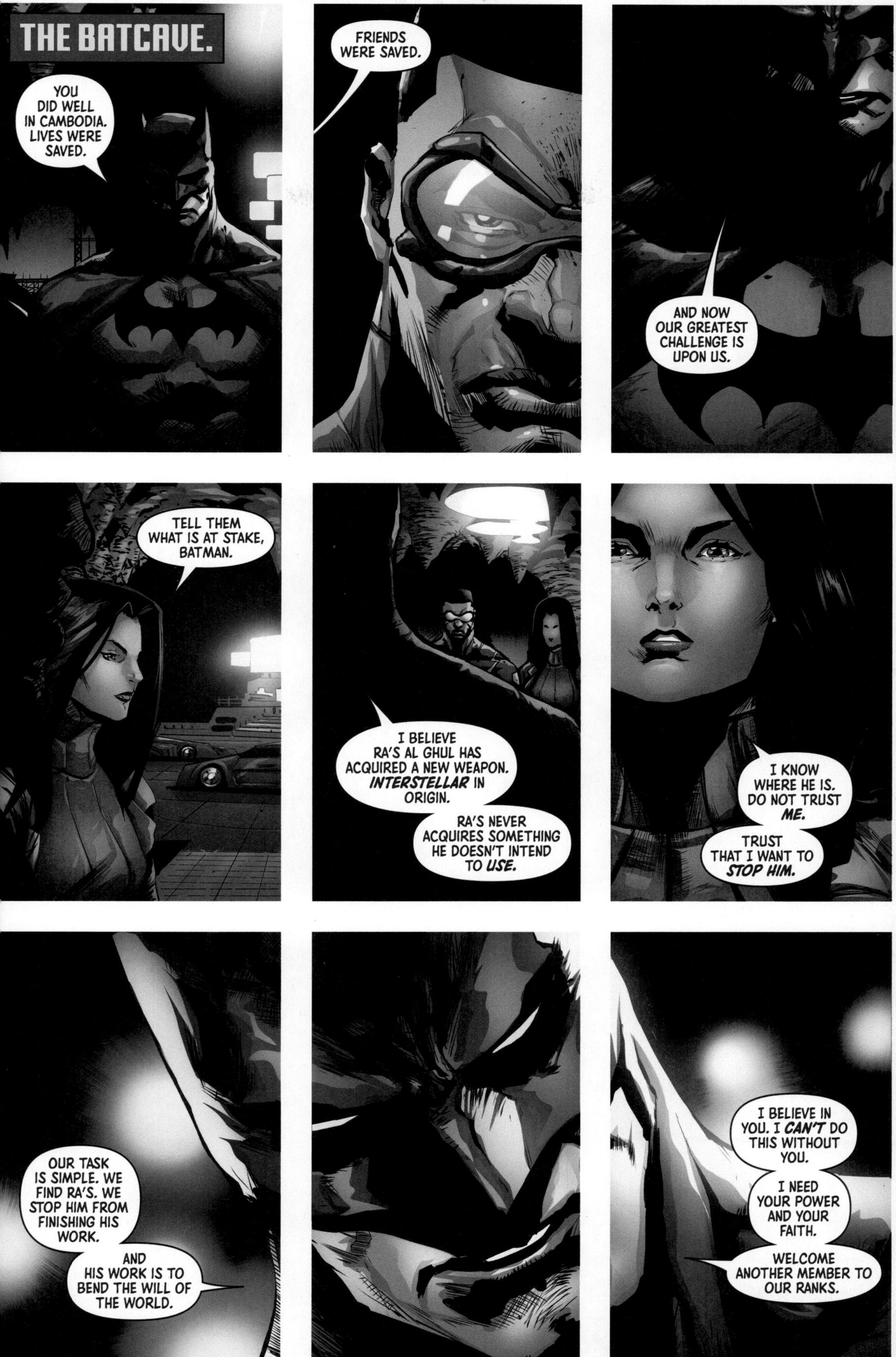
THE BATCAVE.
YOU DID WELL IN CAMBODIA. LIVES WERE SAVED.
FRIENDS WERE SAVED.
AND NOW OUR GREATEST CHALLENGE IS UPON US.
TELL THEM WHAT IS AT STAKE, BATMAN.
I BELIEVE RA'S AL GHUL HAS ACQUIRED A NEW WEAPON. INTERSTELLAR IN ORIGIN.
RA'S NEVER ACQUIRES SOMETHING HE DOESN'T INTEND TO USE.
I KNOW WHERE HE IS. DO NOT TRUST ME.
TRUST THAT I WANT TO STOP HIM.
OUR TASK IS SIMPLE. WE FIND RA'S. WE STOP HIM FROM FINISHING HIS WORK.
AND HIS WORK IS TO BEND THE WILL OF THE WORLD.
I BELIEVE IN YOU. I CAN'T DO THIS WITHOUT YOU.
I NEED YOUR POWER AND YOUR FAITH.
WELCOME ANOTHER MEMBER TO OUR RANKS.

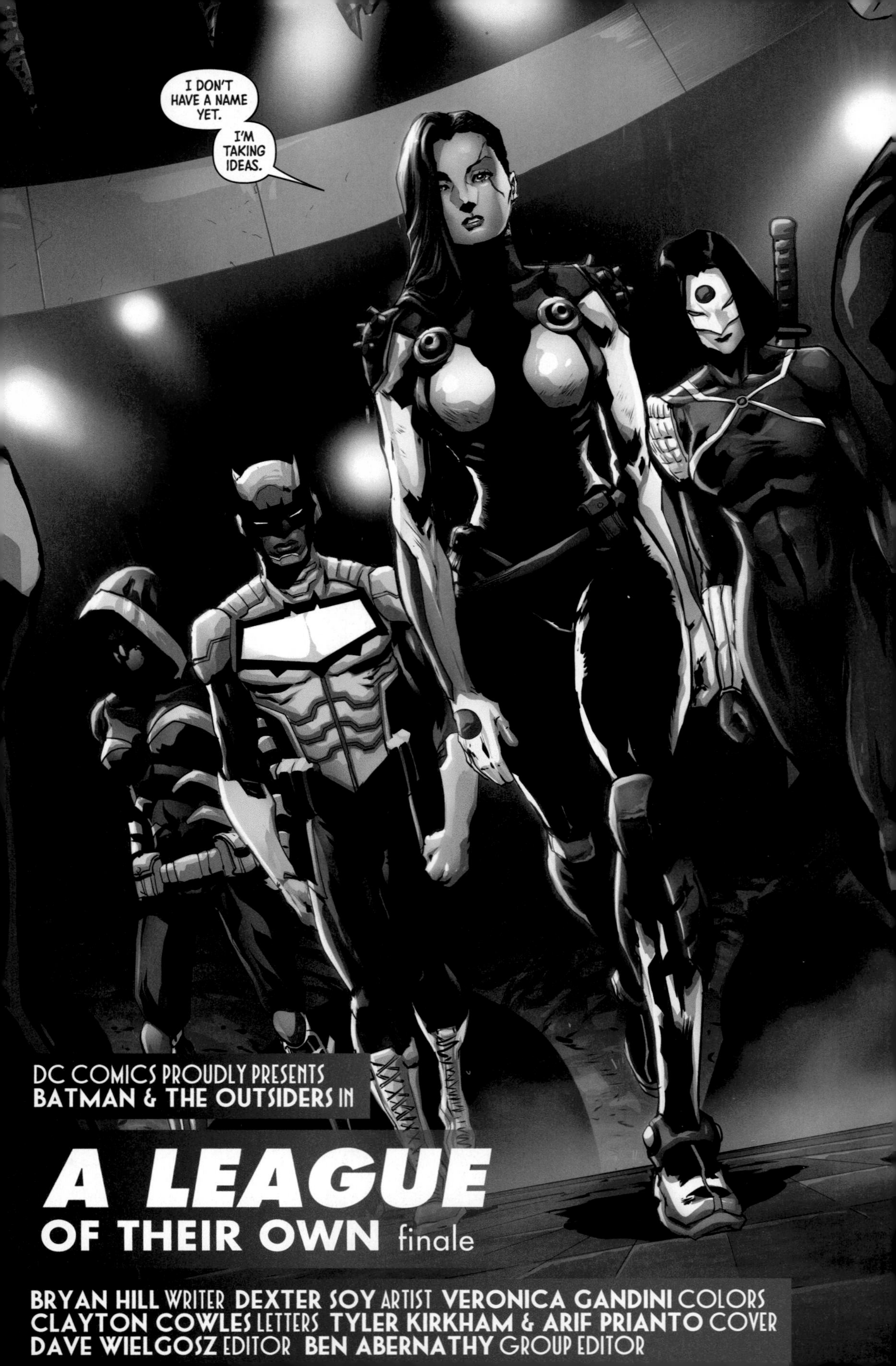
I DON'T HAVE A NAME YET.
I'M TAKING IDEAS.
DC COMICS PROUDLY PRESENTS
BATMAN & THE OUTSIDERS IN
A LEAGUE OF THEIR OWN finale
BRYAN HILL WRITER DEXTER SOY ARTIST VERONICA GANDINI COLORS
CLAYTON COWLES LETTERS TYLER KIRKHAM & ARIF PRIANTO COVER
DAVE WIELGOSZ EDITOR BEN ABERNATHY GROUP EDITOR

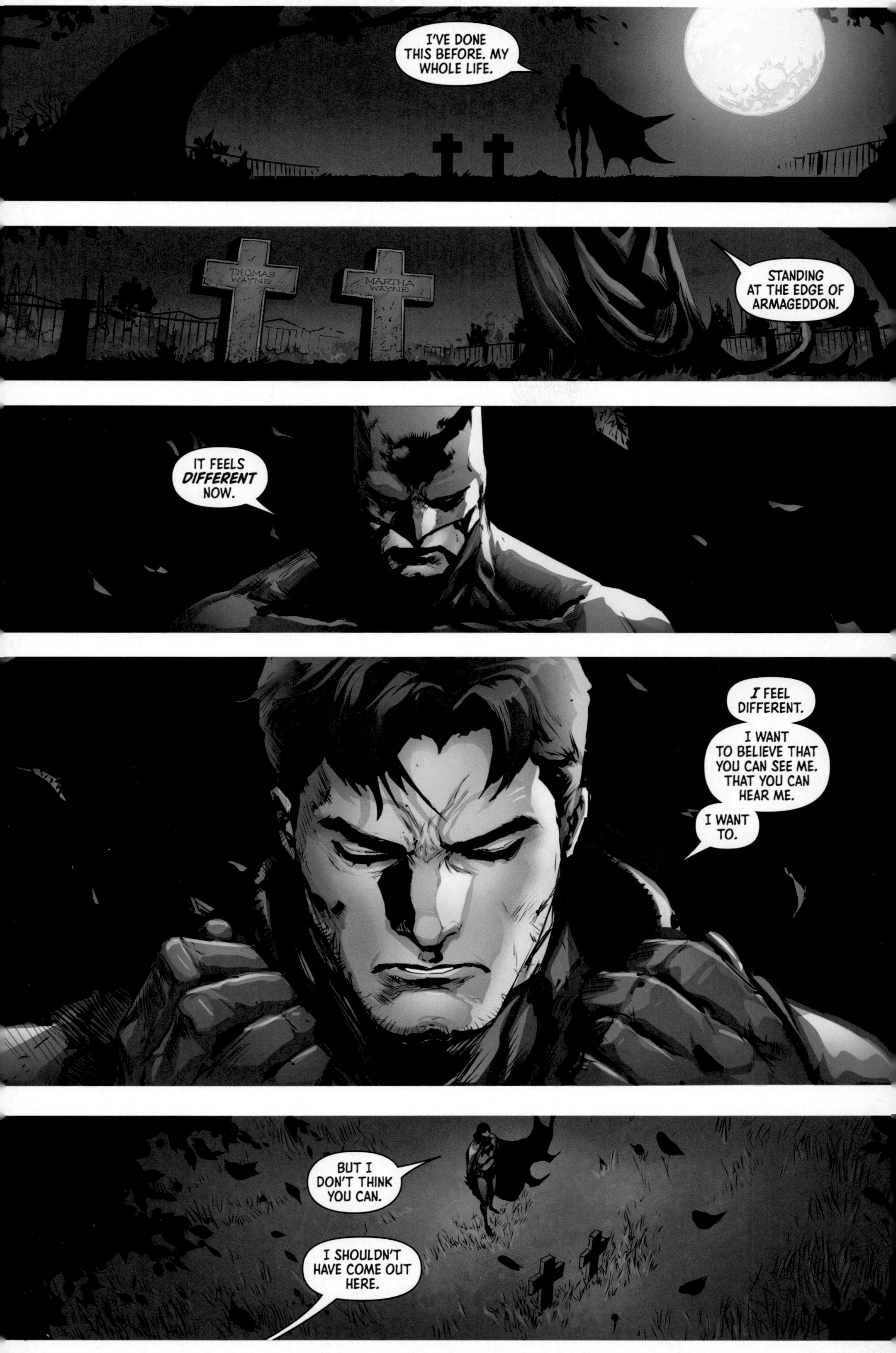
I'VE DONE THIS BEFORE. MY WHOLE LIFE.
THOMAS WAYNE
MARTHA WAYNE
STANDING AT THE EDGE OF ARMAGEDDON.
IT FEELS *DIFFERENT* NOW.
I FEEL DIFFERENT.
I WANT TO BELIEVE THAT YOU CAN SEE ME. THAT YOU CAN HEAR ME.
I WANT TO.
BUT I DON'T THINK YOU CAN.
I SHOULDN'T HAVE COME OUT HERE.

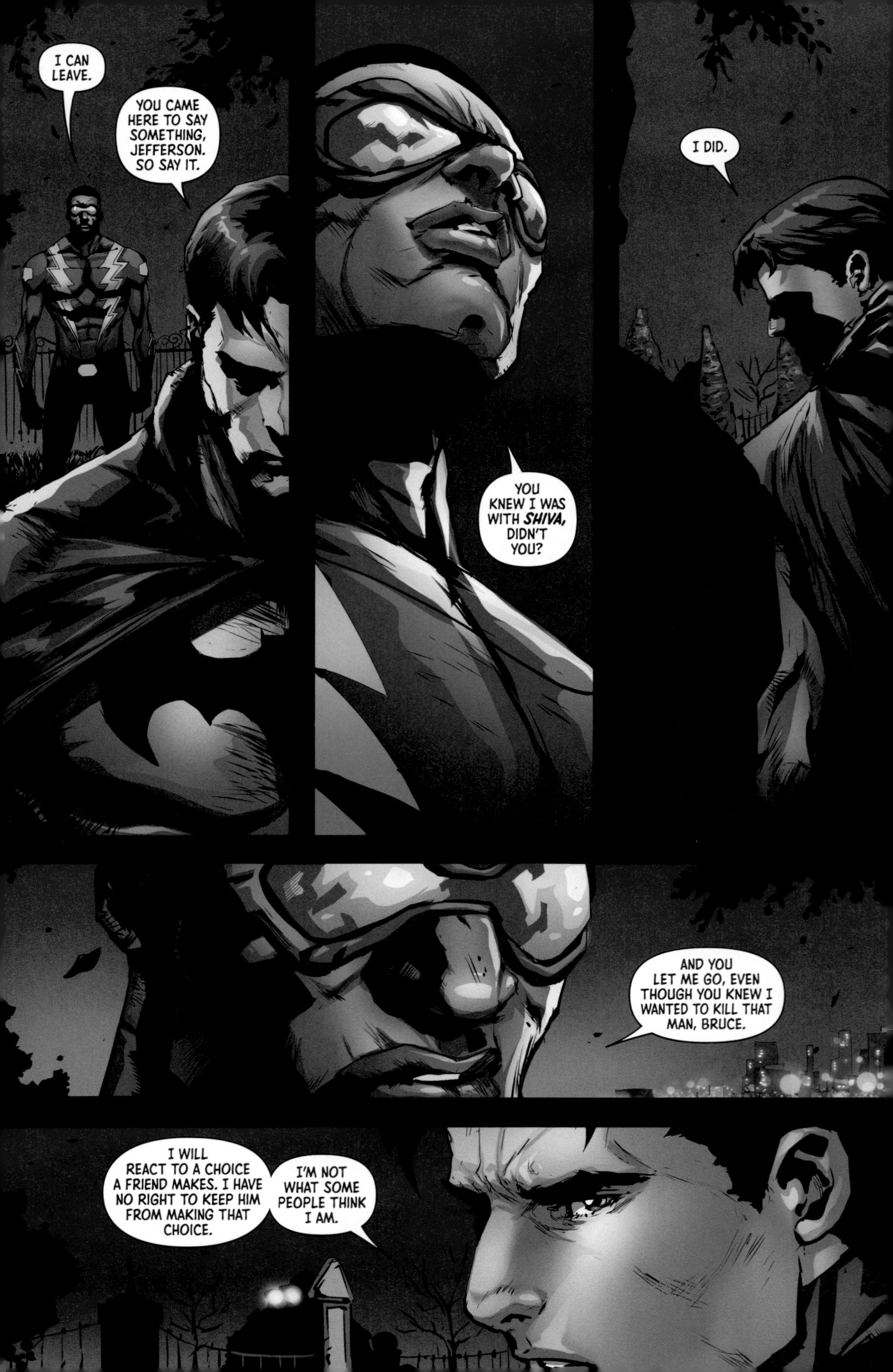
I CAN LEAVE.
YOU CAME HERE TO SAY SOMETHING, JEFFERSON. SO SAY IT.
YOU KNEW I WAS WITH SHIVA, DIDN'T YOU?
I DID.
AND YOU LET ME GO, EVEN THOUGH YOU KNEW I WANTED TO KILL THAT MAN, BRUCE.
I WILL REACT TO A CHOICE A FRIEND MAKES. I HAVE NO RIGHT TO KEEP HIM FROM MAKING THAT CHOICE.
I'M NOT WHAT SOME PEOPLE THINK I AM.

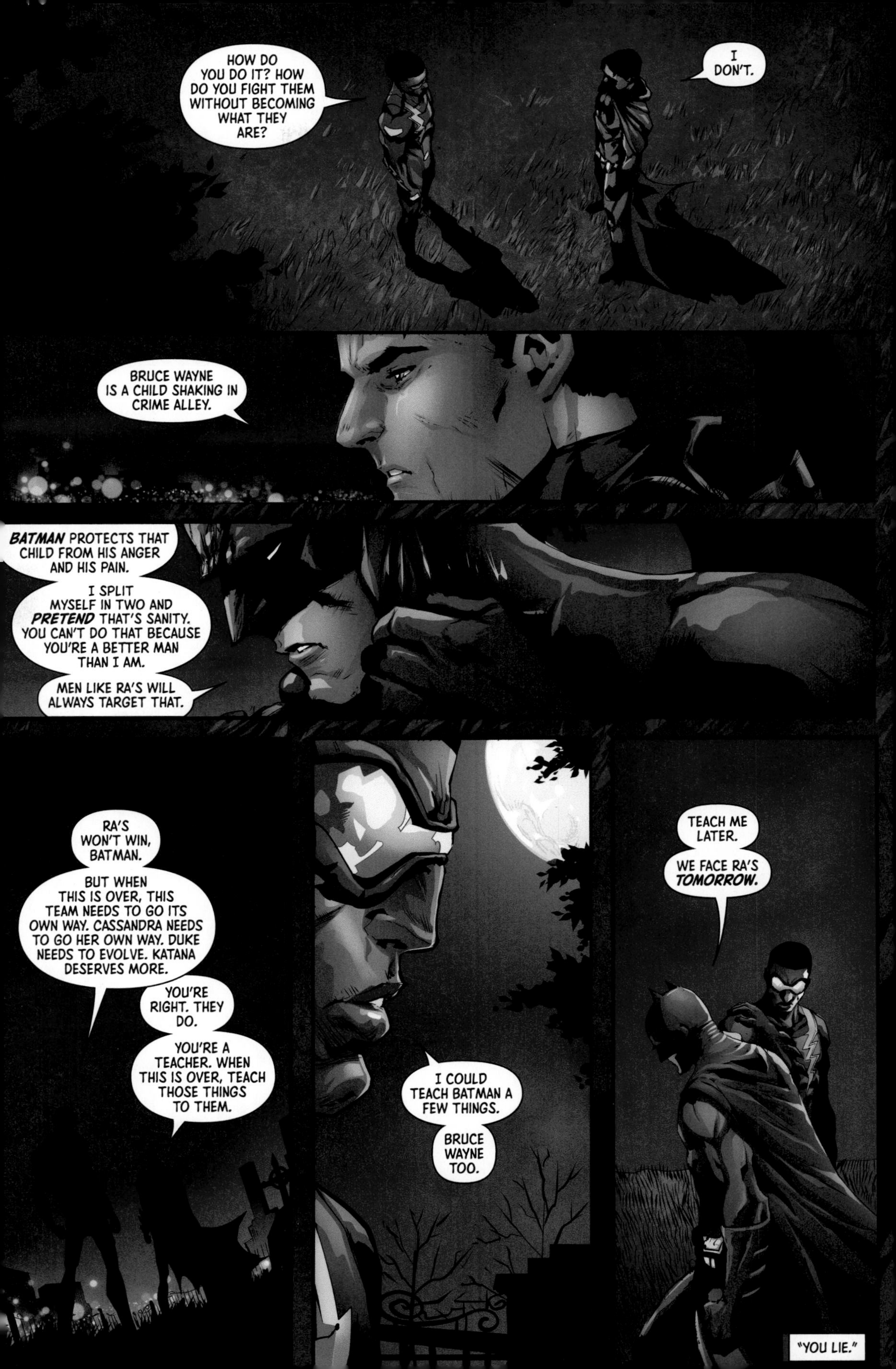
HOW DO YOU DO IT? HOW DO YOU FIGHT THEM WITHOUT BECOMING WHAT THEY ARE?
I DON'T.
BRUCE WAYNE IS A CHILD SHAKING IN CRIME ALLEY.
BATMAN PROTECTS THAT CHILD FROM HIS ANGER AND HIS PAIN.
I SPLIT MYSELF IN TWO AND **PRETEND** THAT'S SANITY. YOU CAN'T DO THAT BECAUSE YOU'RE A BETTER MAN THAN I AM.
MEN LIKE RA'S WILL ALWAYS TARGET THAT.
RA'S WON'T WIN, BATMAN.
BUT WHEN THIS IS OVER, THIS TEAM NEEDS TO GO ITS OWN WAY. CASSANDRA NEEDS TO GO HER OWN WAY. DUKE NEEDS TO EVOLVE. KATANA DESERVES MORE.
YOU'RE RIGHT. THEY DO.
YOU'RE A TEACHER. WHEN THIS IS OVER, TEACH THOSE THINGS TO THEM.
I COULD TEACH BATMAN A FEW THINGS.
BRUCE WAYNE TOO.
TEACH ME LATER.
WE FACE RA'S **TOMORROW.**
"YOU LIE."

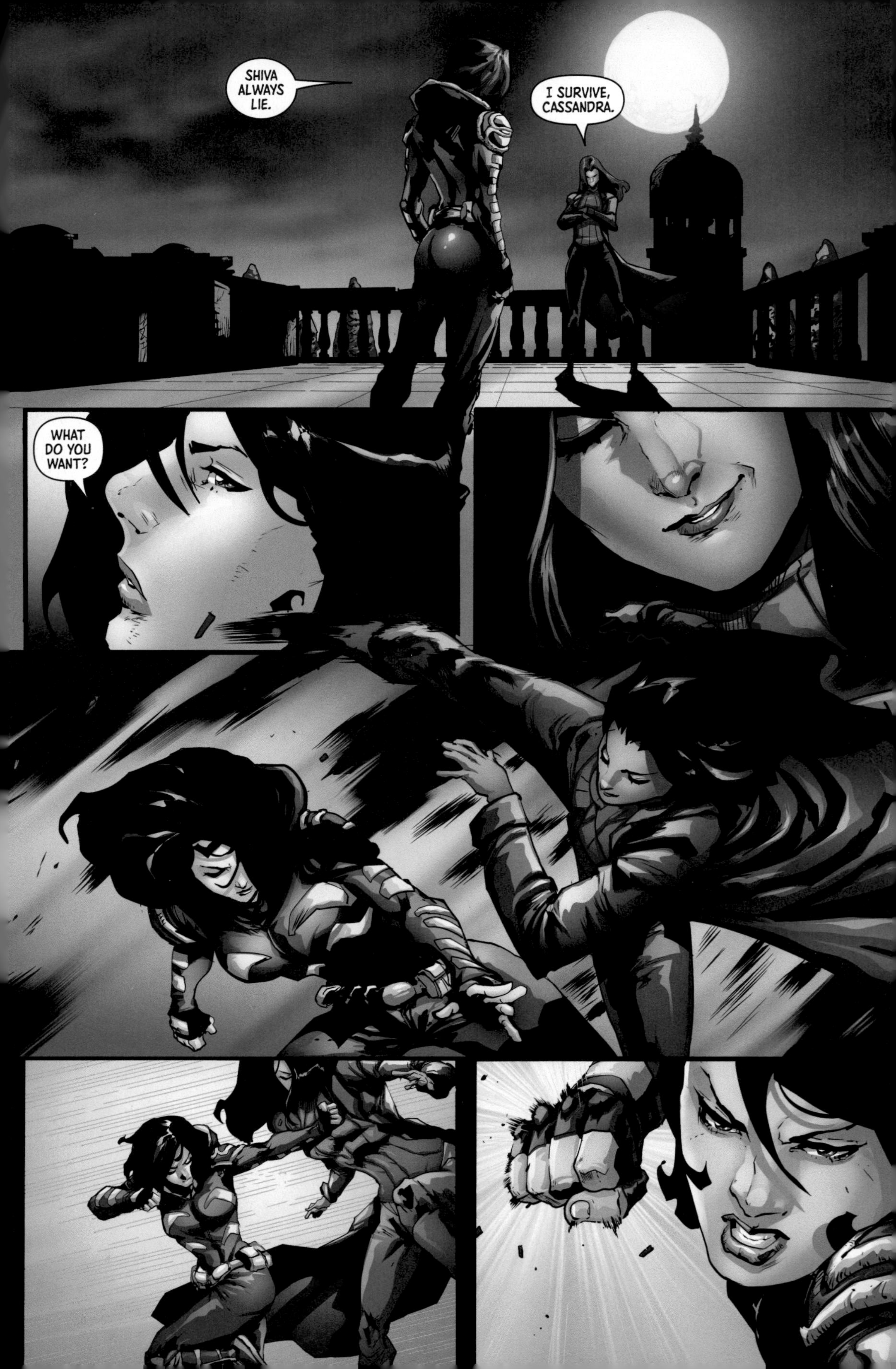
SHIVA ALWAYS LIE.
I SURVIVE, CASSANDRA.
WHAT DO YOU WANT?

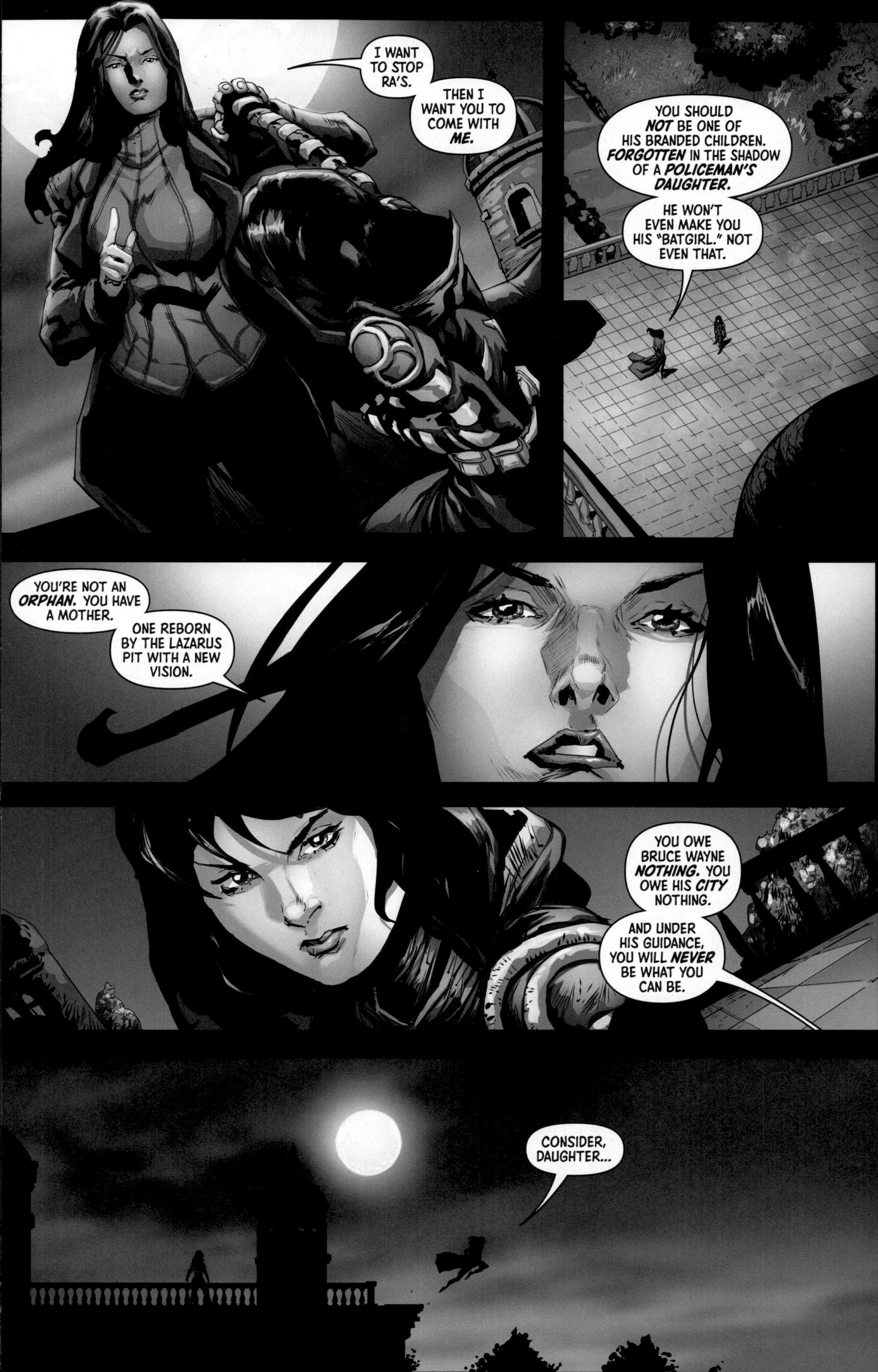
I WANT TO STOP RA'S.
THEN I WANT YOU TO COME WITH ME.
YOU SHOULD NOT BE ONE OF HIS BRANDED CHILDREN. FORGOTTEN IN THE SHADOW OF A POLICEMAN'S DAUGHTER.
HE WON'T EVEN MAKE YOU HIS "BATGIRL." NOT EVEN THAT.
YOU'RE NOT AN ORPHAN. YOU HAVE A MOTHER.
ONE REBORN BY THE LAZARUS PIT WITH A NEW VISION.
YOU OWE BRUCE WAYNE NOTHING. YOU OWE HIS CITY NOTHING.
AND UNDER HIS GUIDANCE, YOU WILL NEVER BE WHAT YOU CAN BE.
CONSIDER, DAUGHTER...

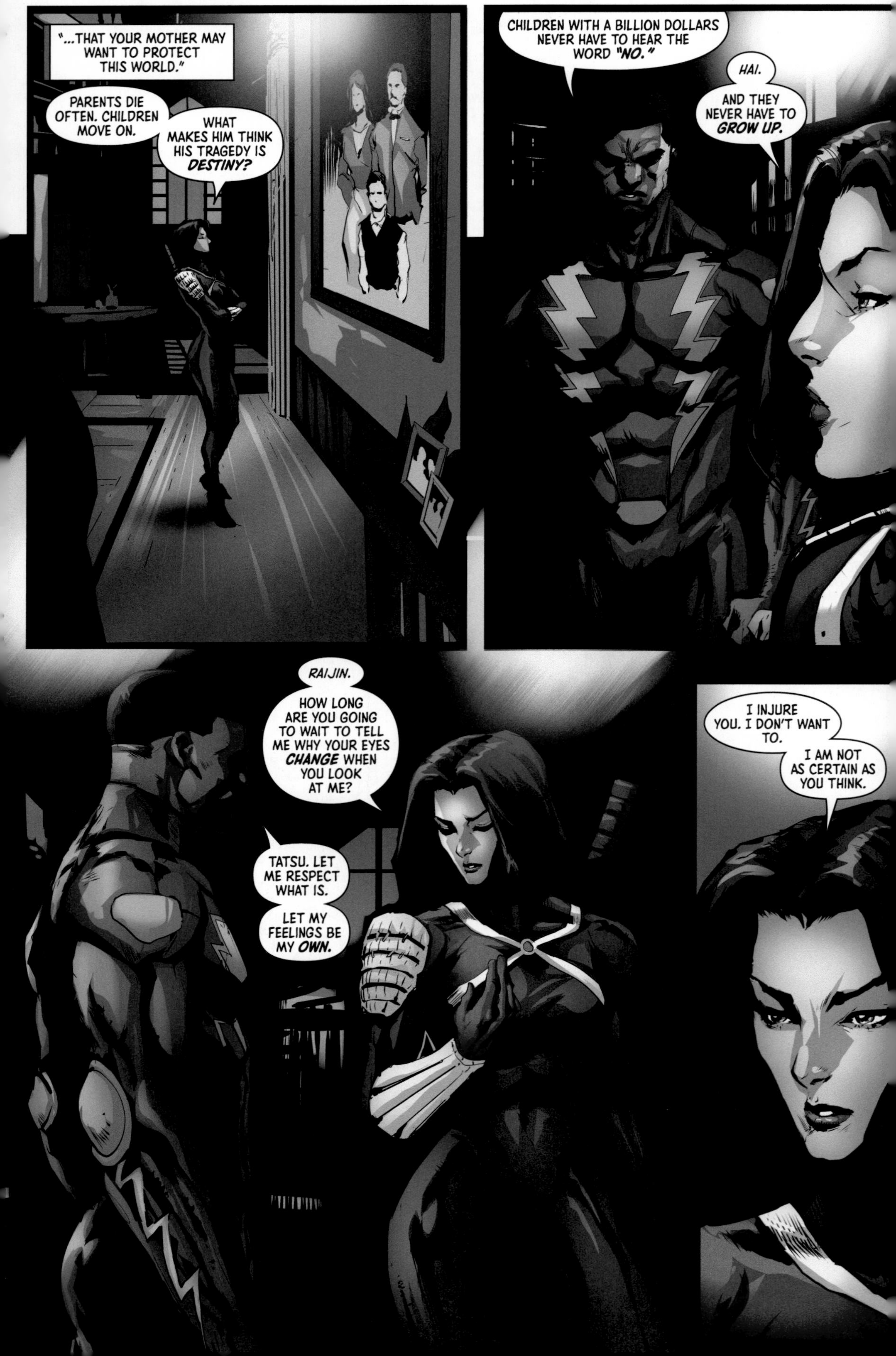
"...THAT YOUR MOTHER MAY WANT TO PROTECT THIS WORLD."
PARENTS DIE OFTEN. CHILDREN MOVE ON.
WHAT MAKES HIM THINK HIS TRAGEDY IS *DESTINY?*
CHILDREN WITH A BILLION DOLLARS NEVER HAVE TO HEAR THE WORD *"NO."*
HAI.
AND THEY NEVER HAVE TO *GROW UP.*
RAIJIN.
HOW LONG ARE YOU GOING TO WAIT TO TELL ME WHY YOUR EYES *CHANGE* WHEN YOU LOOK AT ME?
TATSU. LET ME RESPECT WHAT IS.
LET MY FEELINGS BE MY *OWN.*
I INJURE YOU. I DON'T WANT TO.
I AM NOT AS CERTAIN AS YOU THINK.

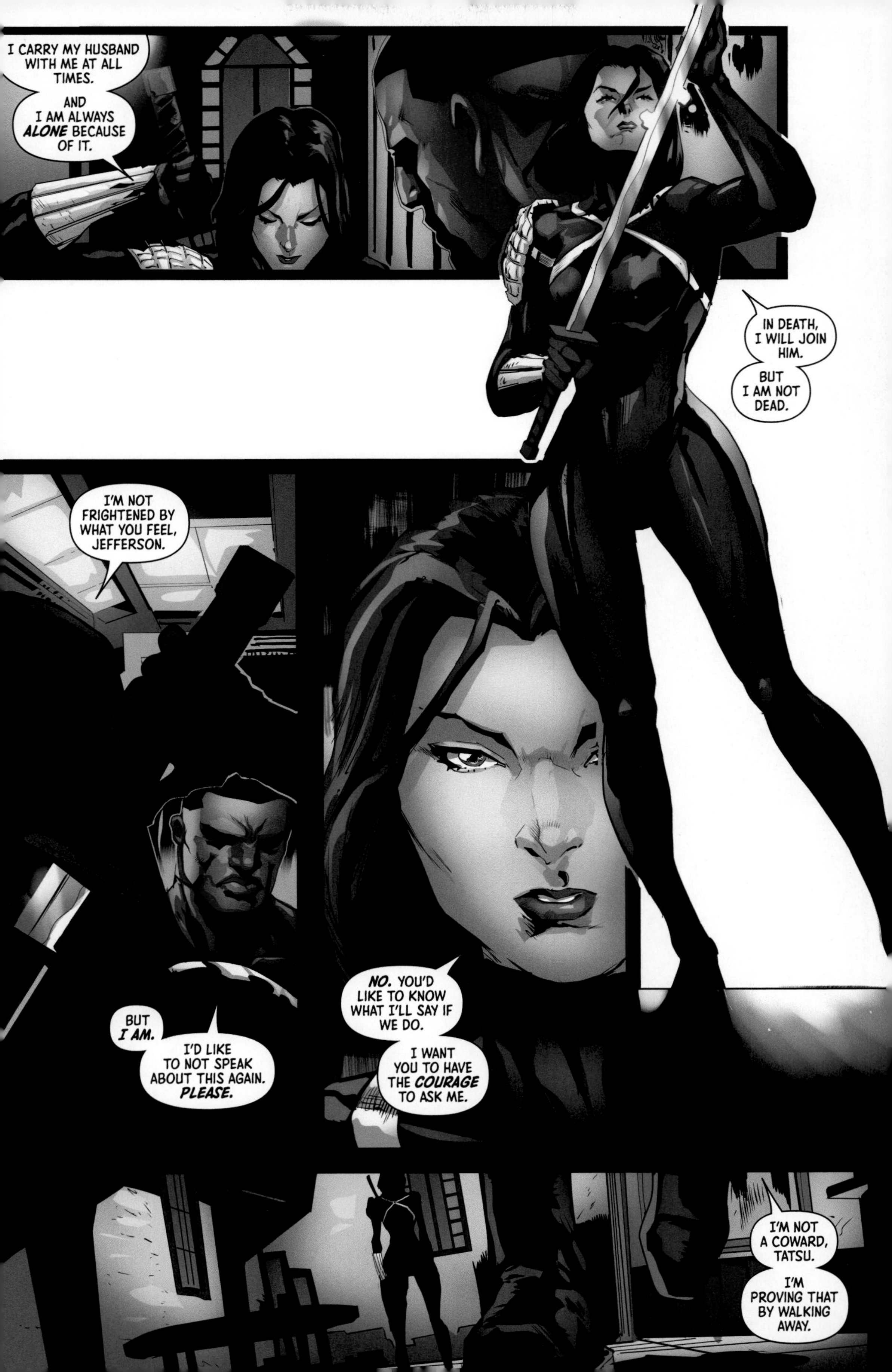
I CARRY MY HUSBAND WITH ME AT ALL TIMES.
AND I AM ALWAYS ALONE BECAUSE OF IT.
IN DEATH, I WILL JOIN HIM.
BUT I AM NOT DEAD.
I'M NOT FRIGHTENED BY WHAT YOU FEEL, JEFFERSON.
BUT I AM.
I'D LIKE TO NOT SPEAK ABOUT THIS AGAIN. PLEASE.
NO. YOU'D LIKE TO KNOW WHAT I'LL SAY IF WE DO.
I WANT YOU TO HAVE THE COURAGE TO ASK ME.
I'M NOT A COWARD, TATSU.
I'M PROVING THAT BY WALKING AWAY.

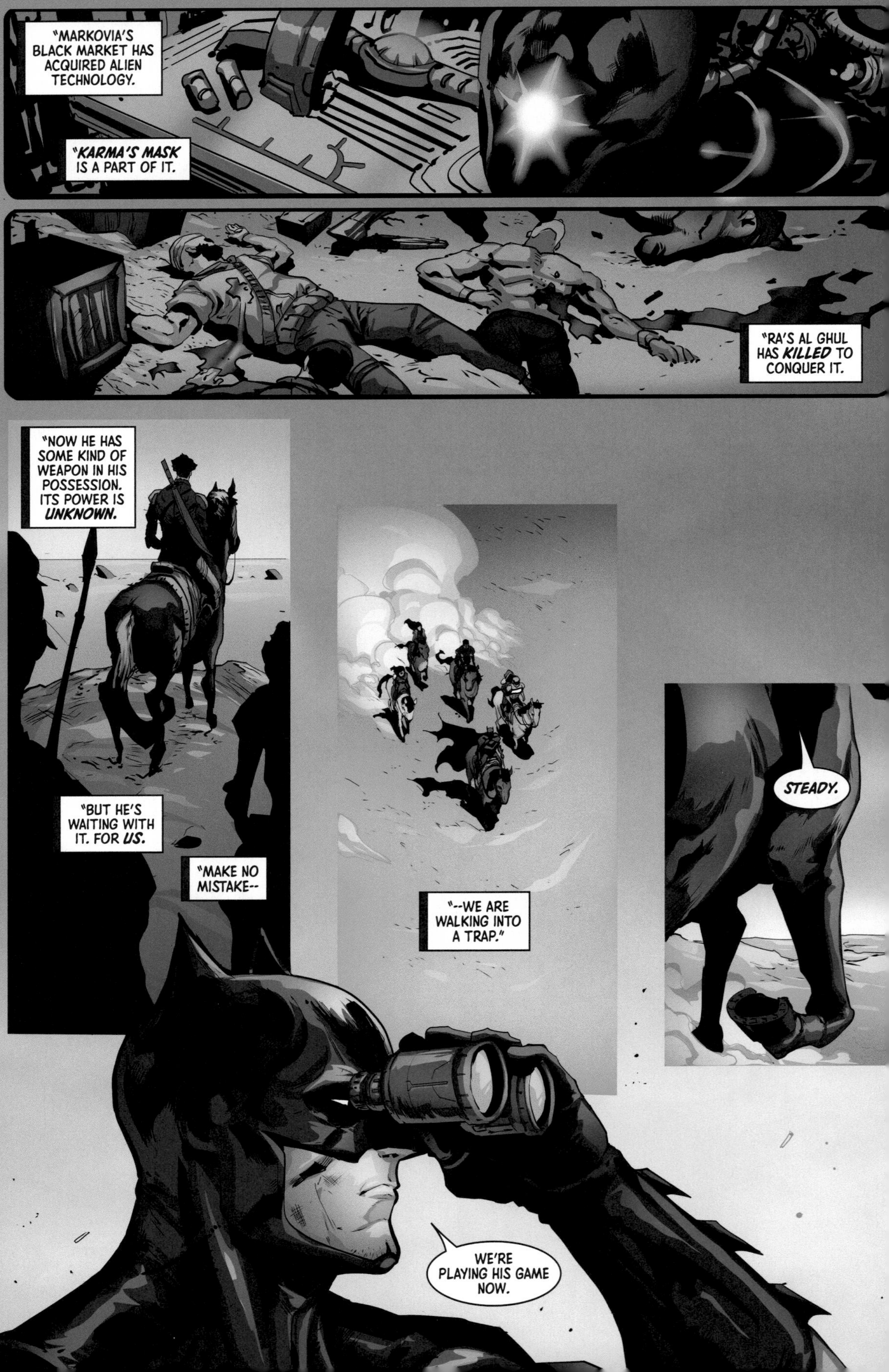
"MARKOVIA'S BLACK MARKET HAS ACQUIRED ALIEN TECHNOLOGY.
"*KARMA'S MASK* IS A PART OF IT.
"RA'S AL GHUL HAS *KILLED* TO CONQUER IT.
"NOW HE HAS SOME KIND OF WEAPON IN HIS POSSESSION. ITS POWER IS *UNKNOWN.*
"BUT HE'S WAITING WITH IT. FOR *US.*
"MAKE NO MISTAKE--
"--WE ARE WALKING INTO A TRAP."
STEADY.
WE'RE PLAYING HIS GAME NOW.

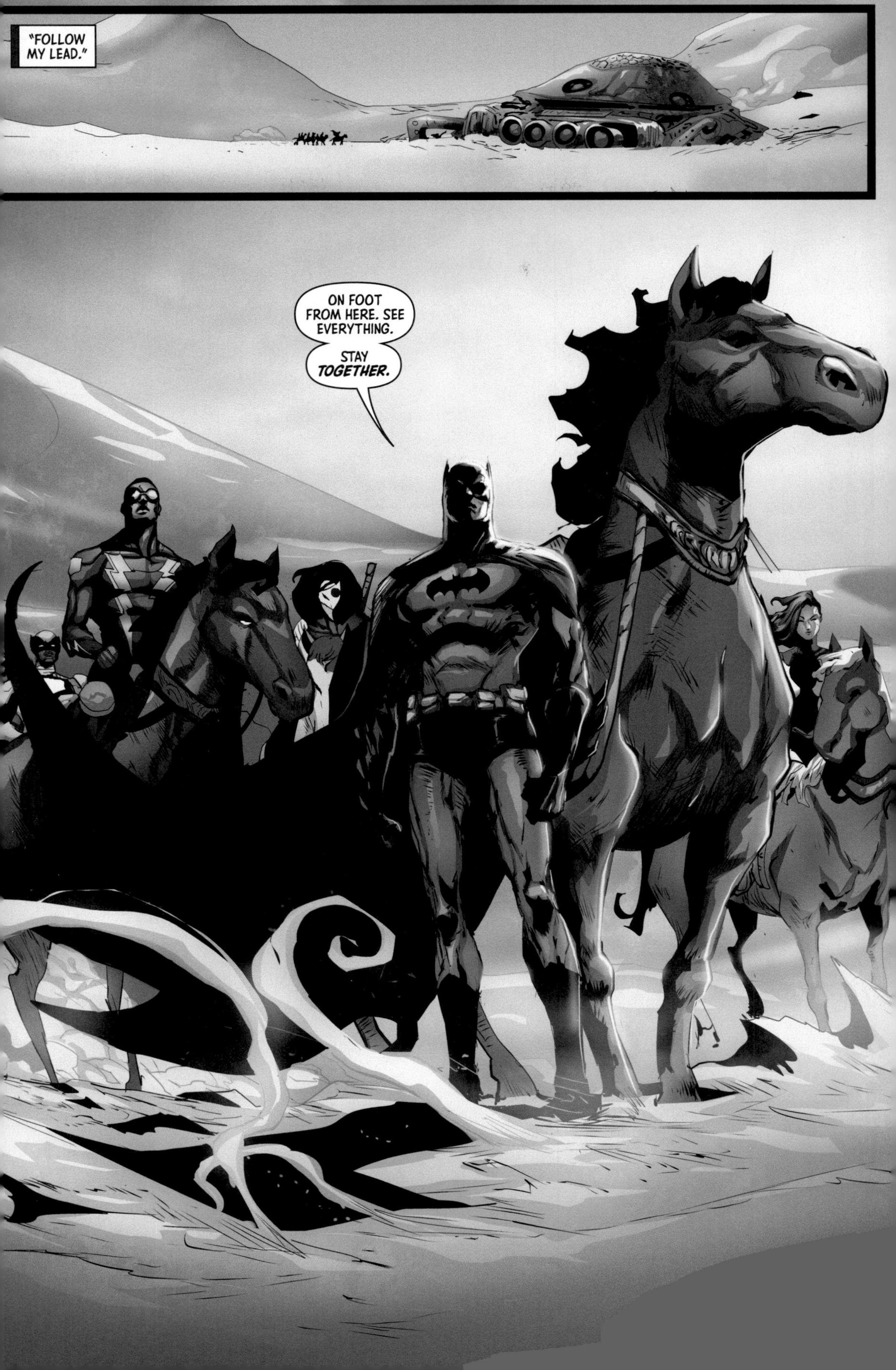
"FOLLOW MY LEAD."
ON FOOT FROM HERE. SEE EVERYTHING.
STAY *TOGETHER*.

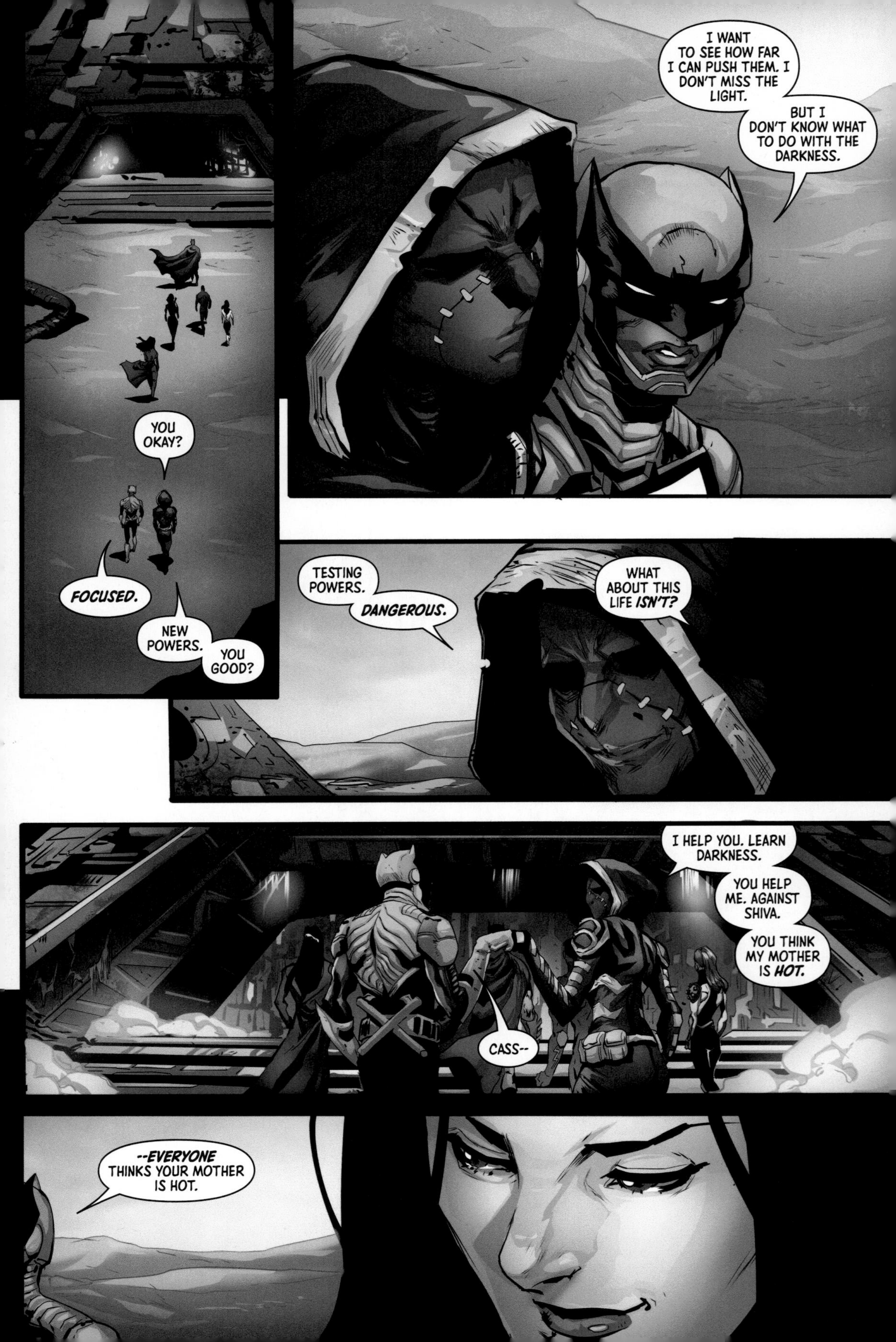
YOU OKAY?
FOCUSED.
NEW POWERS.
YOU GOOD?
I WANT TO SEE HOW FAR I CAN PUSH THEM. I DON'T MISS THE LIGHT.
BUT I DON'T KNOW WHAT TO DO WITH THE DARKNESS.
TESTING POWERS.
DANGEROUS.
WHAT ABOUT THIS LIFE ISN'T?
I HELP YOU. LEARN DARKNESS.
YOU HELP ME. AGAINST SHIVA.
YOU THINK MY MOTHER IS HOT.
CASS--
--EVERYONE THINKS YOUR MOTHER IS HOT.

WHEN YOU ENTER HERE, YOU'RE LEAVING EARTH.
REMEMBER THAT. *FOCUS.*
SOFIA. YOU'RE UP.
ON IT, BATMAN.
SHRAK...OOM

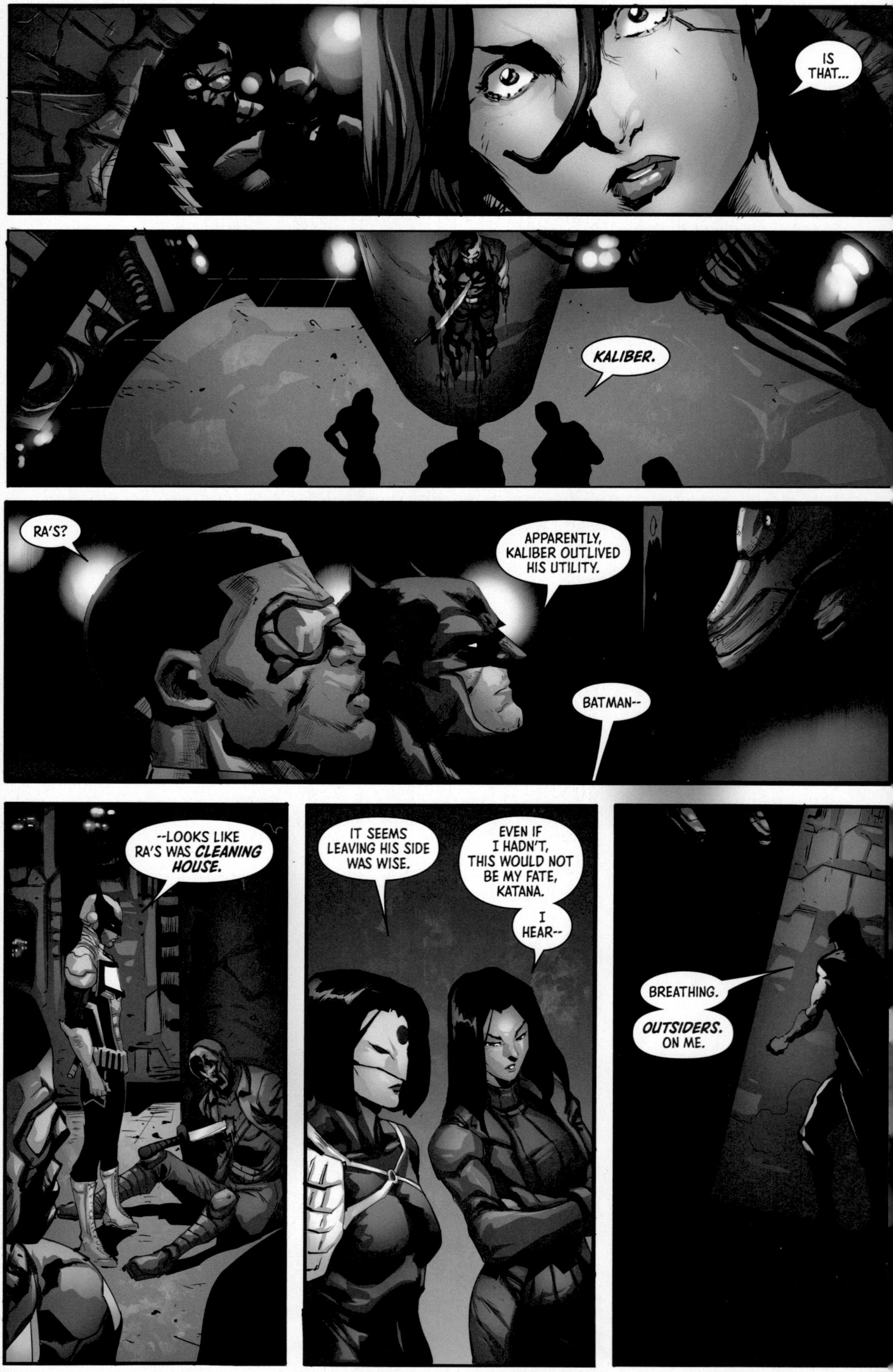
IS THAT...
KALIBER.
RA'S?
APPARENTLY, KALIBER OUTLIVED HIS UTILITY.
BATMAN--
--LOOKS LIKE RA'S WAS *CLEANING HOUSE.*
IT SEEMS LEAVING HIS SIDE WAS WISE.
EVEN IF I HADN'T, THIS WOULD NOT BE MY FATE, KATANA.
I HEAR--
BREATHING.
OUTSIDERS. ON ME.

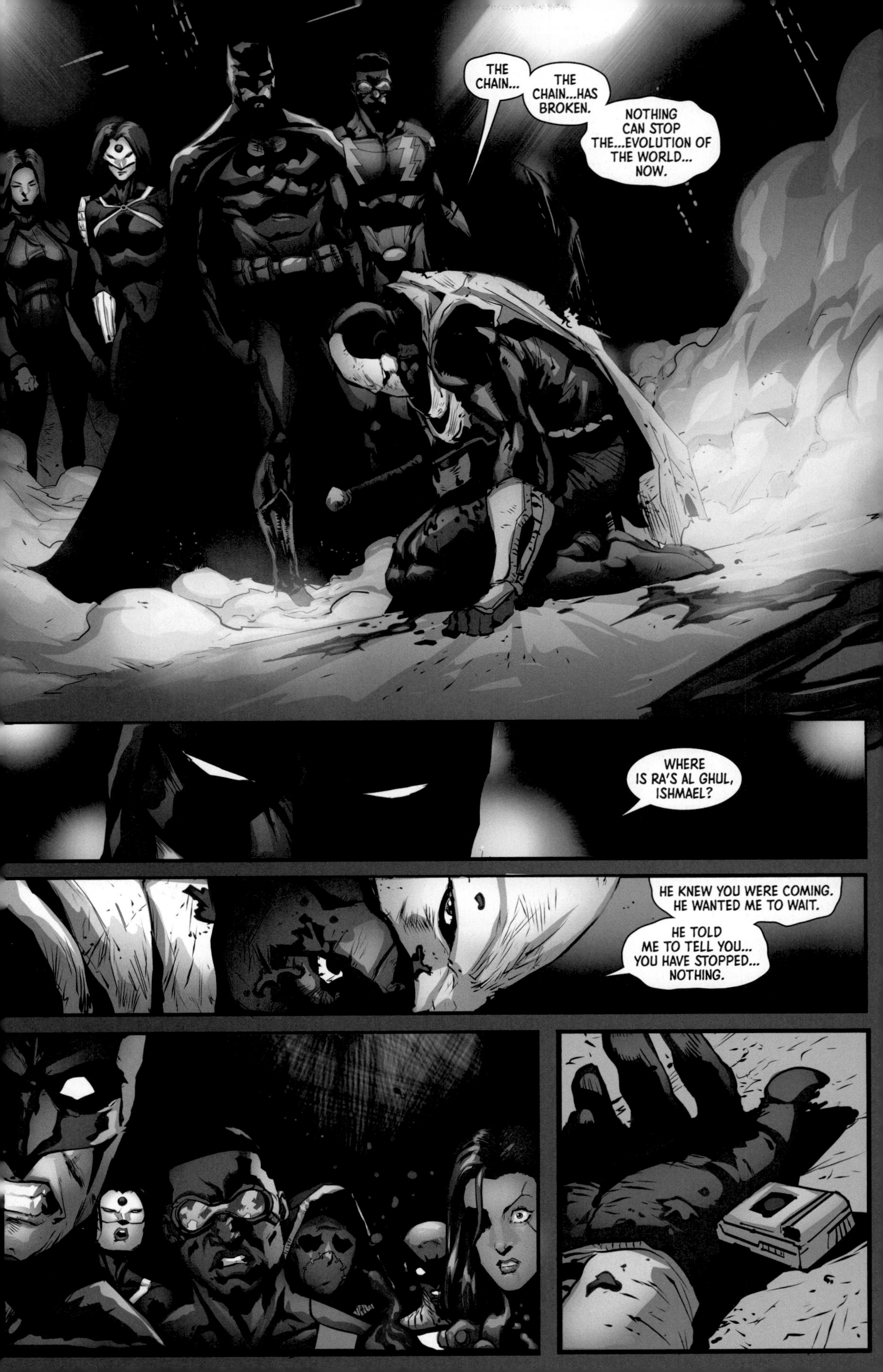
THE CHAIN...
THE CHAIN...HAS BROKEN.
NOTHING CAN STOP THE...EVOLUTION OF THE WORLD... NOW.
WHERE IS RA'S AL GHUL, ISHMAEL?
HE KNEW YOU WERE COMING. HE WANTED ME TO WAIT.
HE TOLD ME TO TELL YOU... YOU HAVE STOPPED... NOTHING.

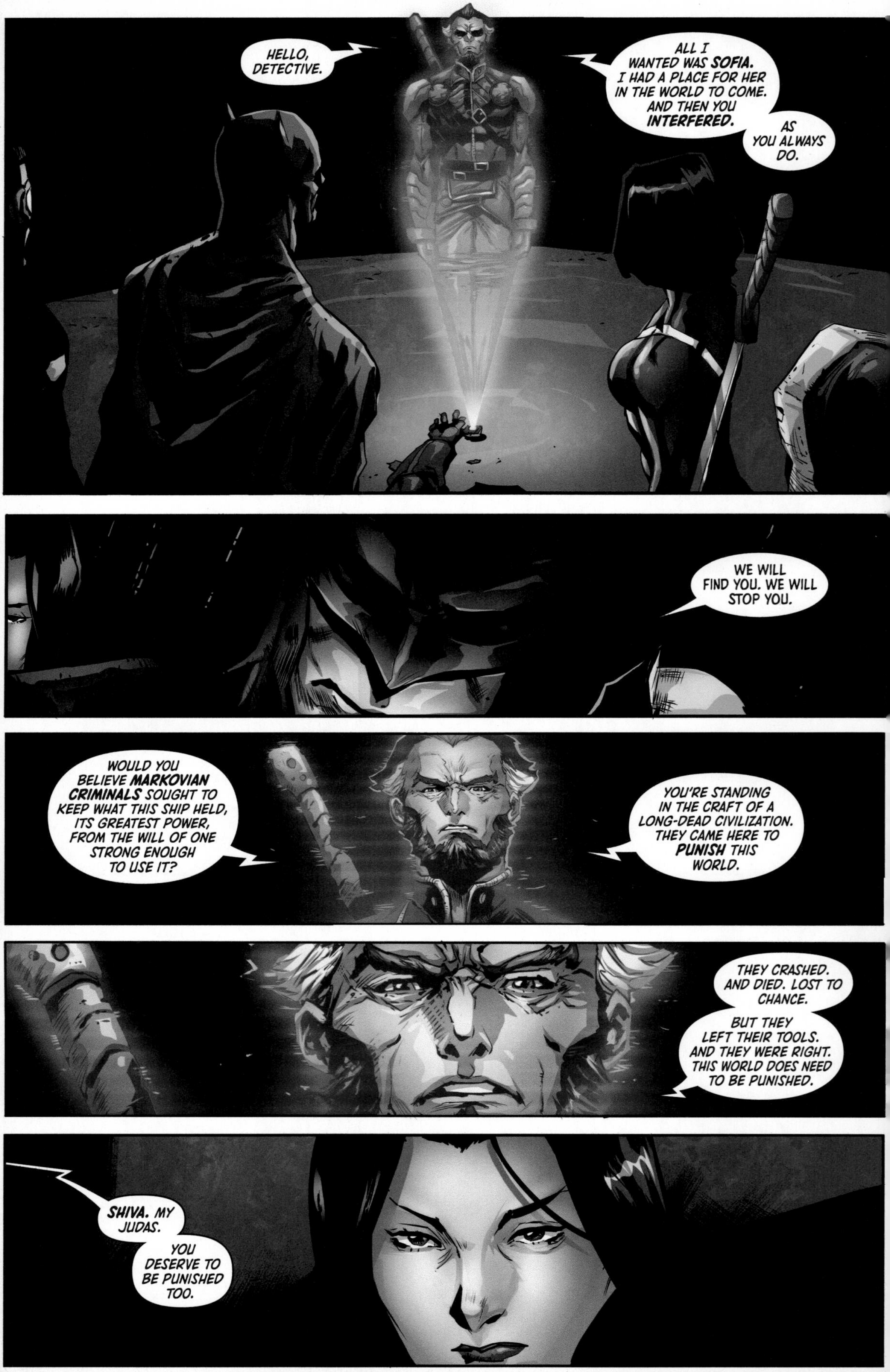
HELLO, DETECTIVE.
ALL I WANTED WAS SOFIA. I HAD A PLACE FOR HER IN THE WORLD TO COME. AND THEN YOU INTERFERED.
AS YOU ALWAYS DO.
WE WILL FIND YOU. WE WILL STOP YOU.
WOULD YOU BELIEVE MARKOVIAN CRIMINALS SOUGHT TO KEEP WHAT THIS SHIP HELD, ITS GREATEST POWER, FROM THE WILL OF ONE STRONG ENOUGH TO USE IT?
YOU'RE STANDING IN THE CRAFT OF A LONG-DEAD CIVILIZATION. THEY CAME HERE TO PUNISH THIS WORLD.
THEY CRASHED. AND DIED. LOST TO CHANCE.
BUT THEY LEFT THEIR TOOLS. AND THEY WERE RIGHT. THIS WORLD DOES NEED TO BE PUNISHED.
SHIVA. MY JUDAS.
YOU DESERVE TO BE PUNISHED TOO.

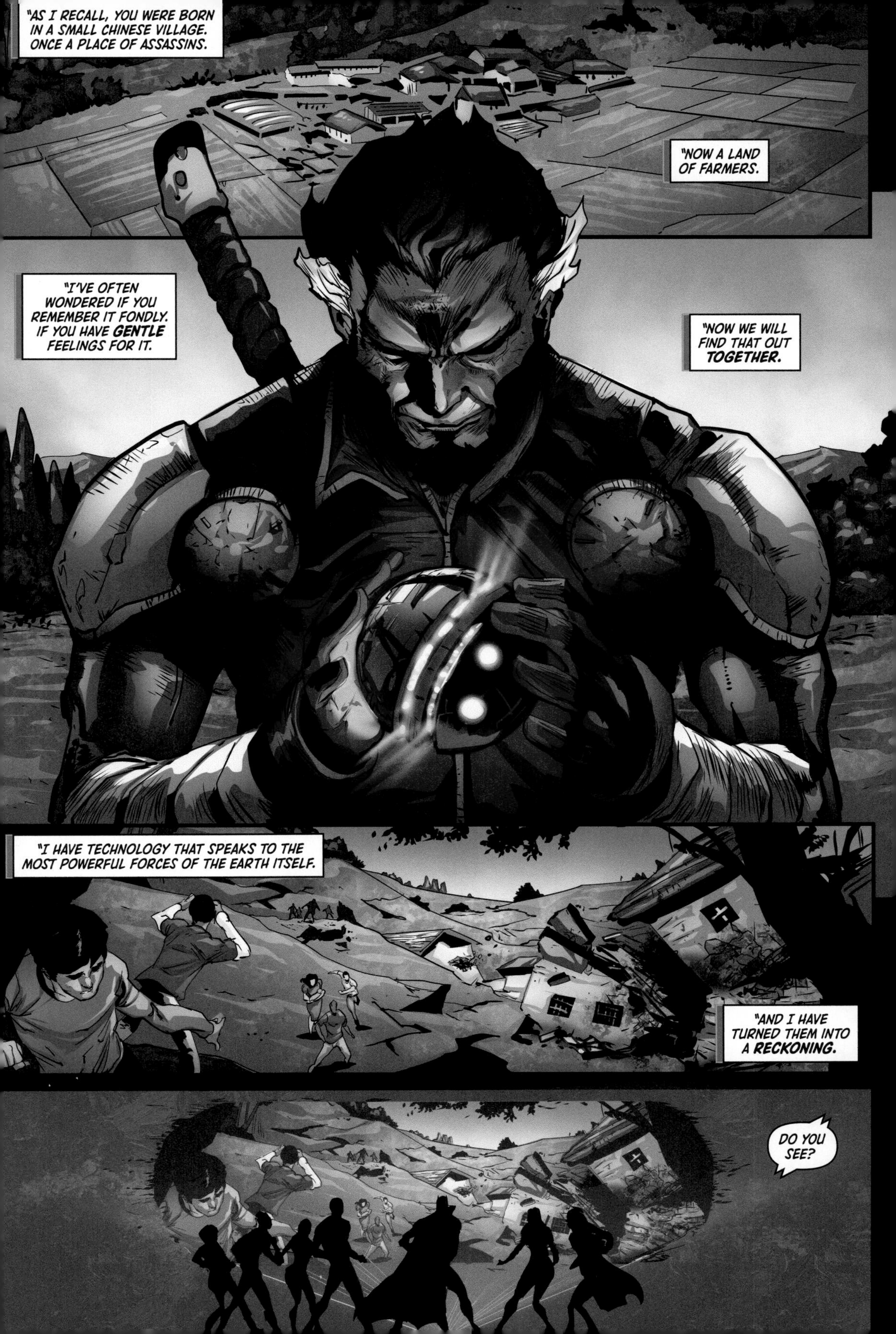
"AS I RECALL, YOU WERE BORN IN A SMALL CHINESE VILLAGE. ONCE A PLACE OF ASSASSINS.
"NOW A LAND OF FARMERS.
"I'VE OFTEN WONDERED IF YOU REMEMBER IT FONDLY. IF YOU HAVE GENTLE FEELINGS FOR IT.
"NOW WE WILL FIND THAT OUT TOGETHER.
"I HAVE TECHNOLOGY THAT SPEAKS TO THE MOST POWERFUL FORCES OF THE EARTH ITSELF.
"AND I HAVE TURNED THEM INTO A RECKONING.
DO YOU SEE?

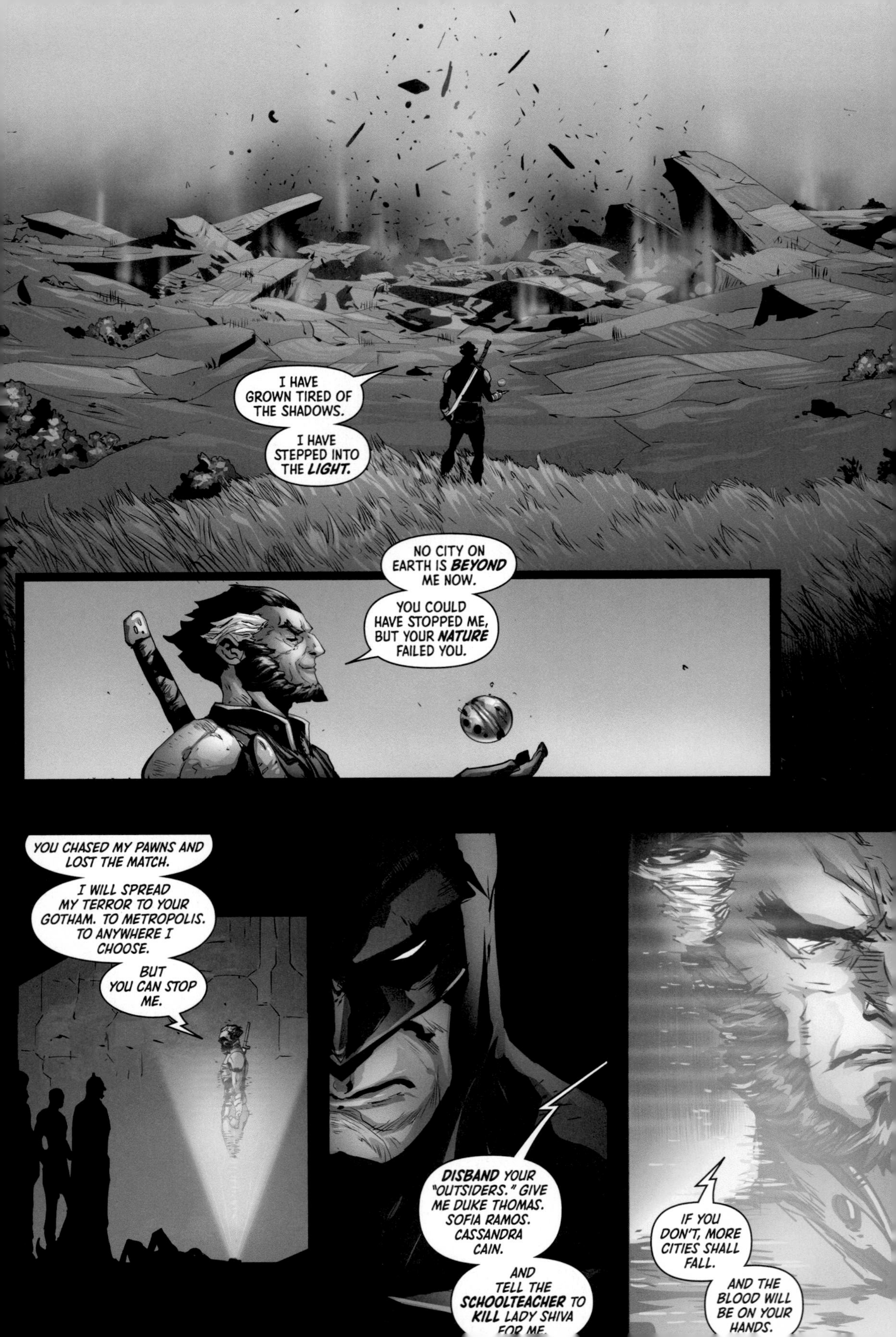
I HAVE GROWN TIRED OF THE SHADOWS.
I HAVE STEPPED INTO THE LIGHT.
NO CITY ON EARTH IS BEYOND ME NOW.
YOU COULD HAVE STOPPED ME, BUT YOUR NATURE FAILED YOU.
YOU CHASED MY PAWNS AND LOST THE MATCH.
I WILL SPREAD MY TERROR TO YOUR GOTHAM. TO METROPOLIS. TO ANYWHERE I CHOOSE.
BUT YOU CAN STOP ME.
DISBAND YOUR "OUTSIDERS." GIVE ME DUKE THOMAS. SOFIA RAMOS. CASSANDRA CAIN.
AND TELL THE SCHOOLTEACHER TO KILL LADY SHIVA FOR ME.
IF YOU DON'T, MORE CITIES SHALL FALL.
AND THE BLOOD WILL BE ON YOUR HANDS.

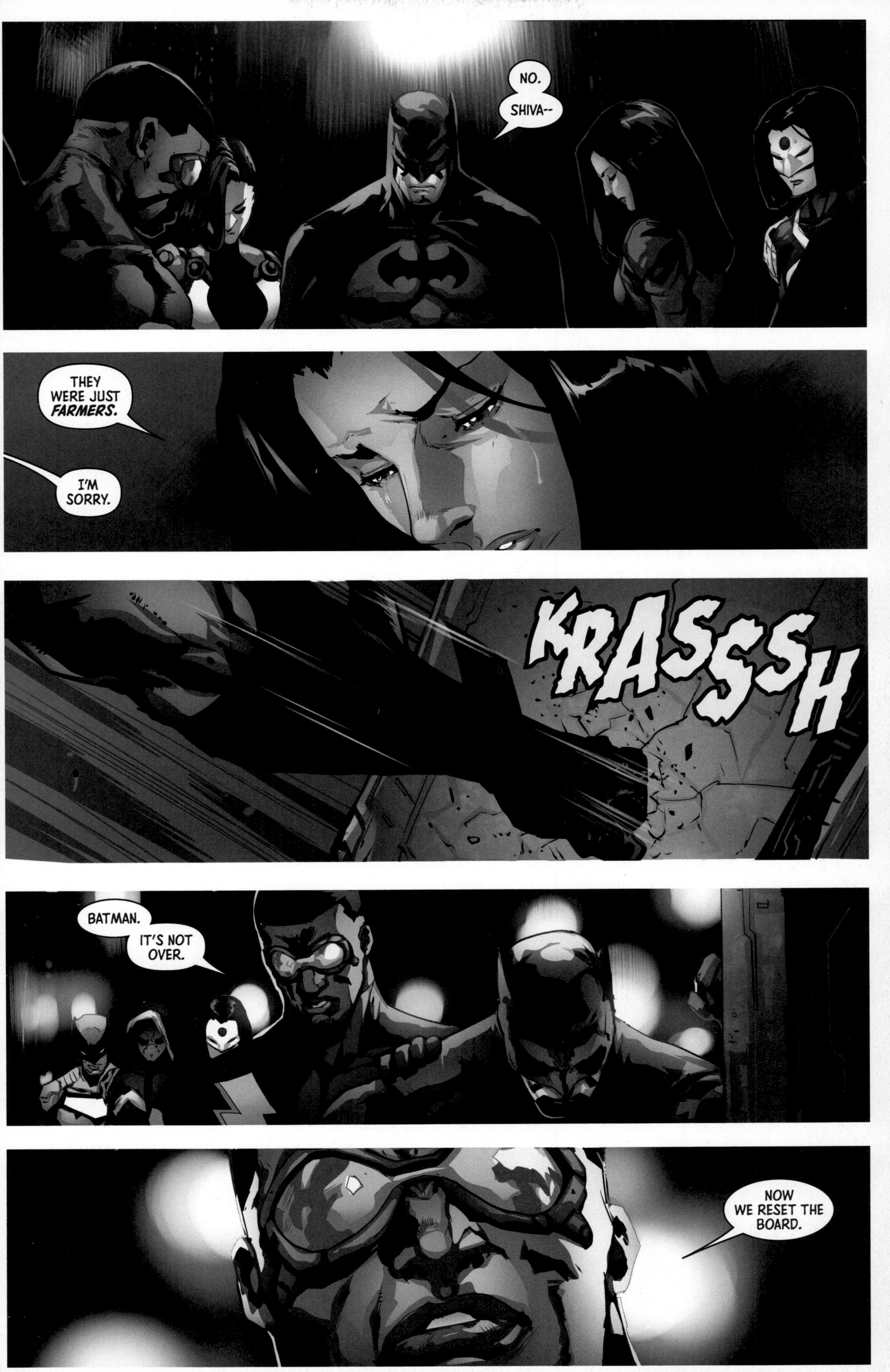
NO.
SHIVA--
THEY WERE JUST FARMERS.
I'M SORRY.
KRASSSH
BATMAN.
IT'S NOT OVER.
NOW WE RESET THE BOARD.

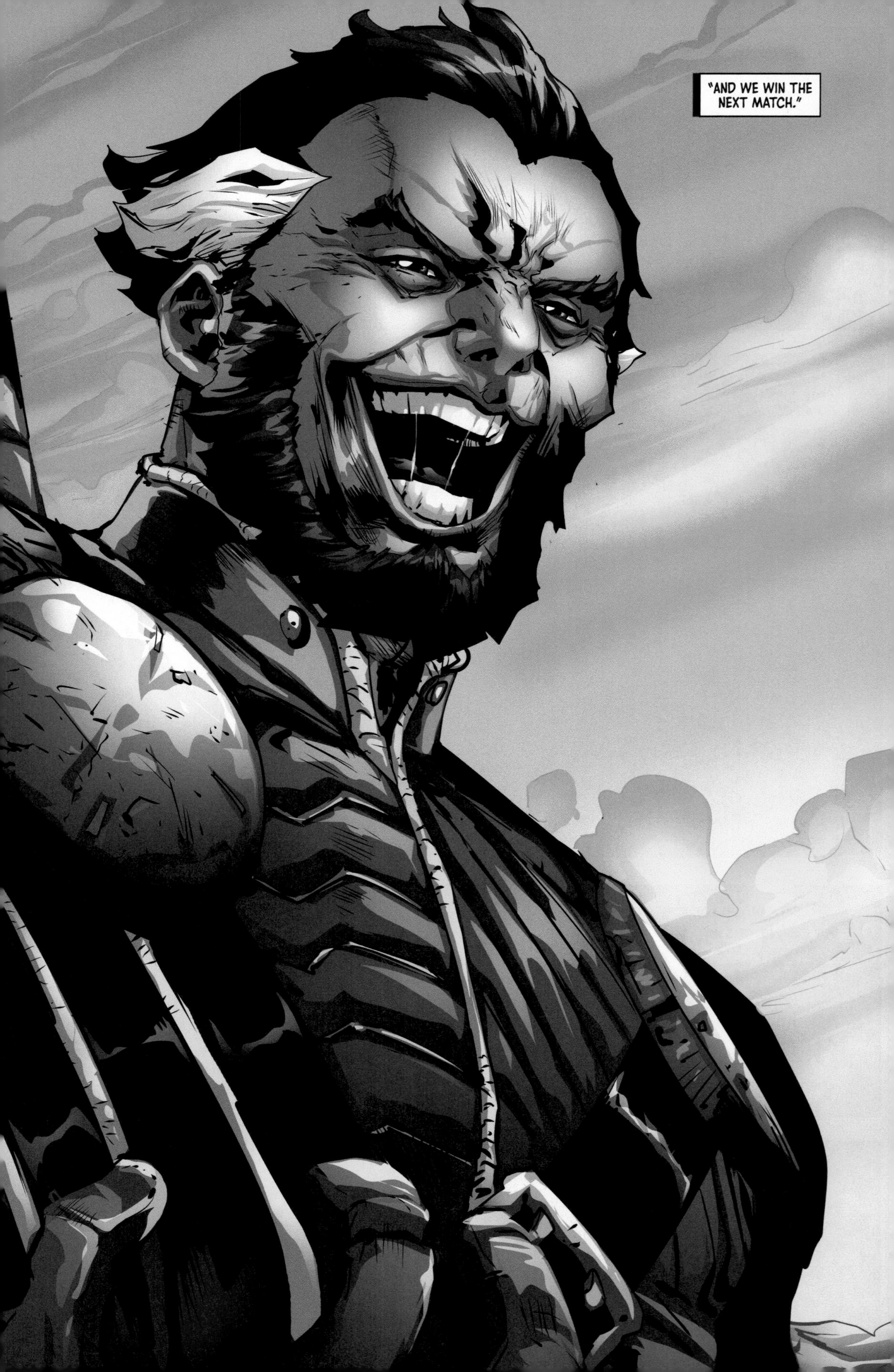
"AND WE WIN THE NEXT MATCH."

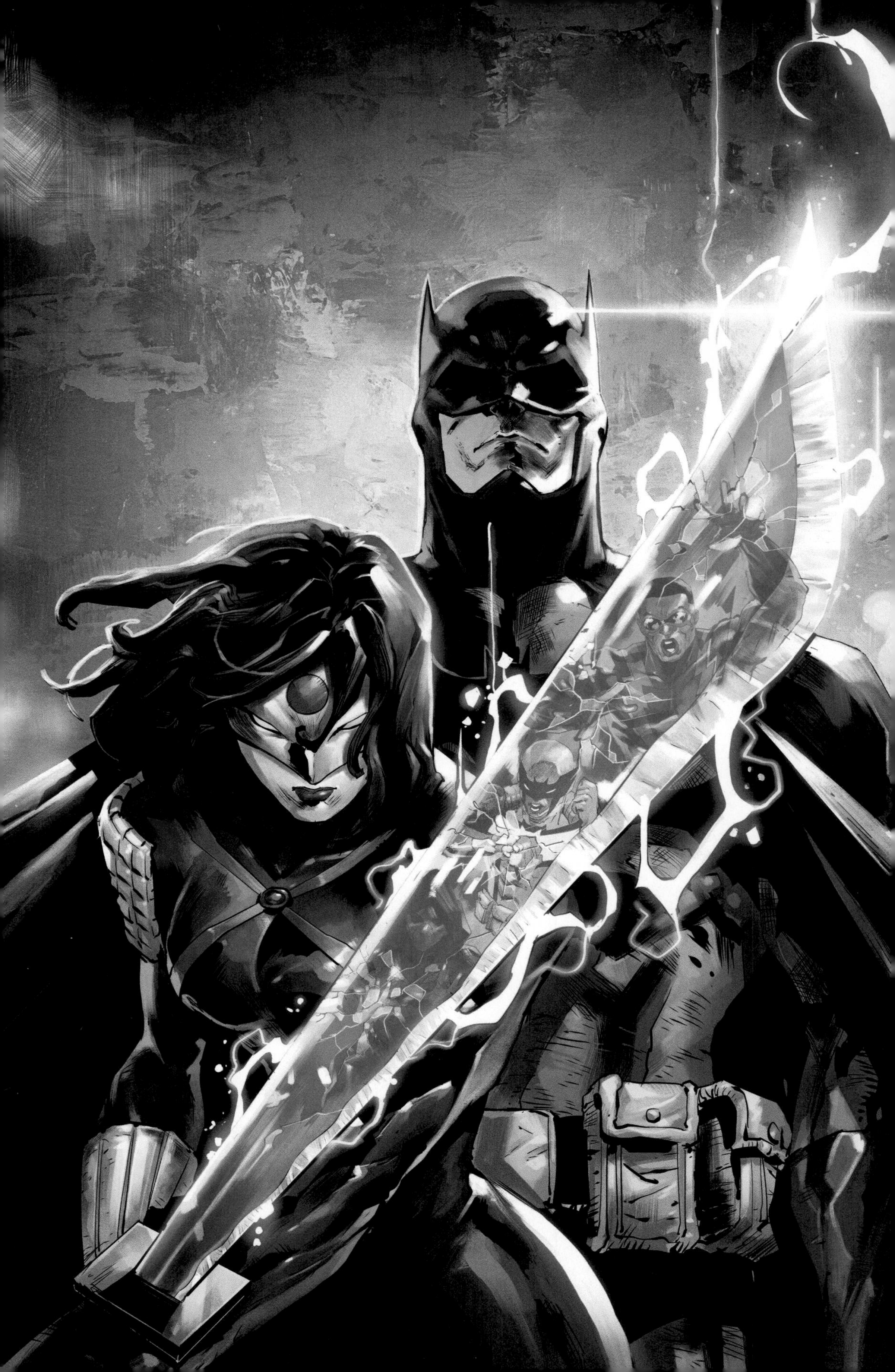

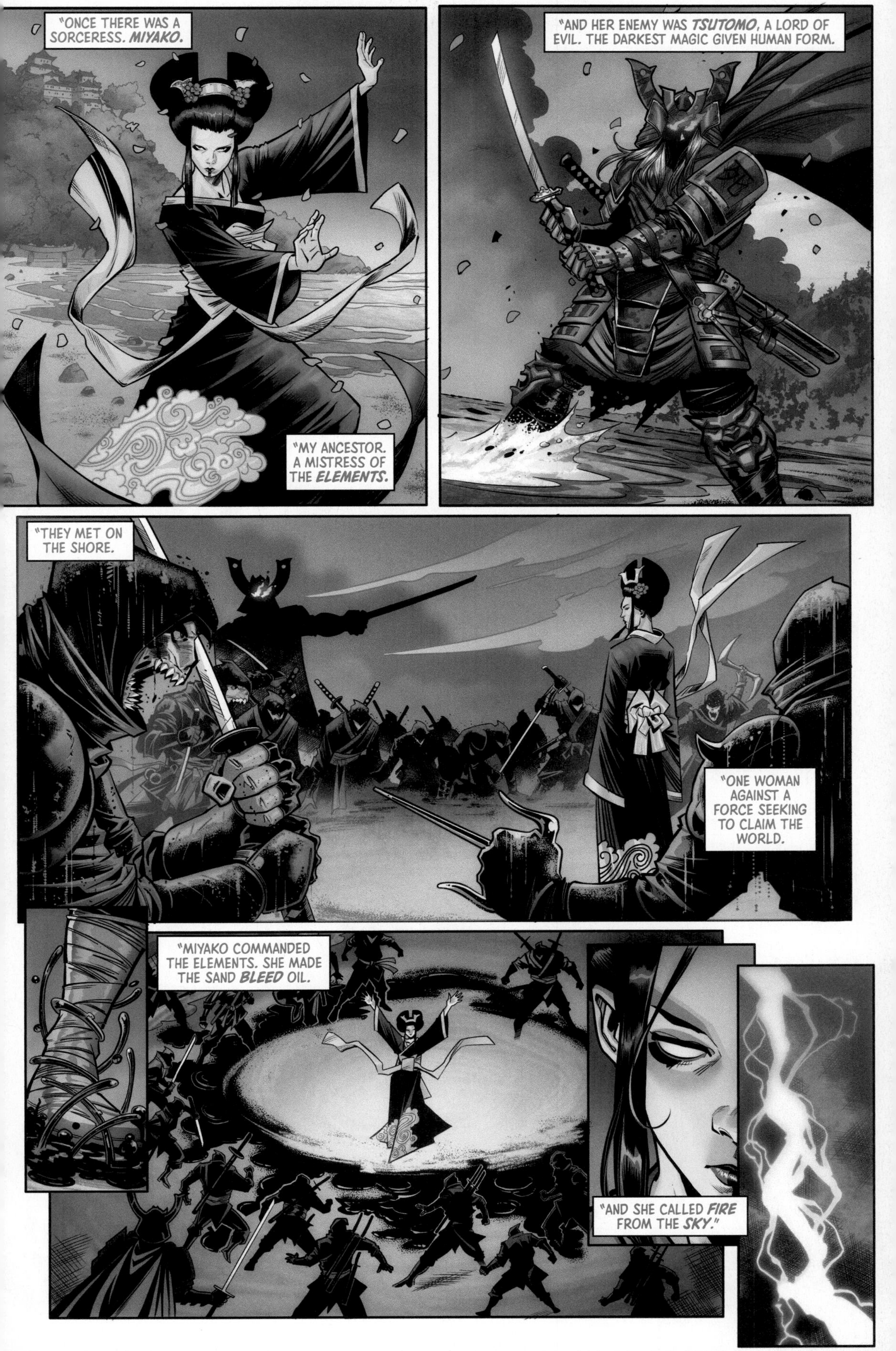
"ONCE THERE WAS A SORCERESS. MIYAKO.
"MY ANCESTOR. A MISTRESS OF THE ELEMENTS.
"AND HER ENEMY WAS TSUTOMO, A LORD OF EVIL. THE DARKEST MAGIC GIVEN HUMAN FORM.
"THEY MET ON THE SHORE.
"ONE WOMAN AGAINST A FORCE SEEKING TO CLAIM THE WORLD.
"MIYAKO COMMANDED THE ELEMENTS. SHE MADE THE SAND BLEED OIL.
"AND SHE CALLED FIRE FROM THE SKY."

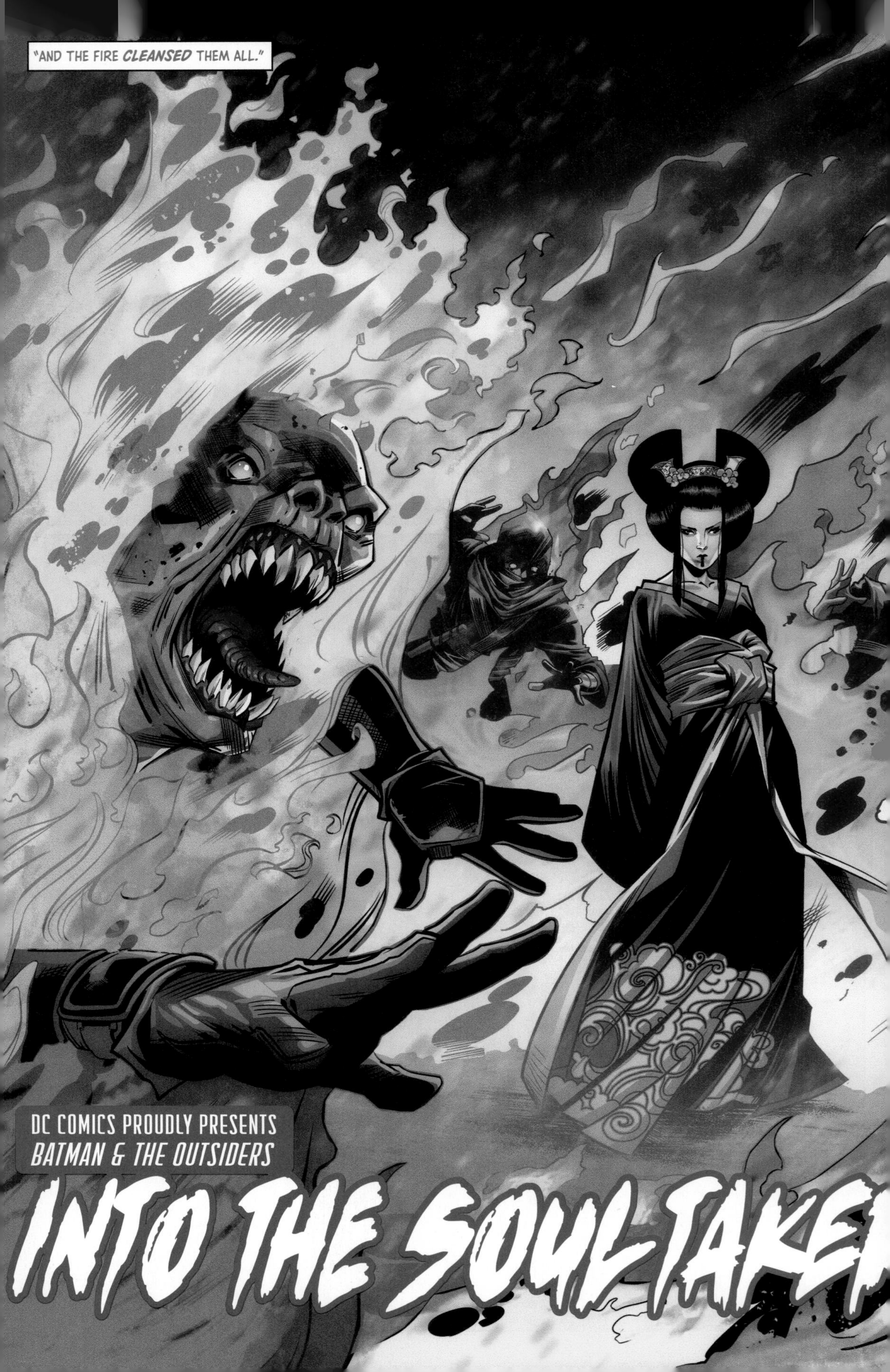
"AND THE FIRE CLEANSED THEM ALL."
DC COMICS PROUDLY PRESENTS
BATMAN & THE OUTSIDERS
INTO THE SOUL TAKE

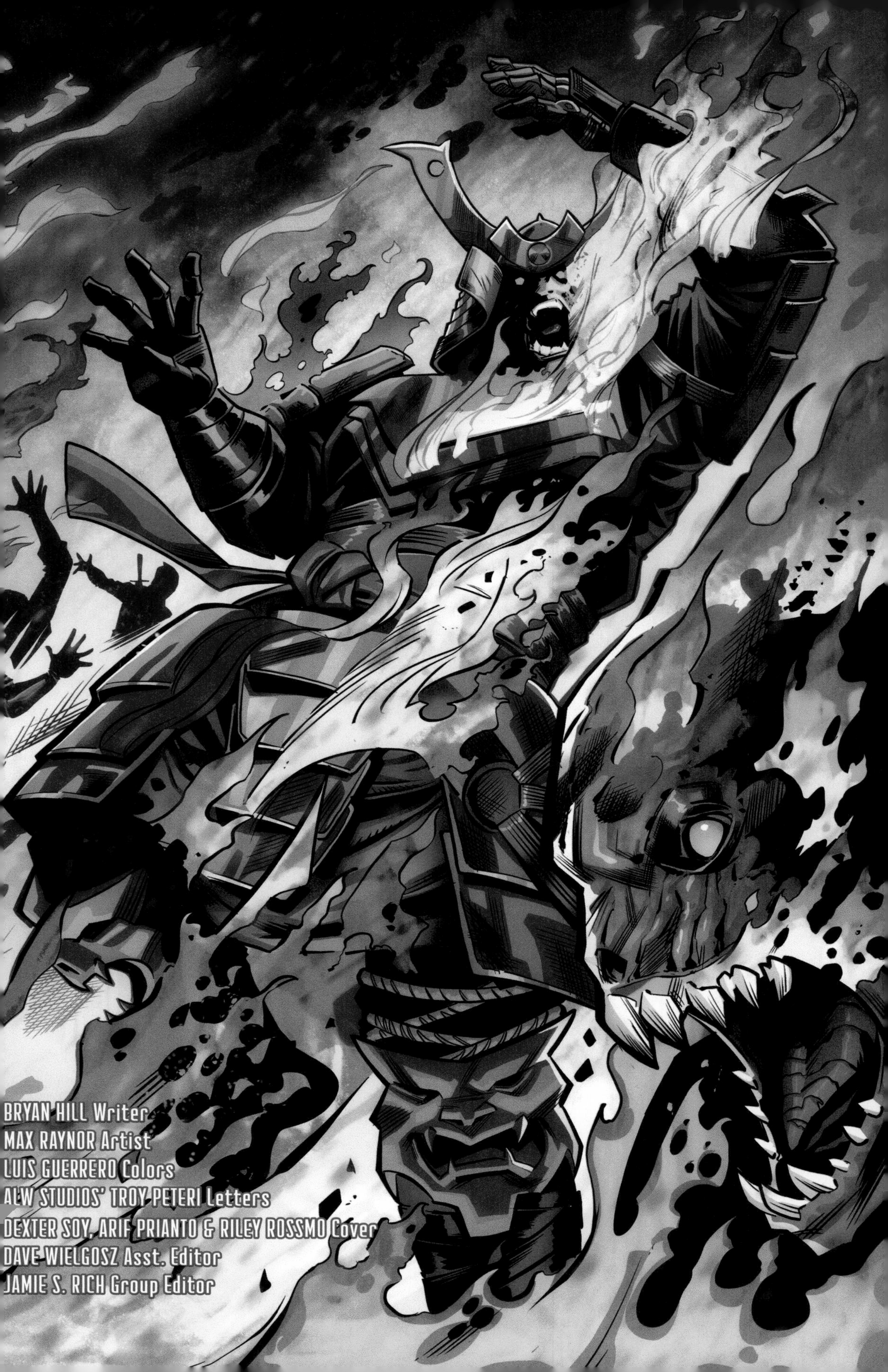
BRYAN HILL Writer
MAX RAYNOR Artist
LUIS GUERRERO Colors
ALW STUDIOS' TROY PETERI Letters
DEXTER SOY, ARIF PRIANTO & RILEY ROSSMO Cover
DAVE WIELGOSZ Asst. Editor
JAMIE S. RICH Group Editor

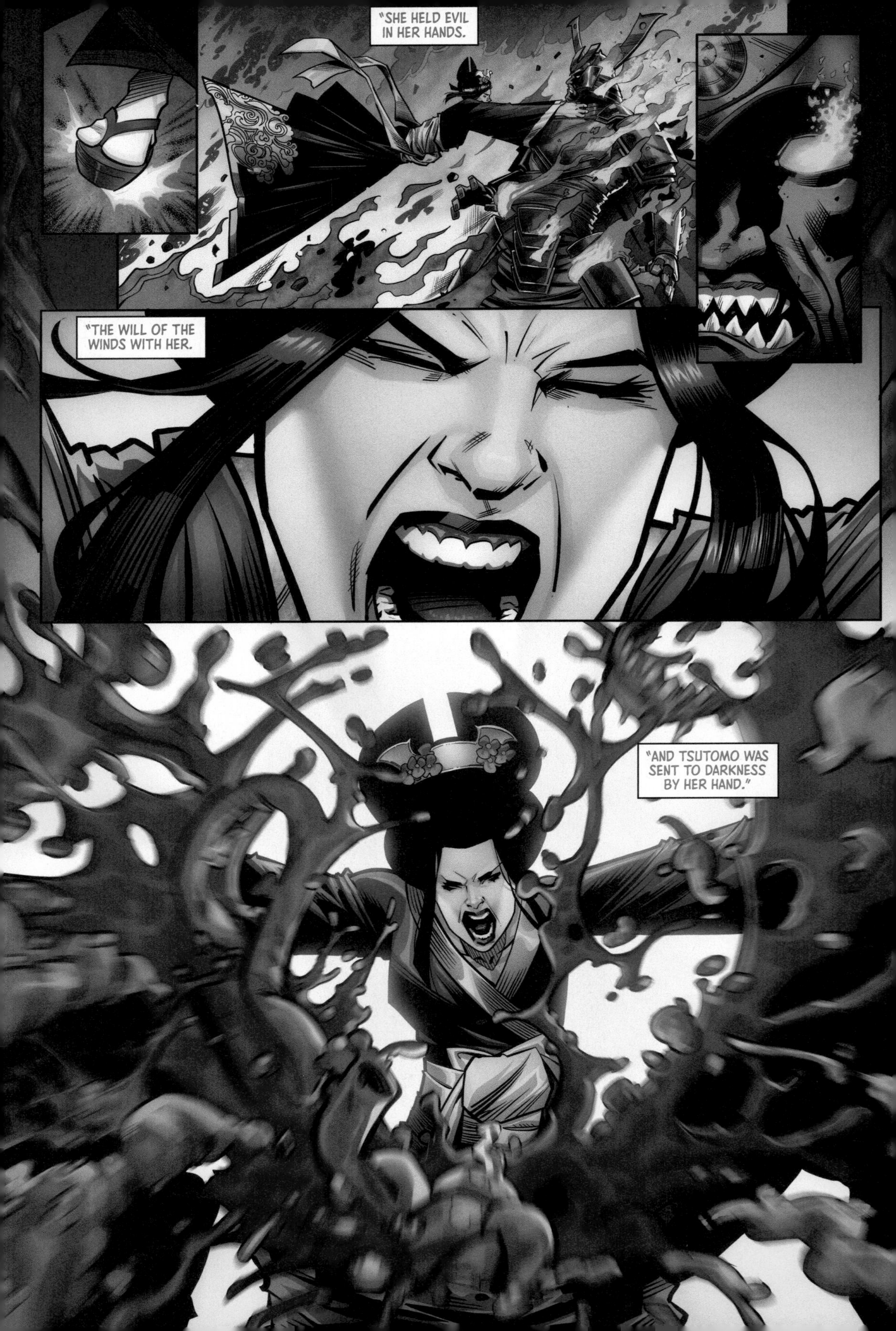
"SHE HELD EVIL IN HER HANDS.
"THE WILL OF THE WINDS WITH HER.
"AND TSUTOMO WAS SENT TO DARKNESS BY HER HAND."

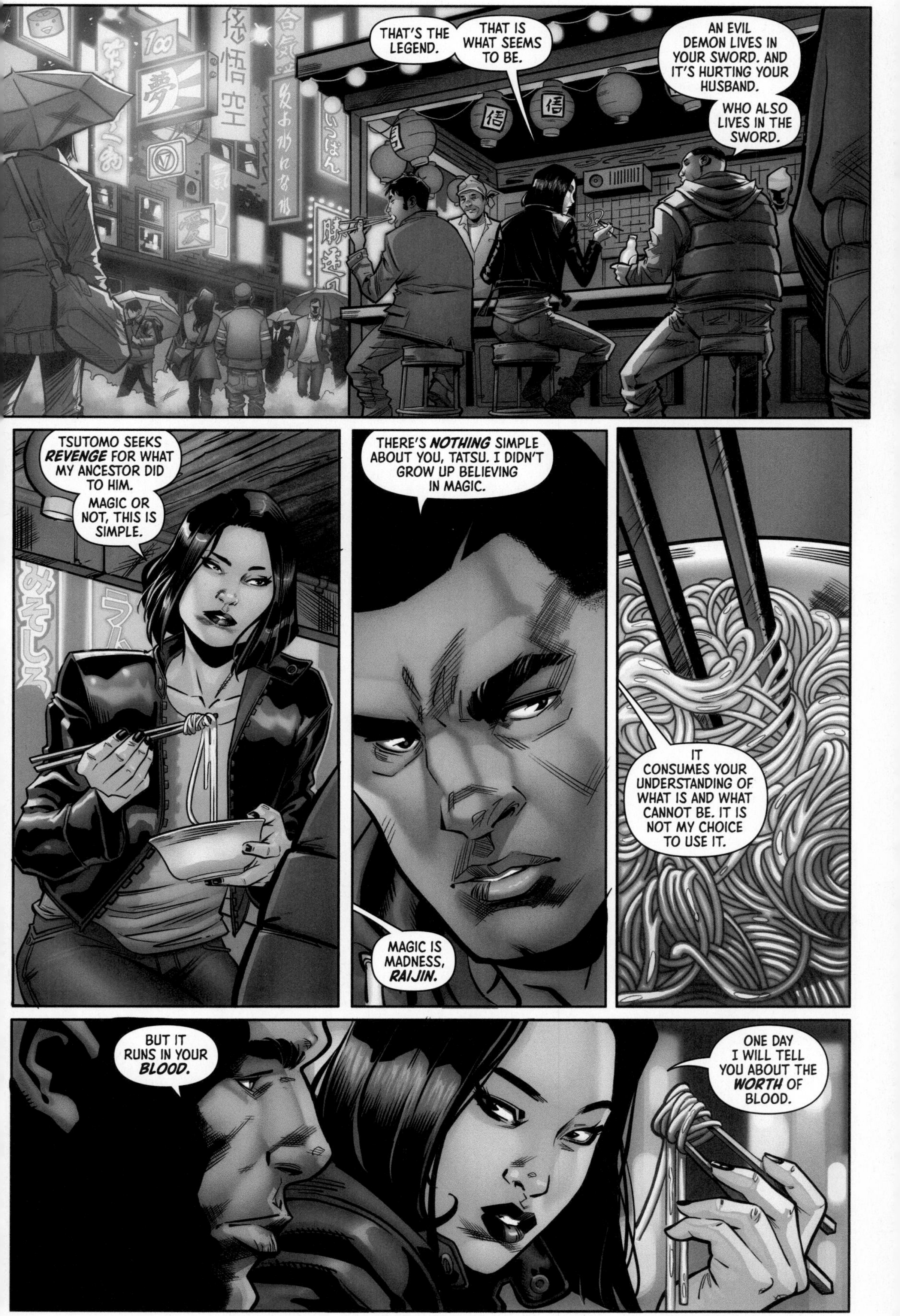
THAT'S THE LEGEND.
THAT IS WHAT SEEMS TO BE.
AN EVIL DEMON LIVES IN YOUR SWORD. AND IT'S HURTING YOUR HUSBAND.
WHO ALSO LIVES IN THE SWORD.
TSUTOMO SEEKS ***REVENGE*** FOR WHAT MY ANCESTOR DID TO HIM.
MAGIC OR NOT, THIS IS SIMPLE.
THERE'S ***NOTHING*** SIMPLE ABOUT YOU, TATSU. I DIDN'T GROW UP BELIEVING IN MAGIC.
MAGIC IS MADNESS, ***RAIJIN.***
IT CONSUMES YOUR UNDERSTANDING OF WHAT IS AND WHAT CANNOT BE. IT IS NOT MY CHOICE TO USE IT.
BUT IT RUNS IN YOUR ***BLOOD.***
ONE DAY I WILL TELL YOU ABOUT THE ***WORTH*** OF BLOOD.

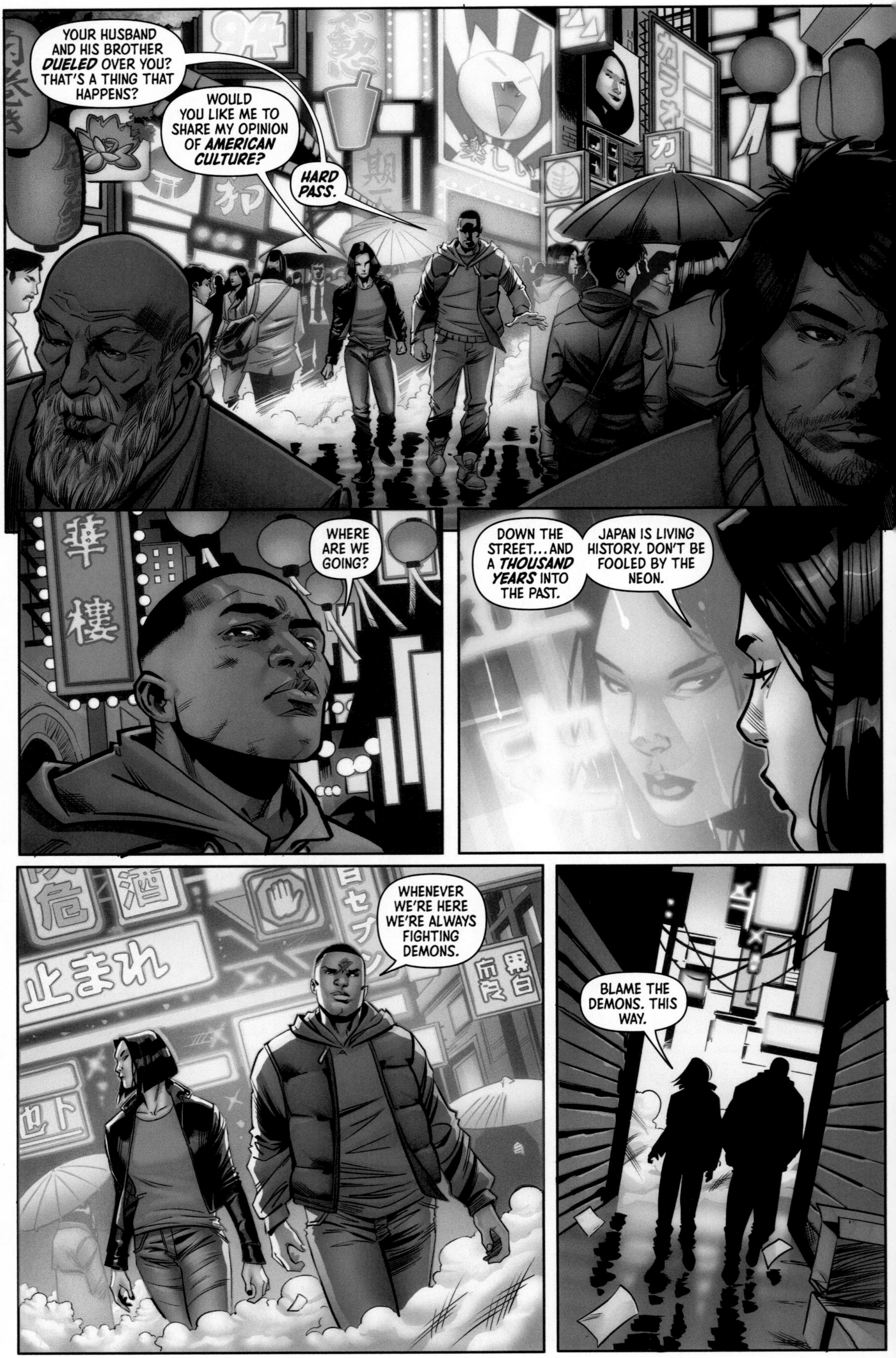

YOUR HUSBAND AND HIS BROTHER DUELED OVER YOU? THAT'S A THING THAT HAPPENS?
WOULD YOU LIKE ME TO SHARE MY OPINION OF AMERICAN CULTURE?
HARD PASS.
WHERE ARE WE GOING?
DOWN THE STREET... AND A THOUSAND YEARS INTO THE PAST.
JAPAN IS LIVING HISTORY. DON'T BE FOOLED BY THE NEON.
WHENEVER WE'RE HERE WE'RE ALWAYS FIGHTING DEMONS.
BLAME THE DEMONS. THIS WAY.

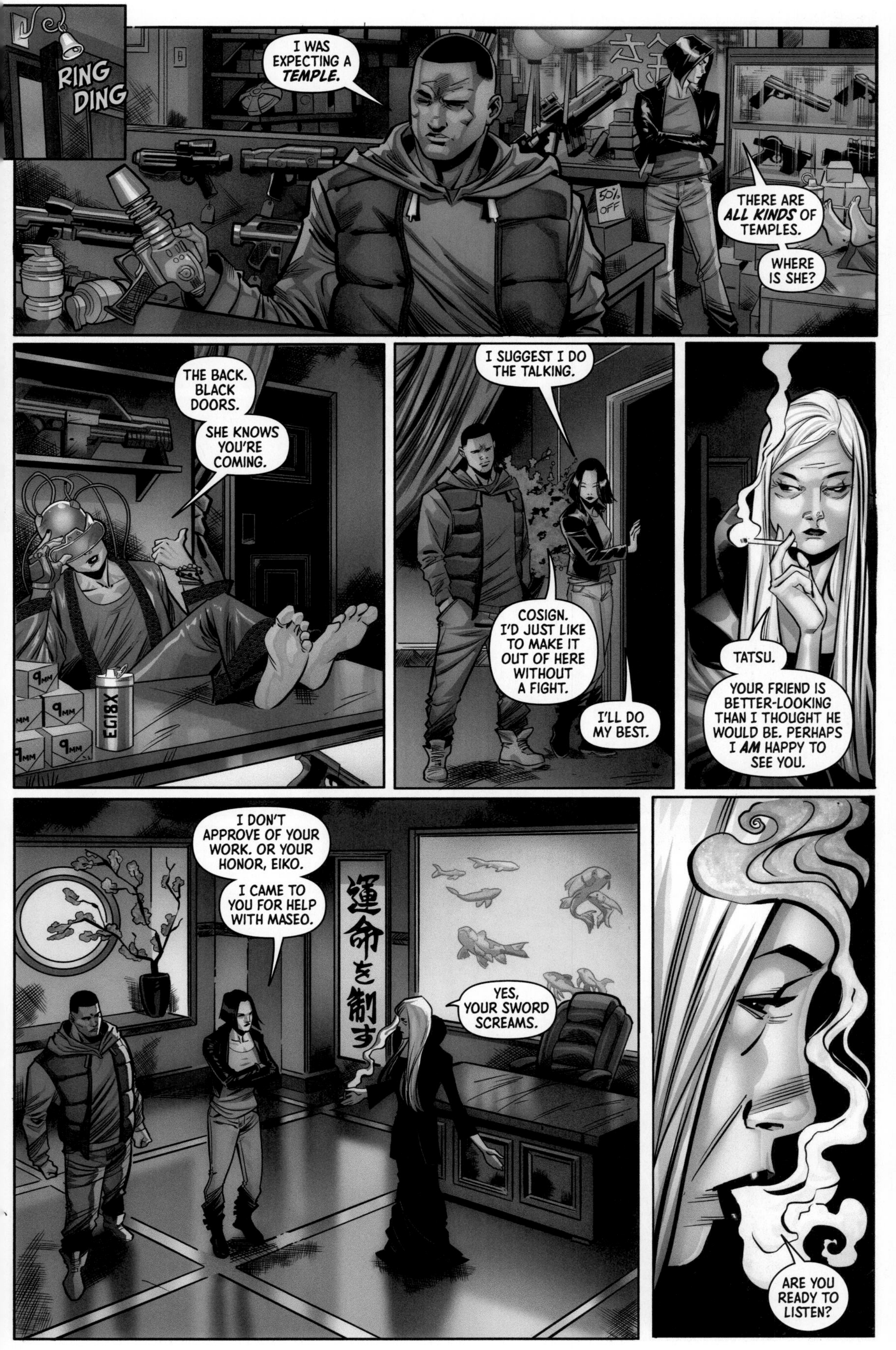

RING DING
I WAS EXPECTING A *TEMPLE.*
50% OFF
THERE ARE ***ALL KINDS*** OF TEMPLES.
WHERE IS SHE?
THE BACK. BLACK DOORS.
SHE KNOWS YOU'RE COMING.
9MM
EG18X
I SUGGEST I DO THE TALKING.
COSIGN. I'D JUST LIKE TO MAKE IT OUT OF HERE WITHOUT A FIGHT.
I'LL DO MY BEST.
TATSU.
YOUR FRIEND IS BETTER-LOOKING THAN I THOUGHT HE WOULD BE. PERHAPS I ***AM*** HAPPY TO SEE YOU.
I DON'T APPROVE OF YOUR WORK. OR YOUR HONOR, EIKO.
I CAME TO YOU FOR HELP WITH MASEO.
運命を制す
YES, YOUR SWORD SCREAMS.
ARE YOU READY TO LISTEN?

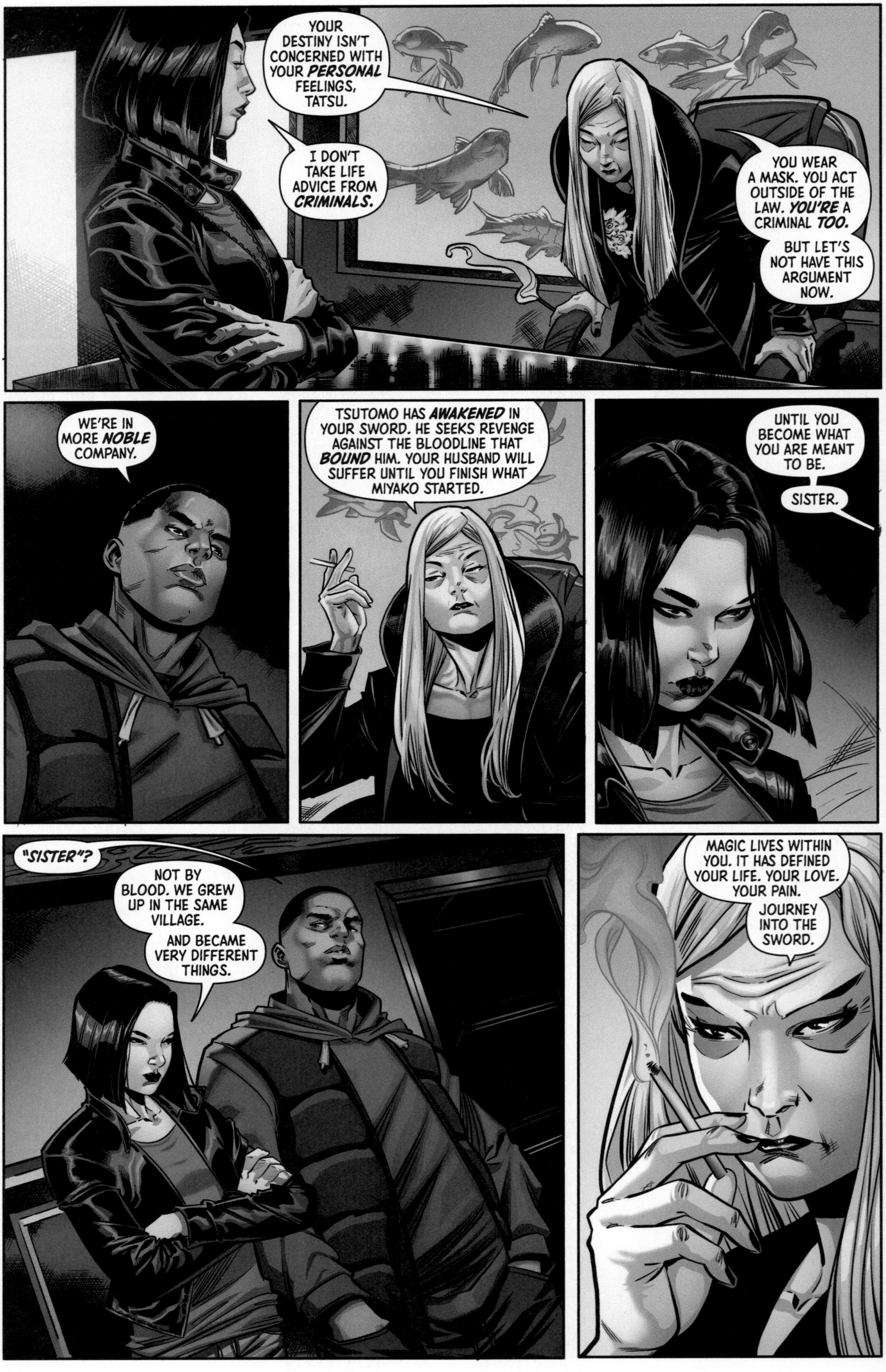
YOUR DESTINY ISN'T CONCERNED WITH YOUR PERSONAL FEELINGS, TATSU.
I DON'T TAKE LIFE ADVICE FROM CRIMINALS.
YOU WEAR A MASK. YOU ACT OUTSIDE OF THE LAW. YOU'RE A CRIMINAL TOO.
BUT LET'S NOT HAVE THIS ARGUMENT NOW.
WE'RE IN MORE NOBLE COMPANY.
TSUTOMO HAS AWAKENED IN YOUR SWORD. HE SEEKS REVENGE AGAINST THE BLOODLINE THAT BOUND HIM. YOUR HUSBAND WILL SUFFER UNTIL YOU FINISH WHAT MIYAKO STARTED.
UNTIL YOU BECOME WHAT YOU ARE MEANT TO BE.
SISTER.
"SISTER"?
NOT BY BLOOD. WE GREW UP IN THE SAME VILLAGE.
AND BECAME VERY DIFFERENT THINGS.
MAGIC LIVES WITHIN YOU. IT HAS DEFINED YOUR LIFE. YOUR LOVE. YOUR PAIN.
JOURNEY INTO THE SWORD.

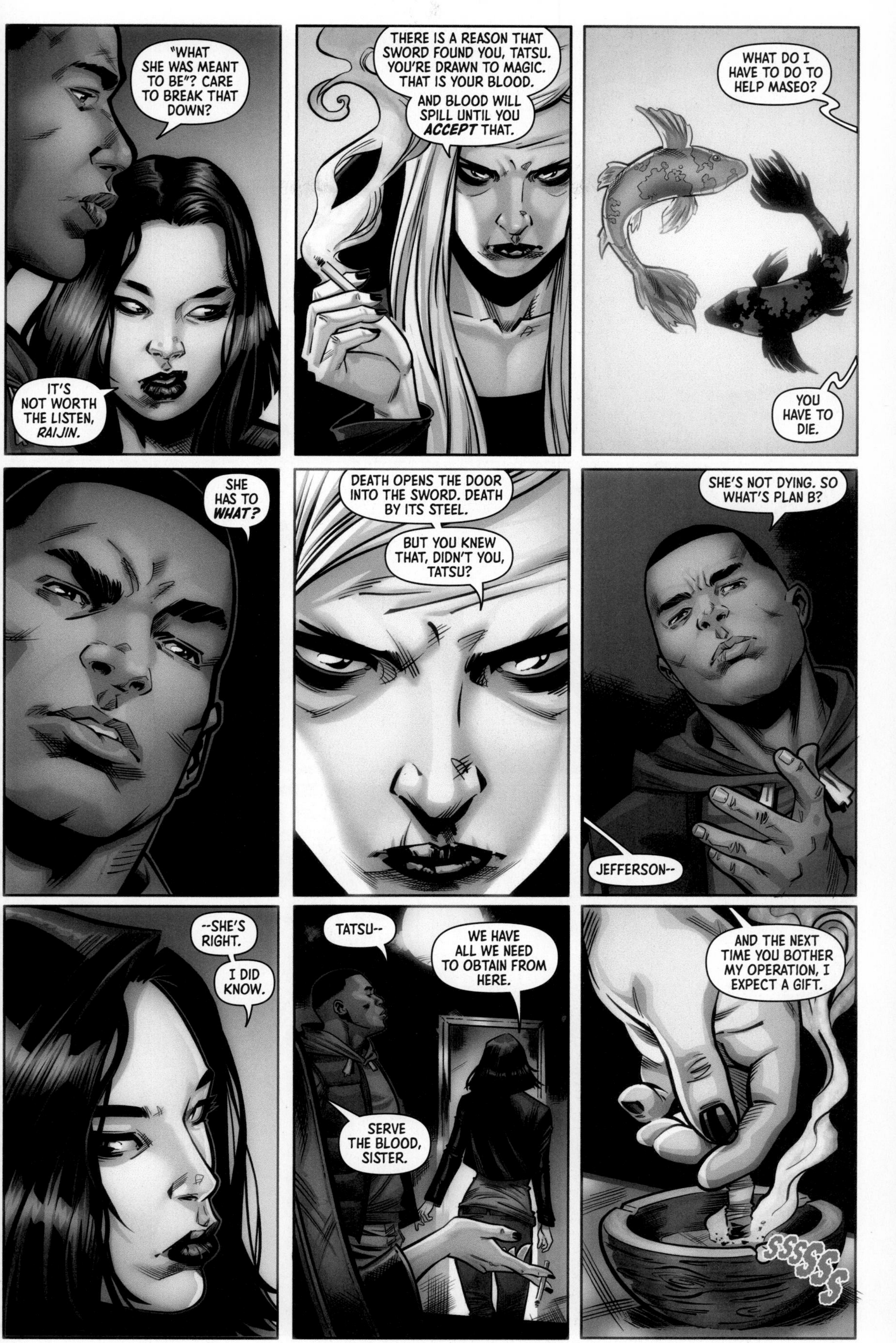

"WHAT SHE WAS MEANT TO BE"? CARE TO BREAK THAT DOWN?
IT'S NOT WORTH THE LISTEN, *RAIJIN.*
THERE IS A REASON THAT SWORD FOUND YOU, TATSU. YOU'RE DRAWN TO MAGIC. THAT IS YOUR BLOOD.
AND BLOOD WILL SPILL UNTIL YOU *ACCEPT* THAT.
WHAT DO I HAVE TO DO TO HELP MASEO?
YOU HAVE TO DIE.
SHE HAS TO *WHAT?*
DEATH OPENS THE DOOR INTO THE SWORD. DEATH BY ITS STEEL.
BUT YOU KNEW THAT, DIDN'T YOU, TATSU?
SHE'S NOT DYING. SO WHAT'S PLAN B?
JEFFERSON--
--SHE'S RIGHT.
I DID KNOW.
TATSU--
WE HAVE ALL WE NEED TO OBTAIN FROM HERE.
SERVE THE BLOOD, SISTER.
AND THE NEXT TIME YOU BOTHER MY OPERATION, I EXPECT A GIFT.
SSSSSS

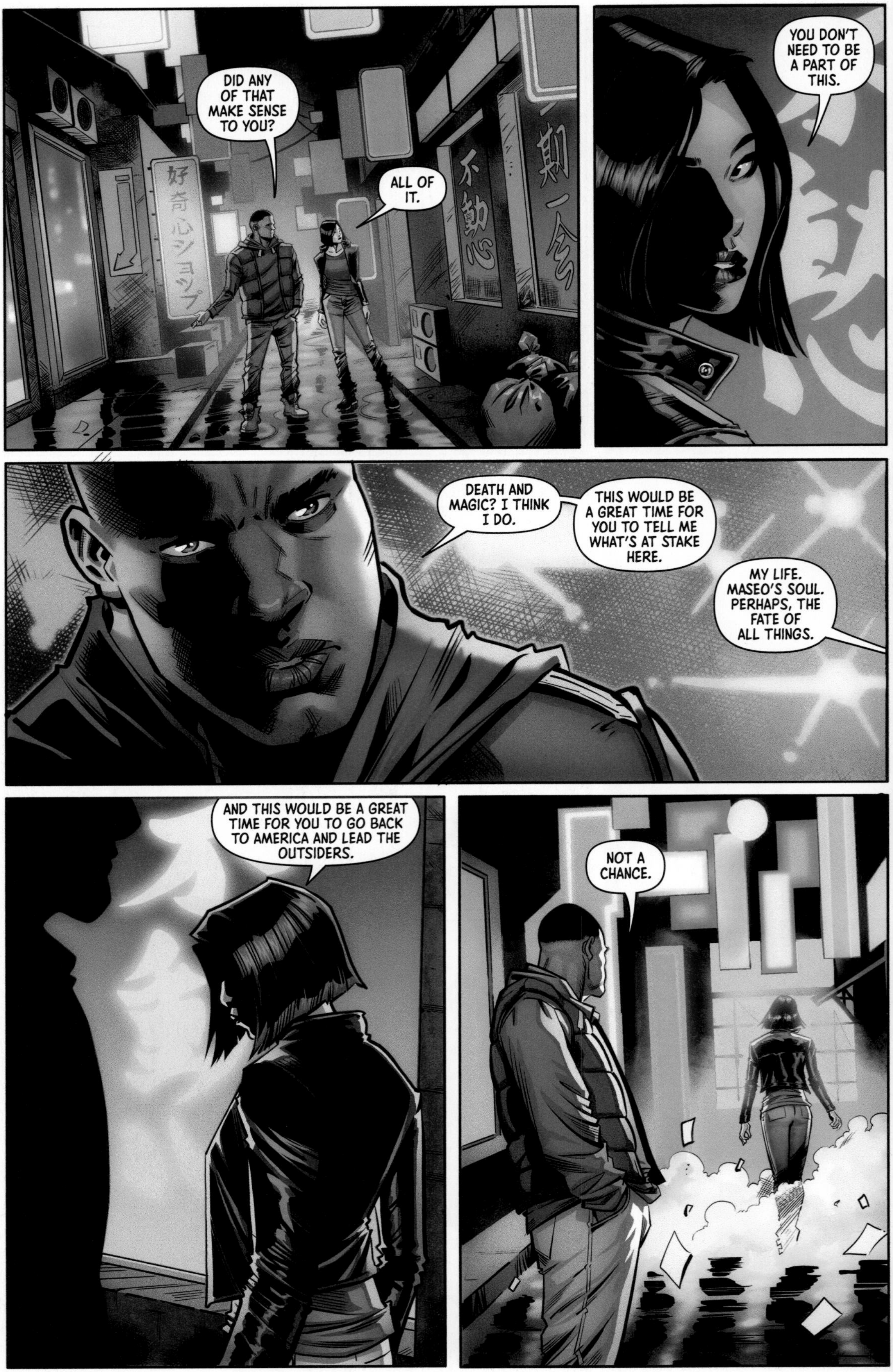
DID ANY OF THAT MAKE SENSE TO YOU?
ALL OF IT.
好奇心ショップ
不動心
YOU DON'T NEED TO BE A PART OF THIS.
DEATH AND MAGIC? I THINK I DO.
THIS WOULD BE A GREAT TIME FOR YOU TO TELL ME WHAT'S AT STAKE HERE.
MY LIFE. MASEO'S SOUL. PERHAPS, THE FATE OF ALL THINGS.
AND THIS WOULD BE A GREAT TIME FOR YOU TO GO BACK TO AMERICA AND LEAD THE OUTSIDERS.
NOT A CHANCE.

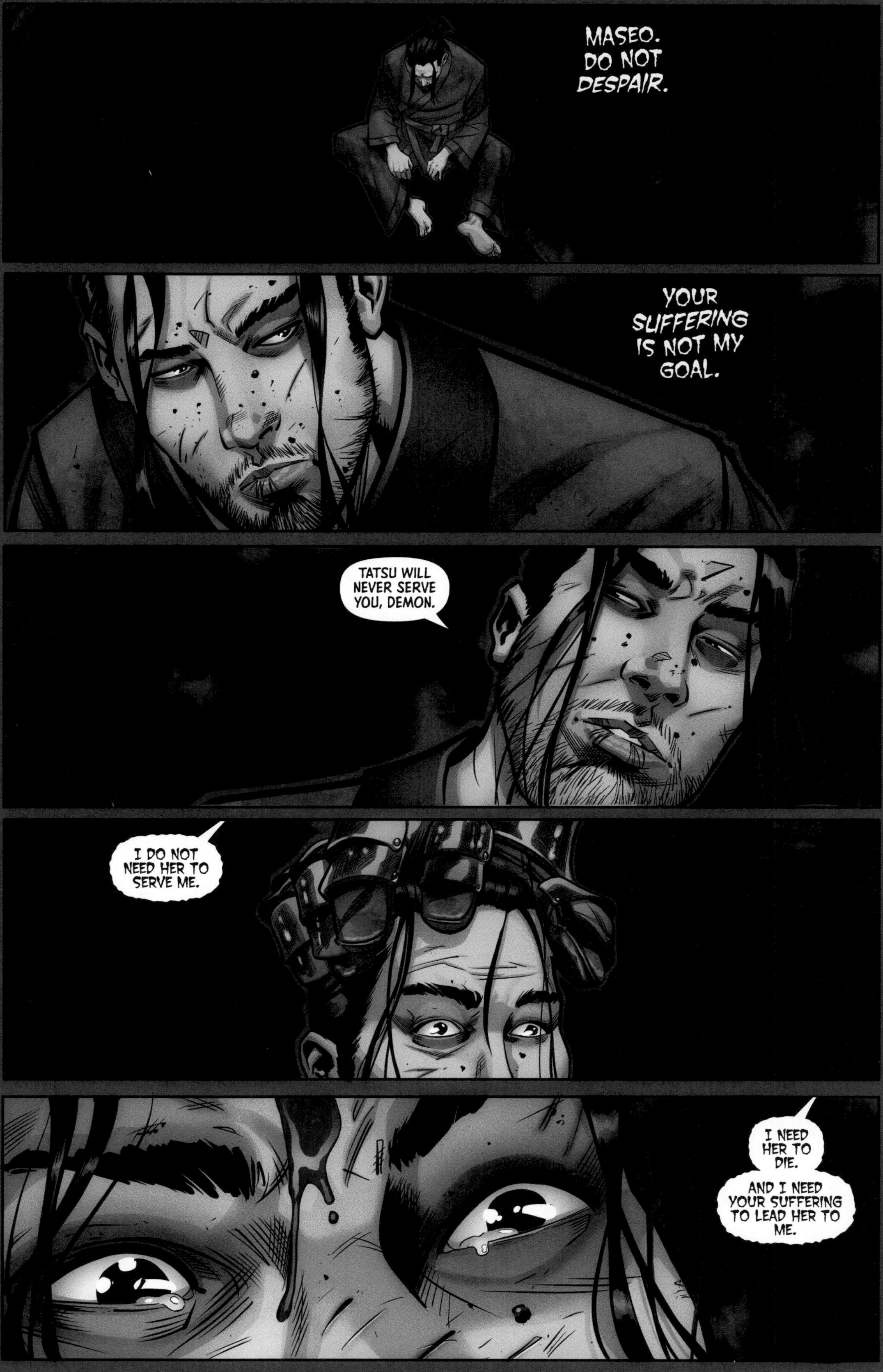
MASEO. DO NOT DESPAIR.
YOUR SUFFERING IS NOT MY GOAL.
TATSU WILL NEVER SERVE YOU, DEMON.
I DO NOT NEED HER TO SERVE ME.
I NEED HER TO DIE.
AND I NEED YOUR SUFFERING TO LEAD HER TO ME.

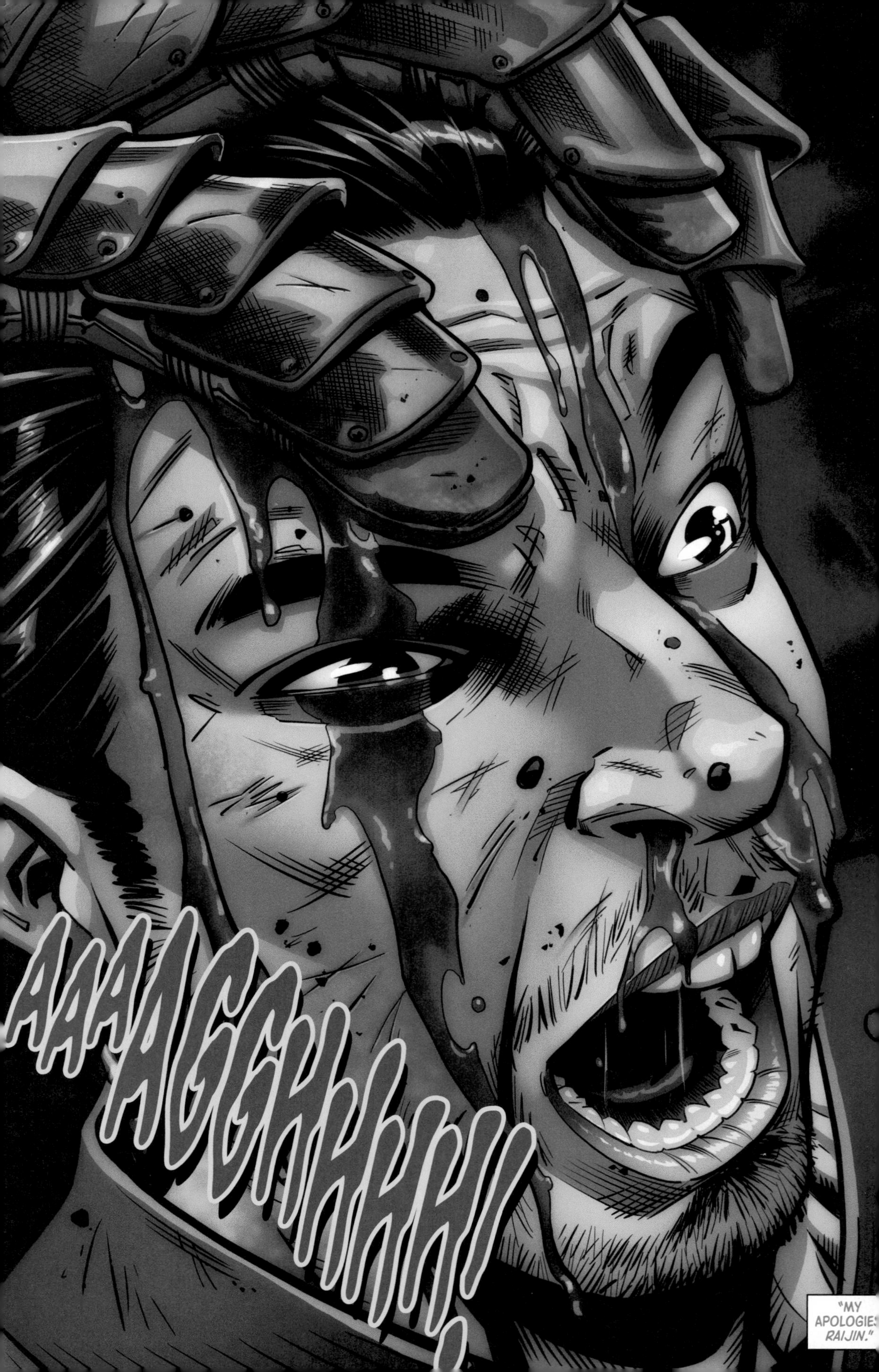
AAAAGGHHHHH!
"MY APOLOGIES RAIJIN."

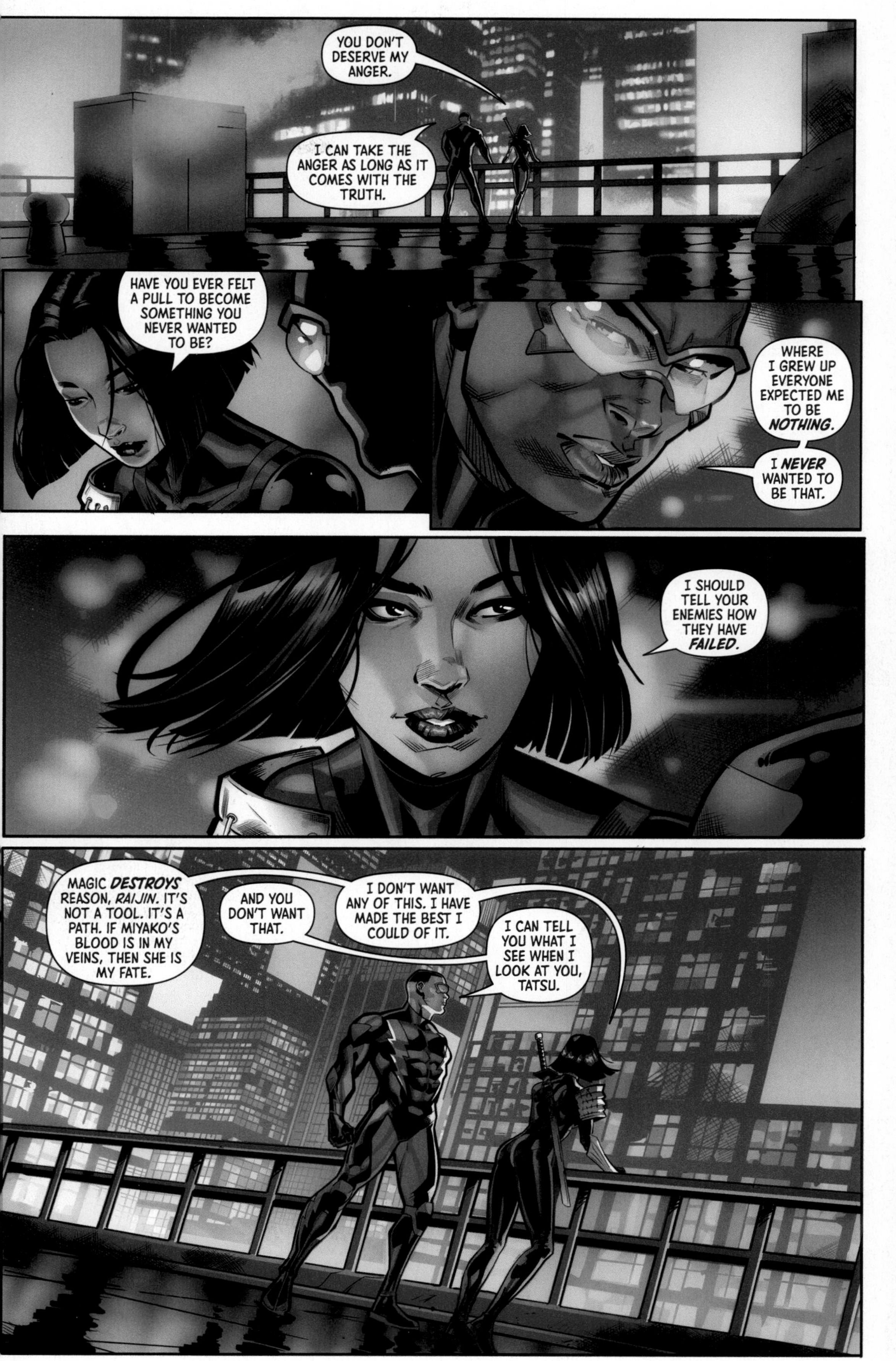
YOU DON'T DESERVE MY ANGER.
I CAN TAKE THE ANGER AS LONG AS IT COMES WITH THE TRUTH.
HAVE YOU EVER FELT A PULL TO BECOME SOMETHING YOU NEVER WANTED TO BE?
WHERE I GREW UP EVERYONE EXPECTED ME TO BE NOTHING.
I NEVER WANTED TO BE THAT.
I SHOULD TELL YOUR ENEMIES HOW THEY HAVE FAILED.
MAGIC DESTROYS REASON, RAIJIN. IT'S NOT A TOOL. IT'S A PATH. IF MIYAKO'S BLOOD IS IN MY VEINS, THEN SHE IS MY FATE.
AND YOU DON'T WANT THAT.
I DON'T WANT ANY OF THIS. I HAVE MADE THE BEST I COULD OF IT.
I CAN TELL YOU WHAT I SEE WHEN I LOOK AT YOU, TATSU.

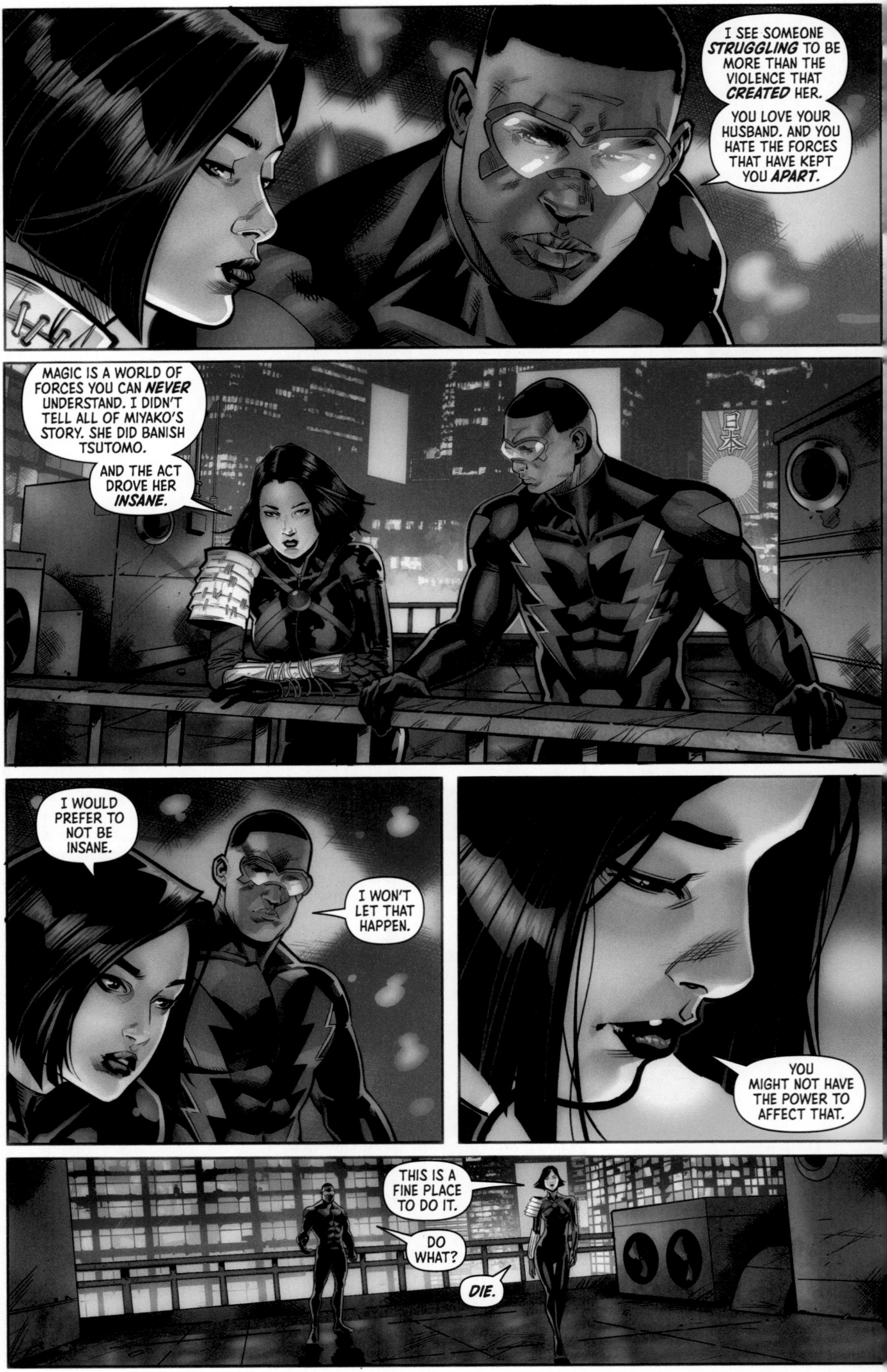
I SEE SOMEONE *STRUGGLING* TO BE MORE THAN THE VIOLENCE THAT *CREATED* HER.
YOU LOVE YOUR HUSBAND. AND YOU HATE THE FORCES THAT HAVE KEPT YOU *APART*.
MAGIC IS A WORLD OF FORCES YOU CAN *NEVER* UNDERSTAND. I DIDN'T TELL ALL OF MIYAKO'S STORY. SHE DID BANISH TSUTOMO.
AND THE ACT DROVE HER *INSANE*.
日本
I WOULD PREFER TO NOT BE INSANE.
I WON'T LET THAT HAPPEN.
YOU MIGHT NOT HAVE THE POWER TO AFFECT THAT.
THIS IS A FINE PLACE TO DO IT.
DO WHAT?
DIE.

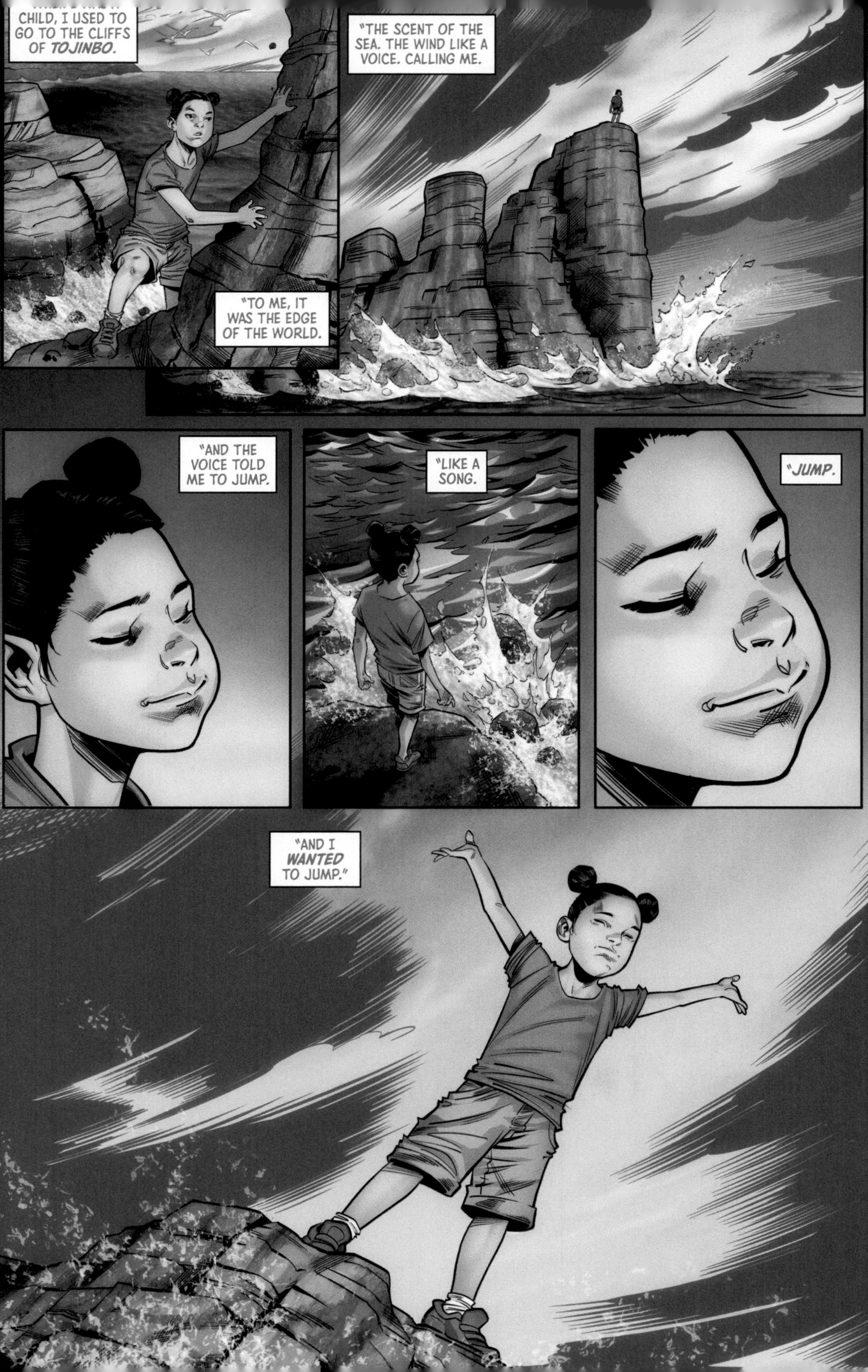
CHILD, I USED TO GO TO THE CLIFFS OF *TOJINBO.*
"THE SCENT OF THE SEA. THE WIND LIKE A VOICE. CALLING ME.
"TO ME, IT WAS THE EDGE OF THE WORLD.
"AND THE VOICE TOLD ME TO JUMP.
"LIKE A SONG.
"*JUMP.*
"AND I *WANTED* TO JUMP."

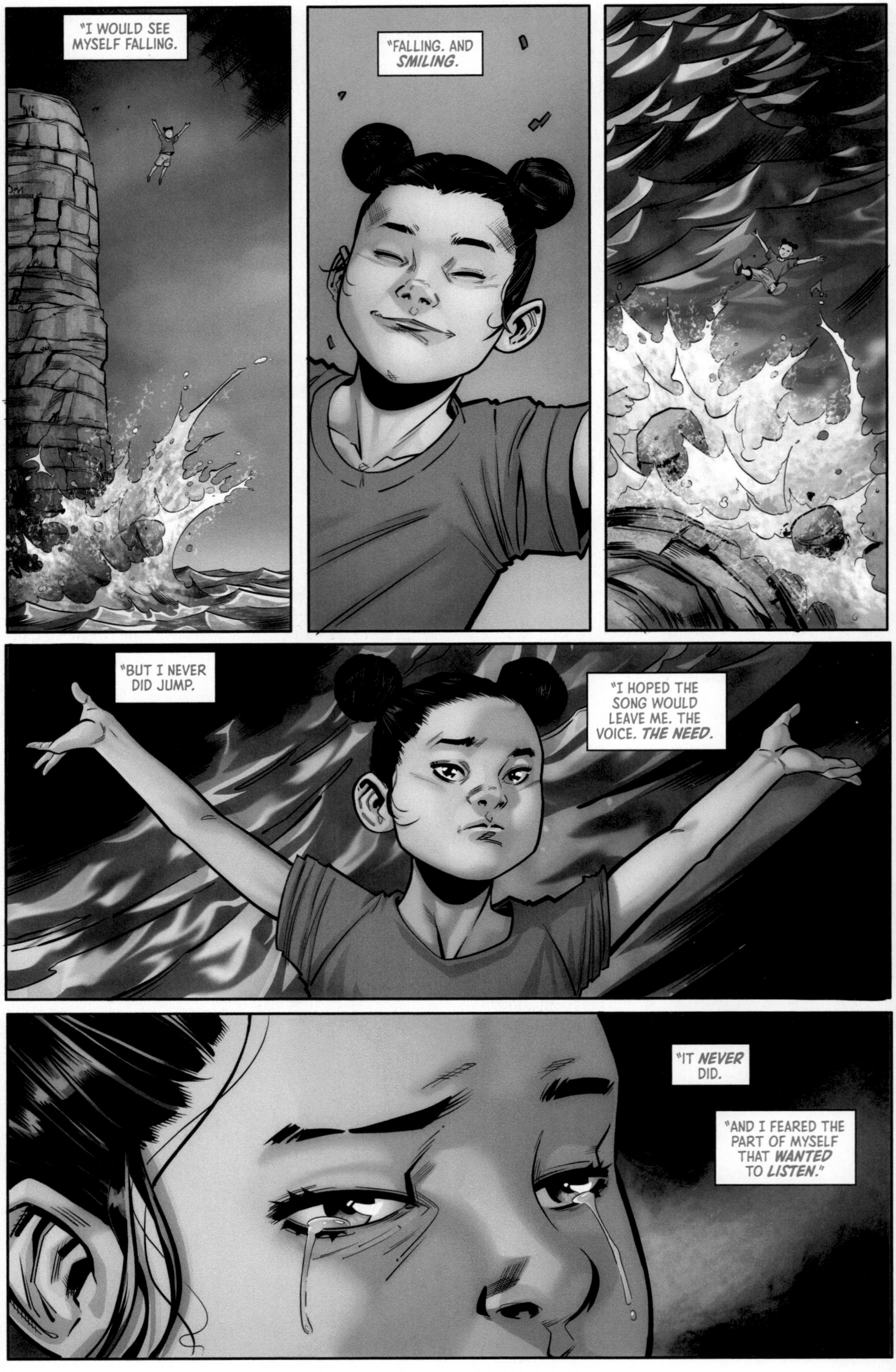
"I WOULD SEE MYSELF FALLING.
"FALLING. AND *SMILING.*
"BUT I NEVER DID JUMP.
"I HOPED THE SONG WOULD LEAVE ME. THE VOICE. ***THE NEED.***
"IT *NEVER* DID.
"AND I FEARED THE PART OF MYSELF THAT *WANTED* TO *LISTEN.*"

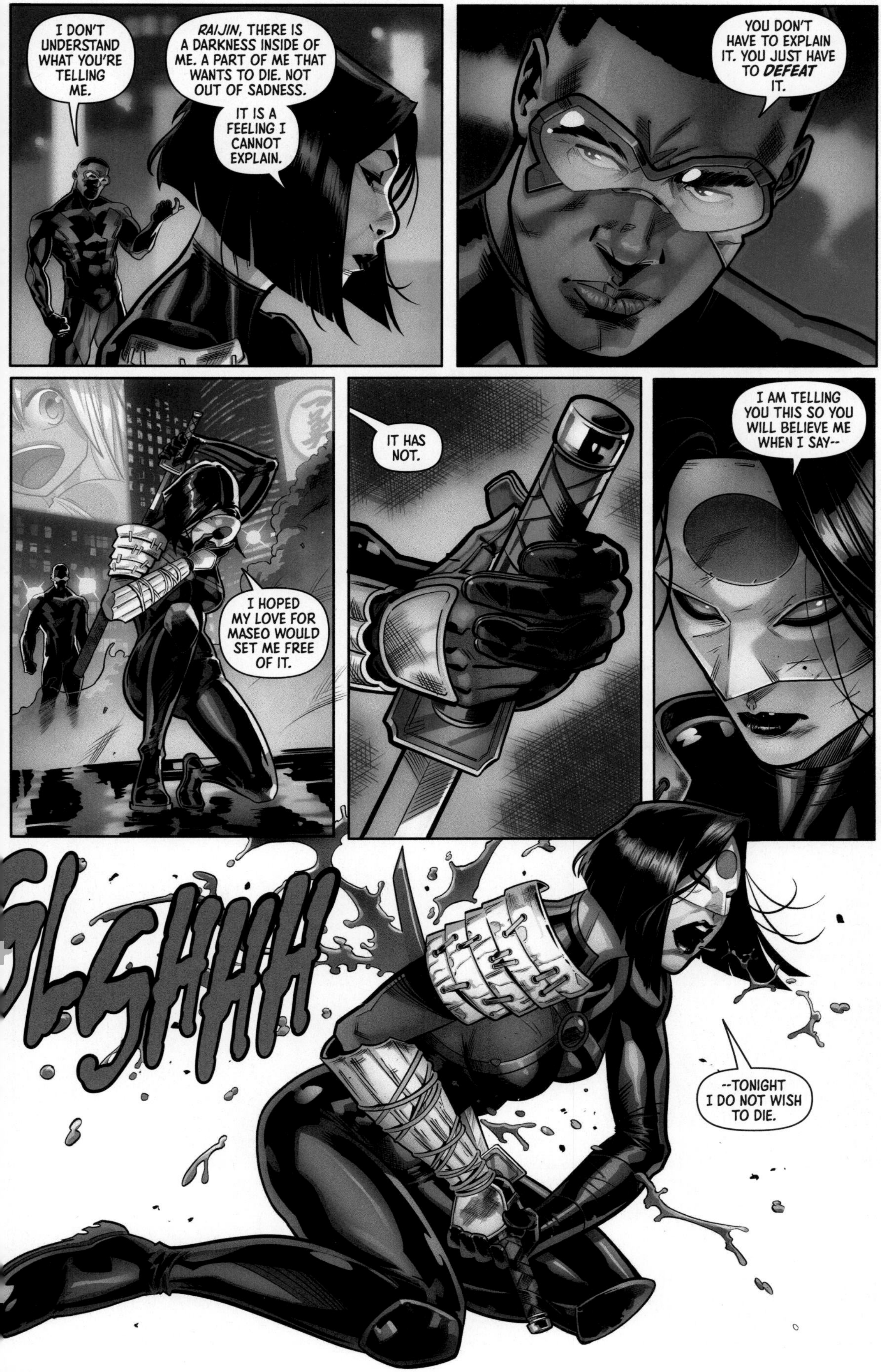
I DON'T UNDERSTAND WHAT YOU'RE TELLING ME.
RAIJIN, THERE IS A DARKNESS INSIDE OF ME. A PART OF ME THAT WANTS TO DIE. NOT OUT OF SADNESS.
IT IS A FEELING I CANNOT EXPLAIN.
YOU DON'T HAVE TO EXPLAIN IT. YOU JUST HAVE TO ***DEFEAT*** IT.
I HOPED MY LOVE FOR MASEO WOULD SET ME FREE OF IT.
IT HAS NOT.
I AM TELLING YOU THIS SO YOU WILL BELIEVE ME WHEN I SAY--
GLSHHH
--TONIGHT I DO NOT WISH TO DIE.

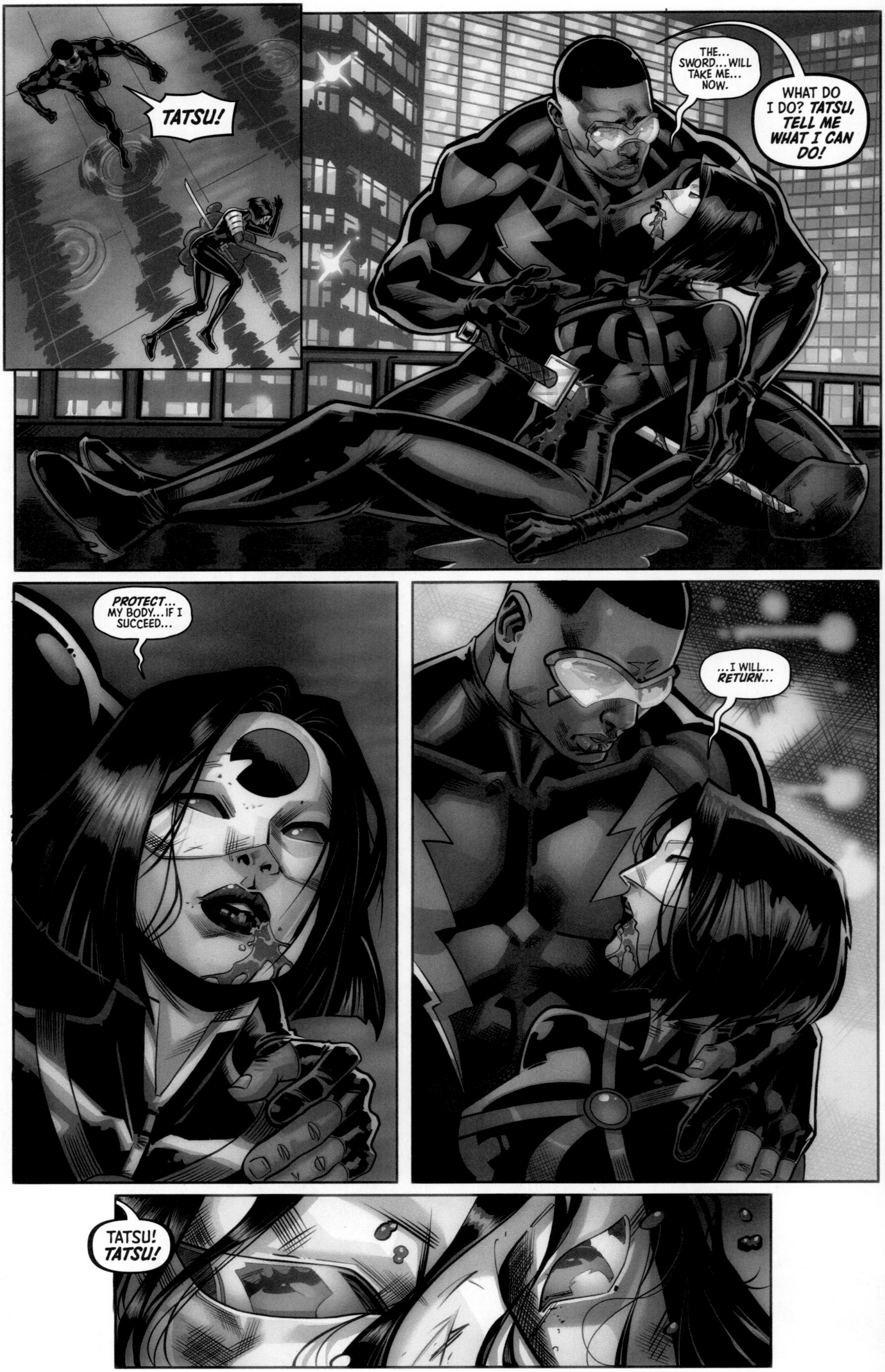
TATSU!
THE... SWORD...WILL TAKE ME... NOW.
WHAT DO I DO? TATSU, TELL ME WHAT I CAN DO!
PROTECT... MY BODY...IF I SUCCEED...
...I WILL... RETURN...
TATSU! TATSU!

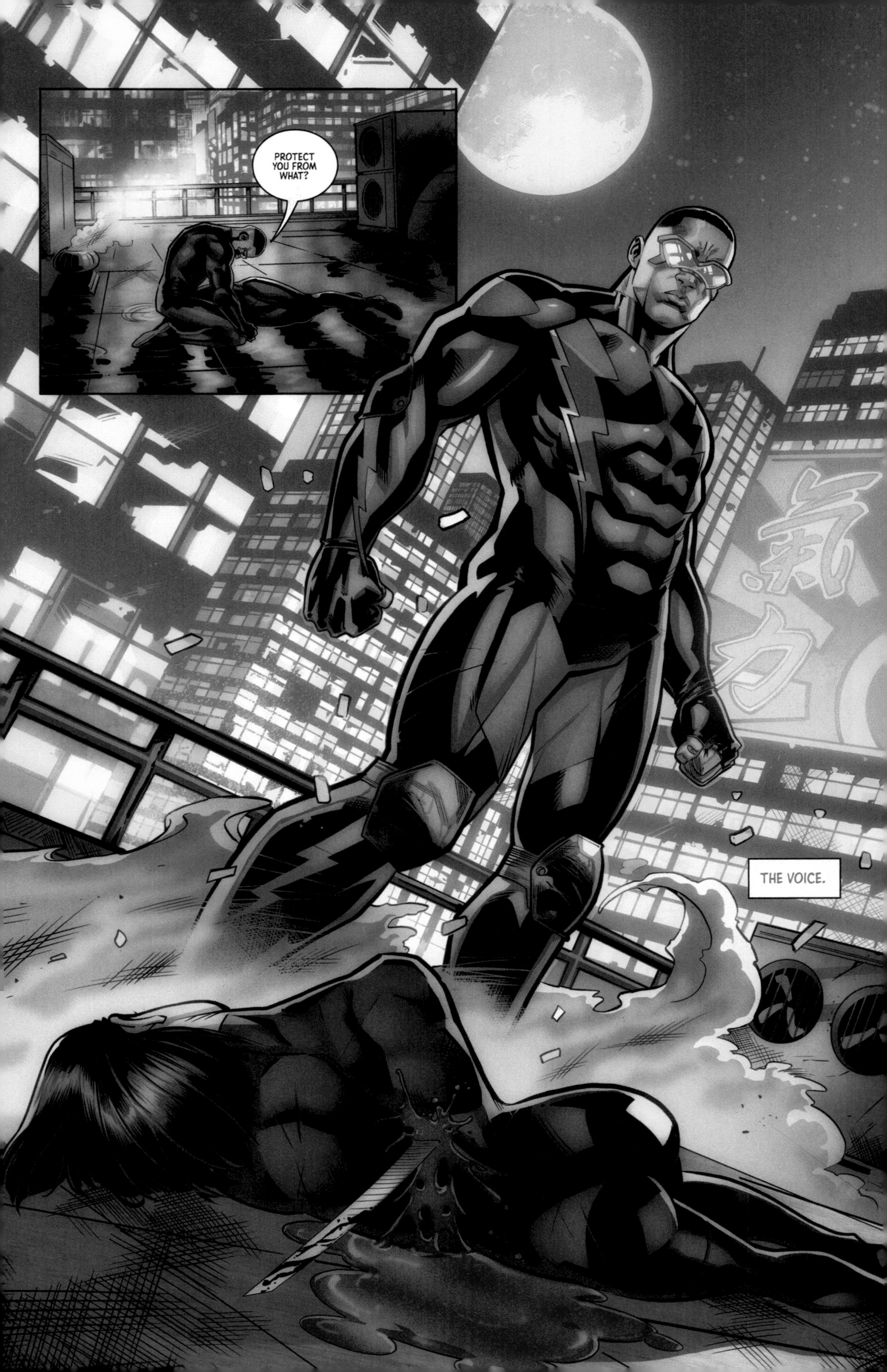
PROTECT YOU FROM WHAT?
THE VOICE.
氣力

THE SONG.

I HEAR IT.

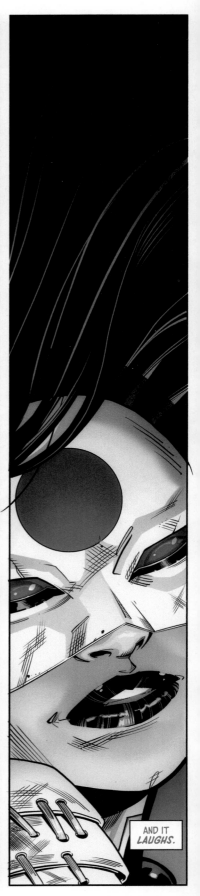

AND IT *LAUGHS.*

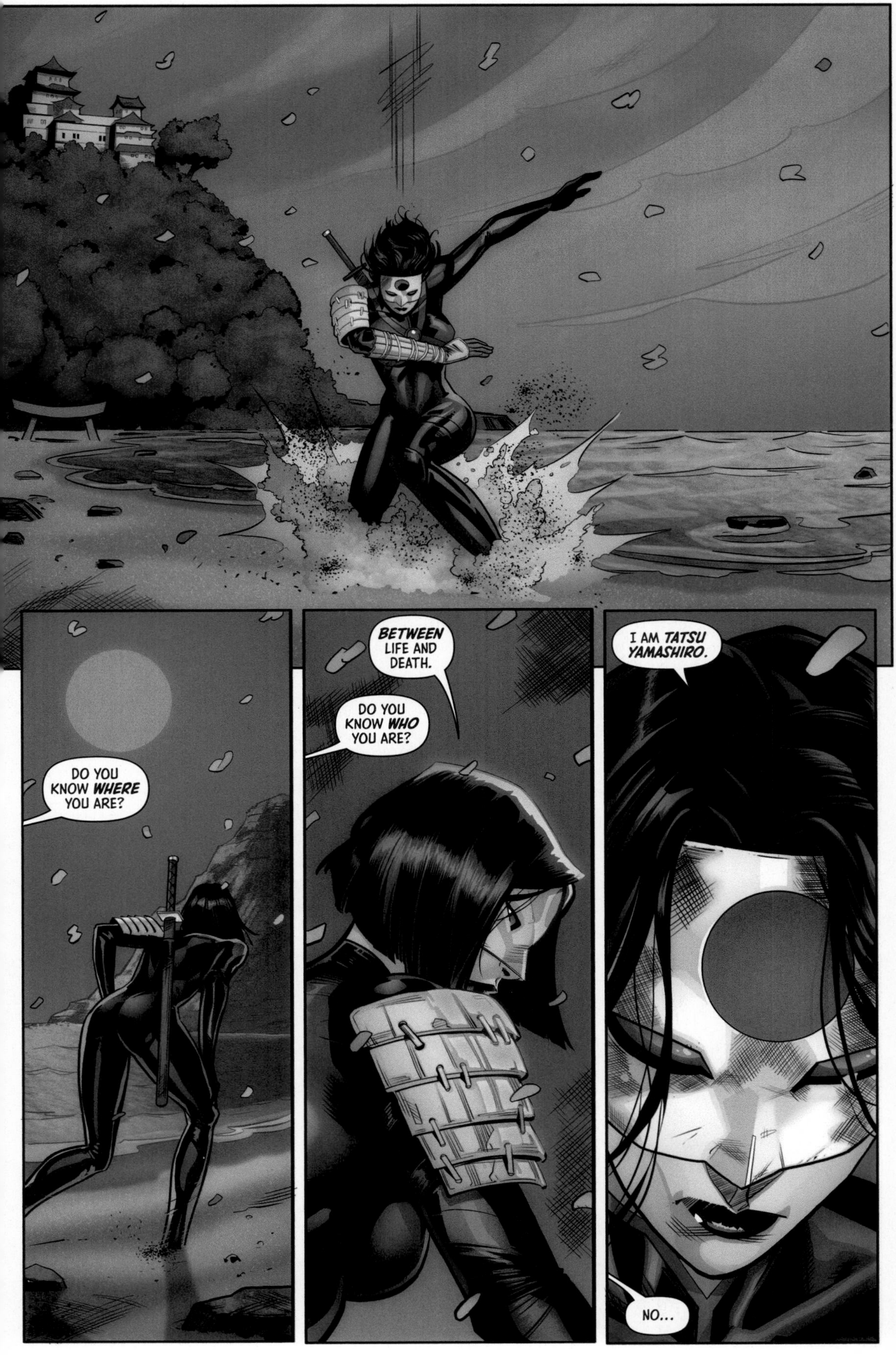
DO YOU KNOW *WHERE* YOU ARE?
BETWEEN LIFE AND DEATH.
DO YOU KNOW *WHO* YOU ARE?
I AM *TATSU YAMASHIRO.*
NO...

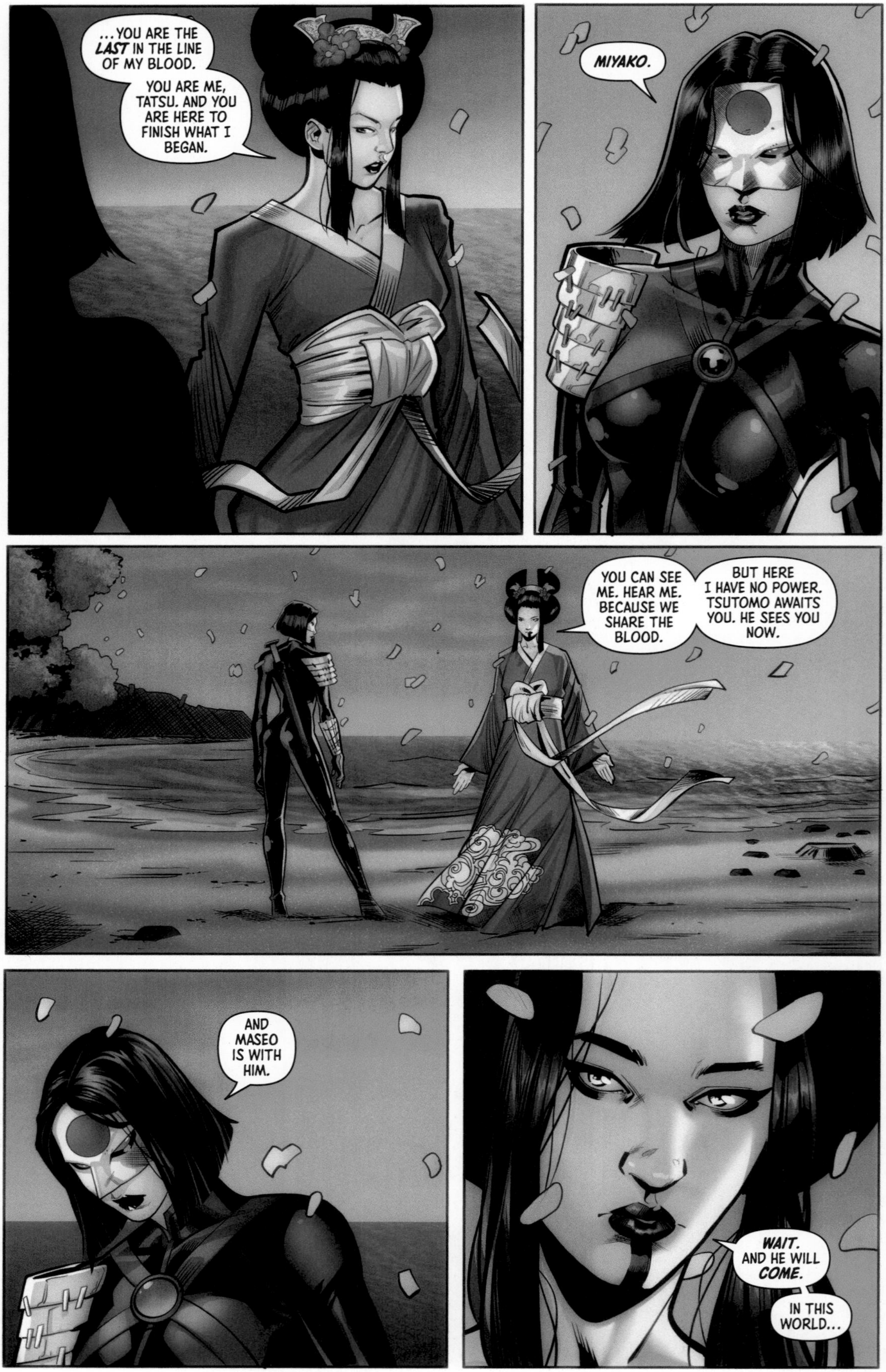
...YOU ARE THE LAST IN THE LINE OF MY BLOOD.
YOU ARE ME, TATSU. AND YOU ARE HERE TO FINISH WHAT I BEGAN.
MIYAKO.
YOU CAN SEE ME. HEAR ME. BECAUSE WE SHARE THE BLOOD.
BUT HERE I HAVE NO POWER. TSUTOMO AWAITS YOU. HE SEES YOU NOW.
AND MASEO IS WITH HIM.
WAIT. AND HE WILL COME.
IN THIS WORLD...

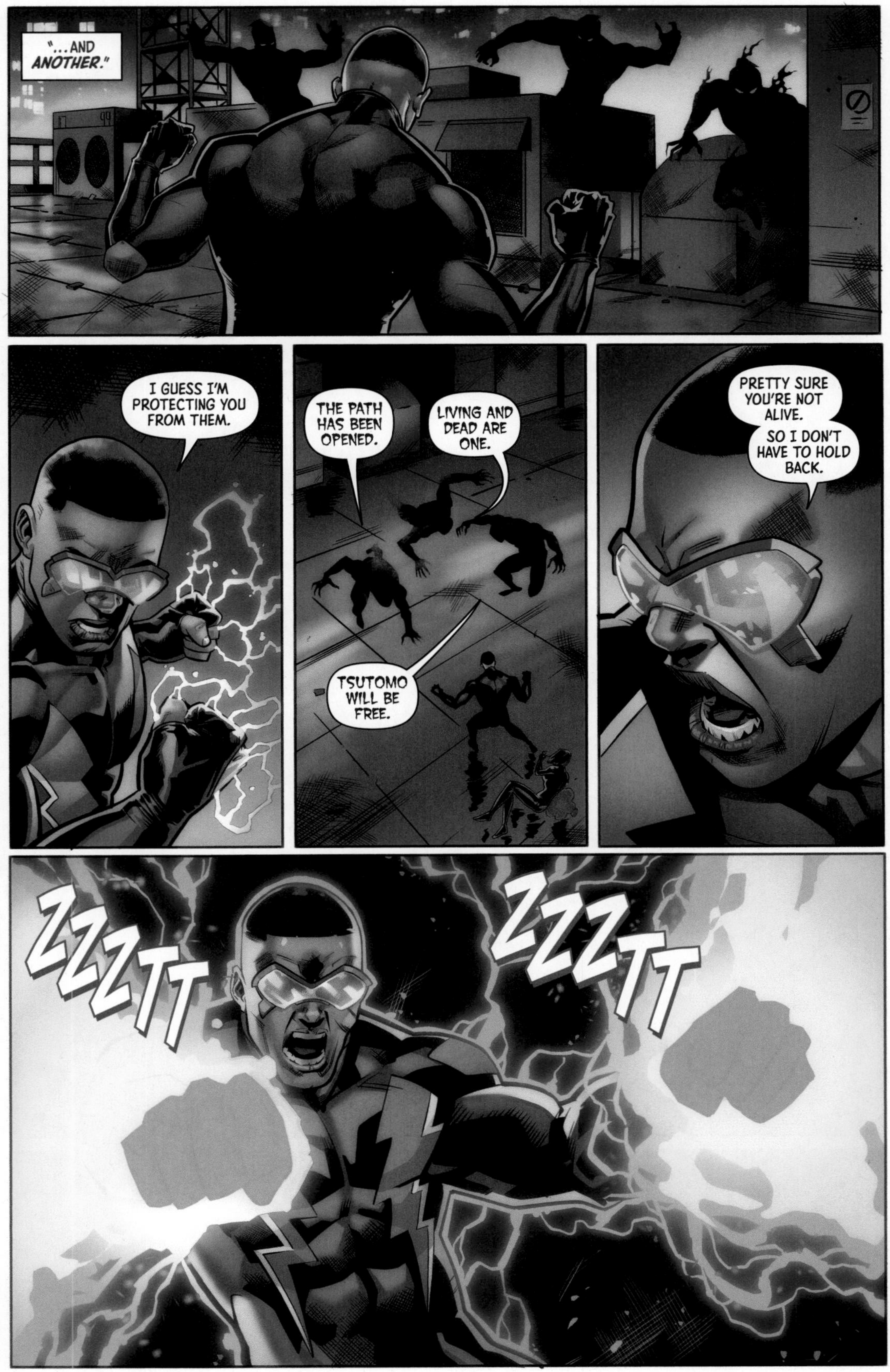
"...AND ANOTHER."
I GUESS I'M PROTECTING YOU FROM THEM.
THE PATH HAS BEEN OPENED.
LIVING AND DEAD ARE ONE.
TSUTOMO WILL BE FREE.
PRETTY SURE YOU'RE NOT ALIVE.
SO I DON'T HAVE TO HOLD BACK.
ZZZTT
ZZZTT

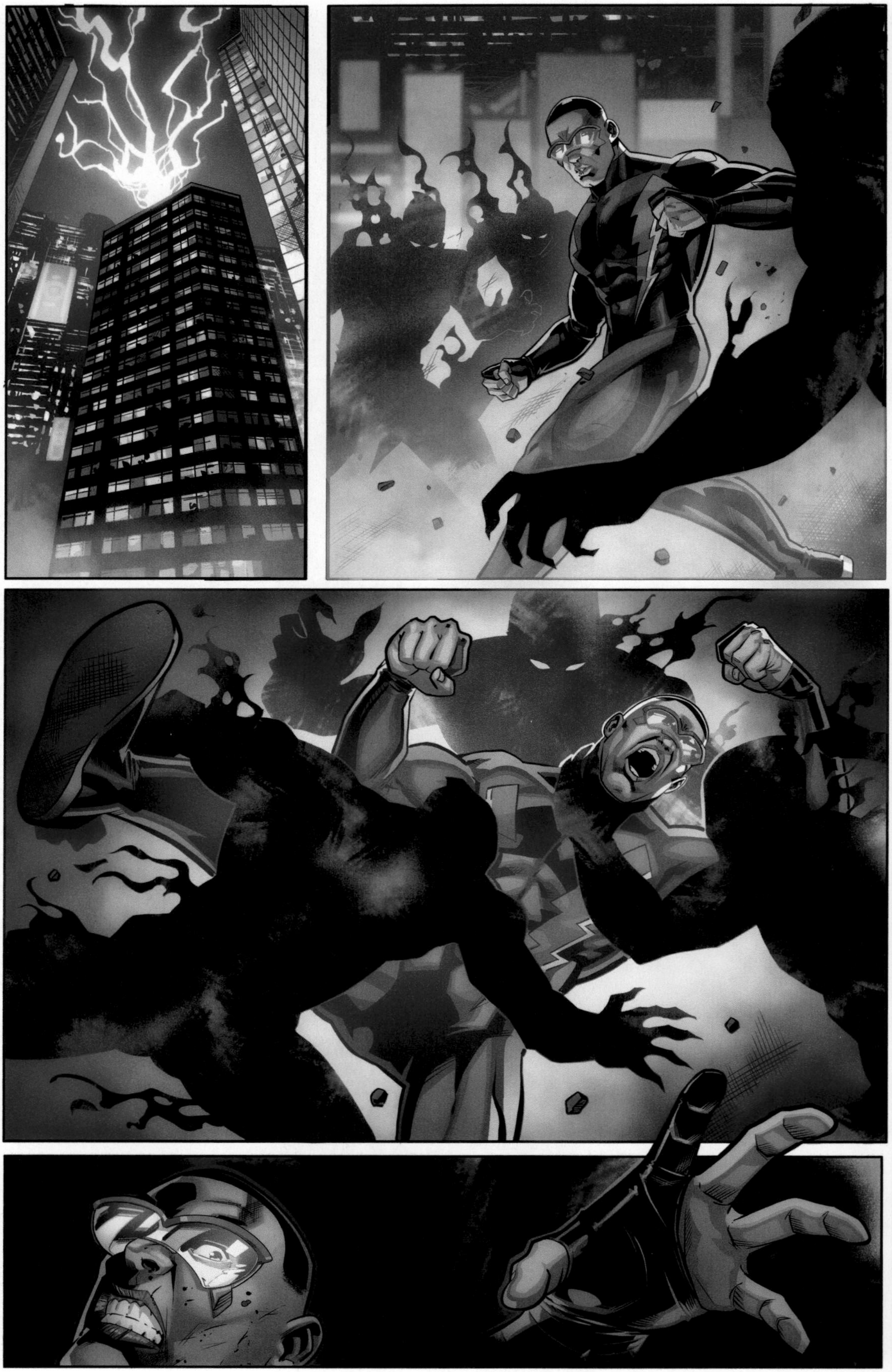

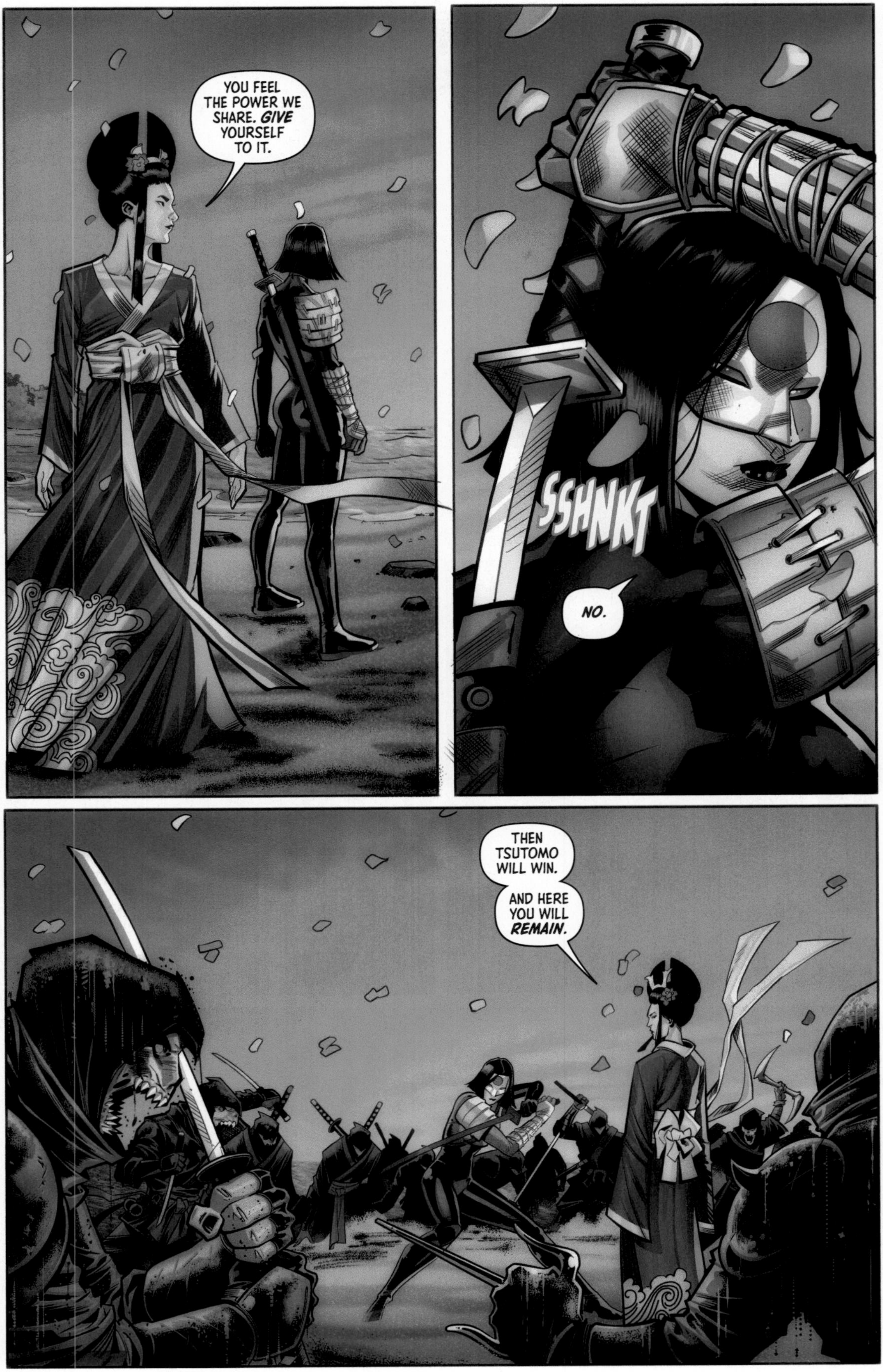
YOU FEEL THE POWER WE SHARE. GIVE YOURSELF TO IT.
SSHNKT
NO.
THEN TSUTOMO WILL WIN.
AND HERE YOU WILL REMAIN.

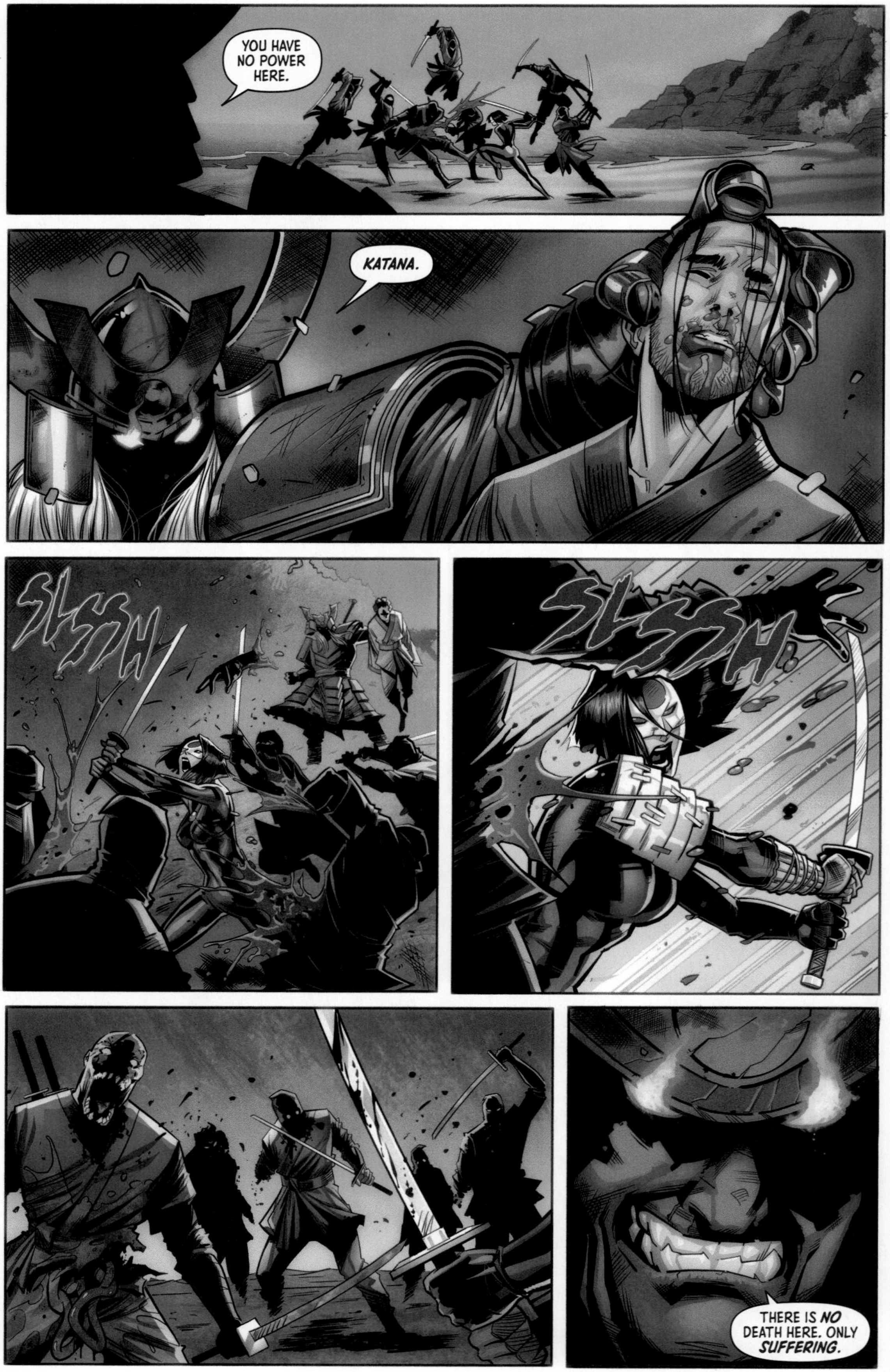
YOU HAVE NO POWER HERE.
KATANA.
SLSSH
SLSSH
THERE IS NO DEATH HERE. ONLY SUFFERING.

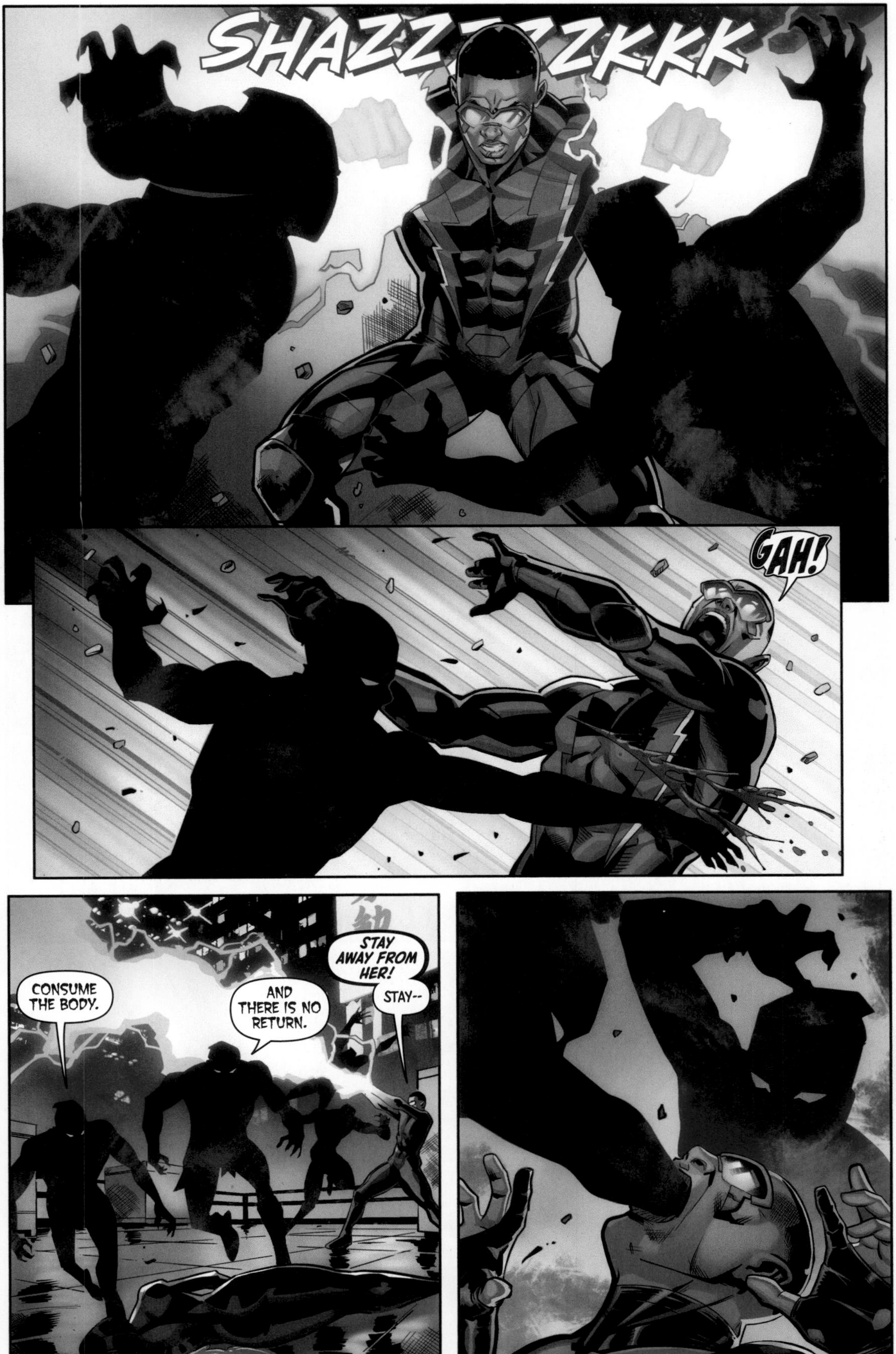
SHAZZZZZKKK
GAH!
CONSUME THE BODY.
AND THERE IS NO RETURN.
STAY AWAY FROM HER!
STAY--

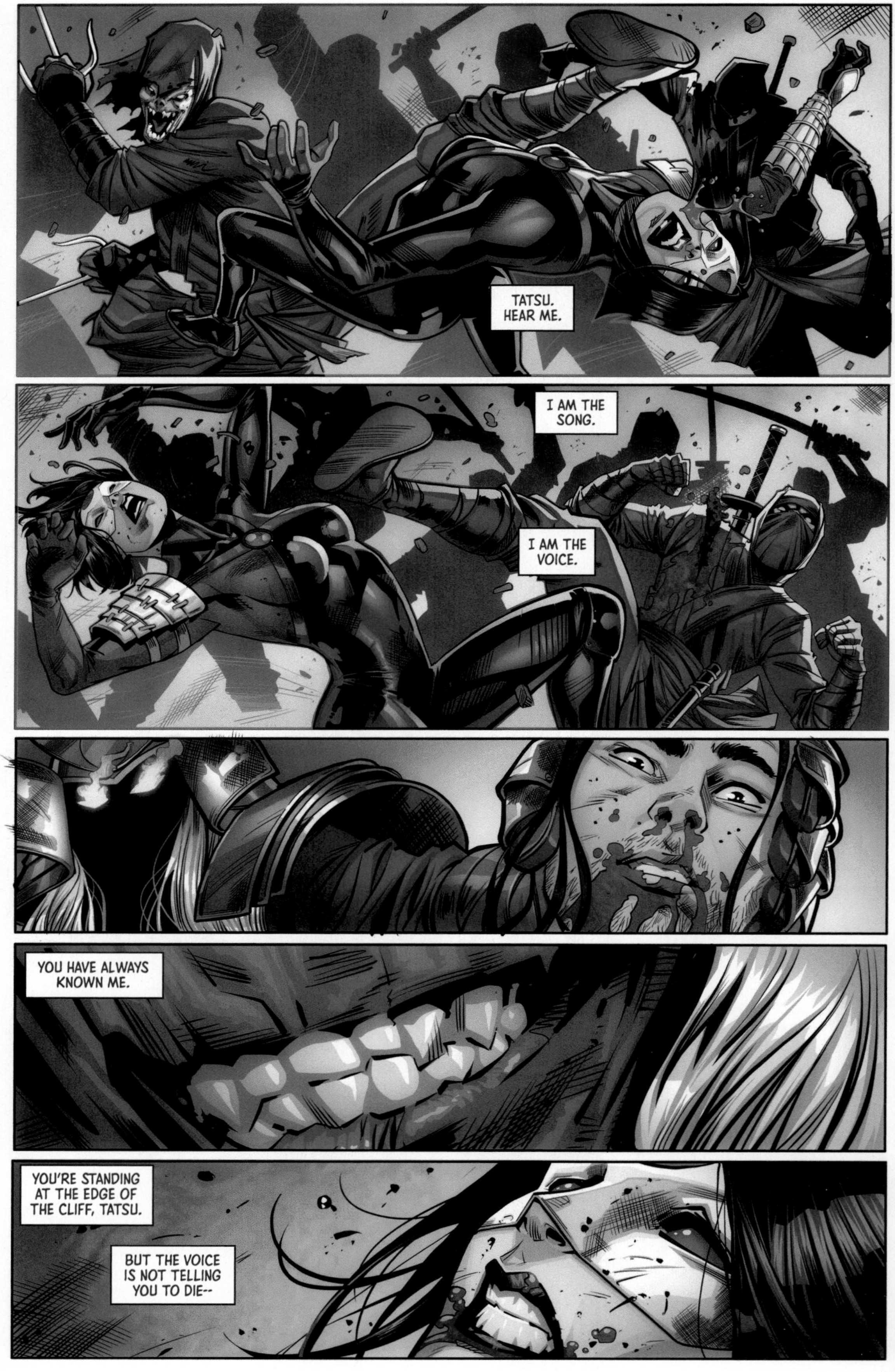
TATSU. HEAR ME.
I AM THE SONG.
I AM THE VOICE.
YOU HAVE ALWAYS KNOWN ME.
YOU'RE STANDING AT THE EDGE OF THE CLIFF, TATSU.
BUT THE VOICE IS NOT TELLING YOU TO DIE--

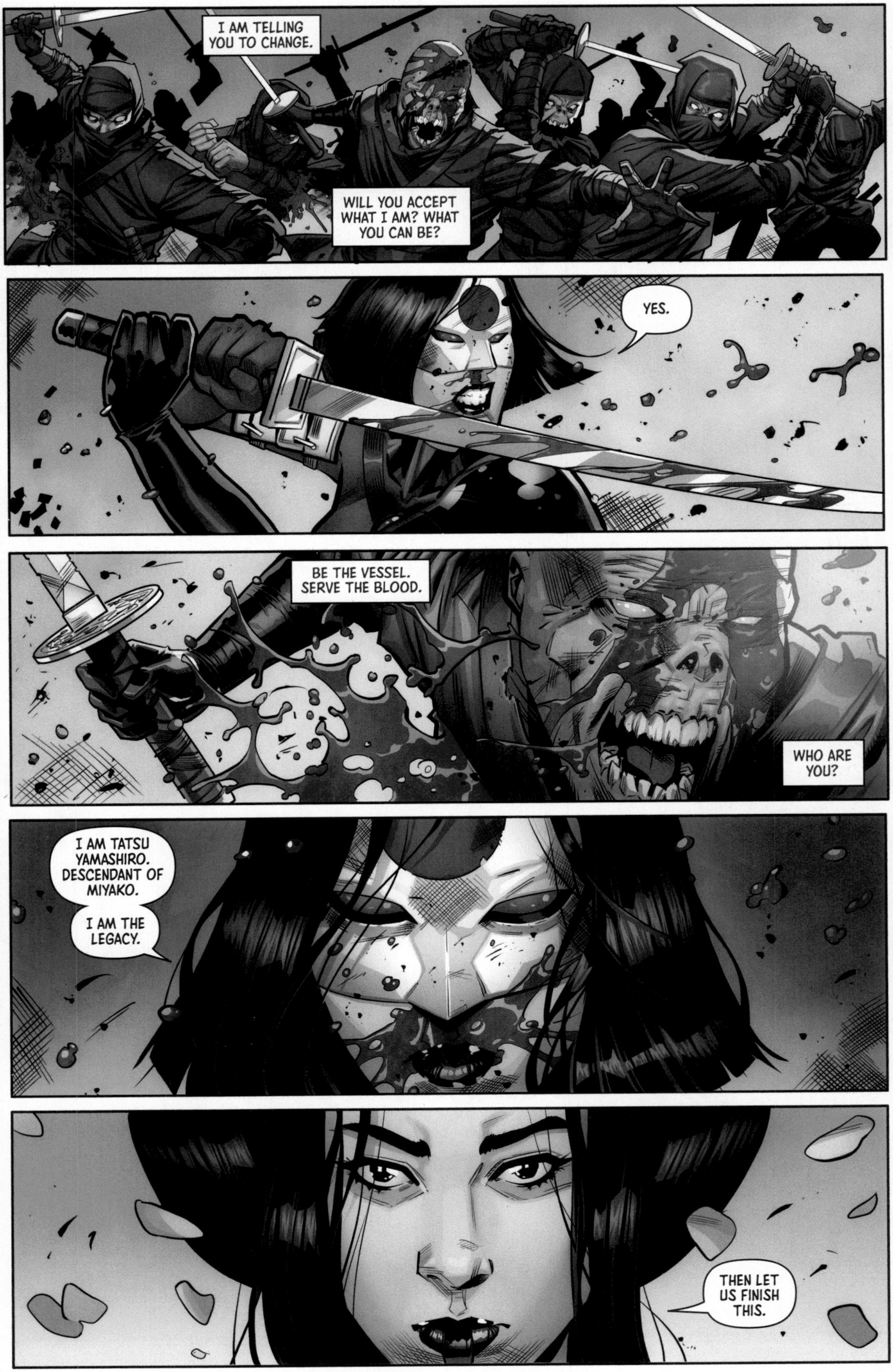

I AM TELLING YOU TO CHANGE.
WILL YOU ACCEPT WHAT I AM? WHAT YOU CAN BE?
YES.
BE THE VESSEL. SERVE THE BLOOD.
WHO ARE YOU?
I AM TATSU YAMASHIRO. DESCENDANT OF MIYAKO.
I AM THE LEGACY.
THEN LET US FINISH THIS.

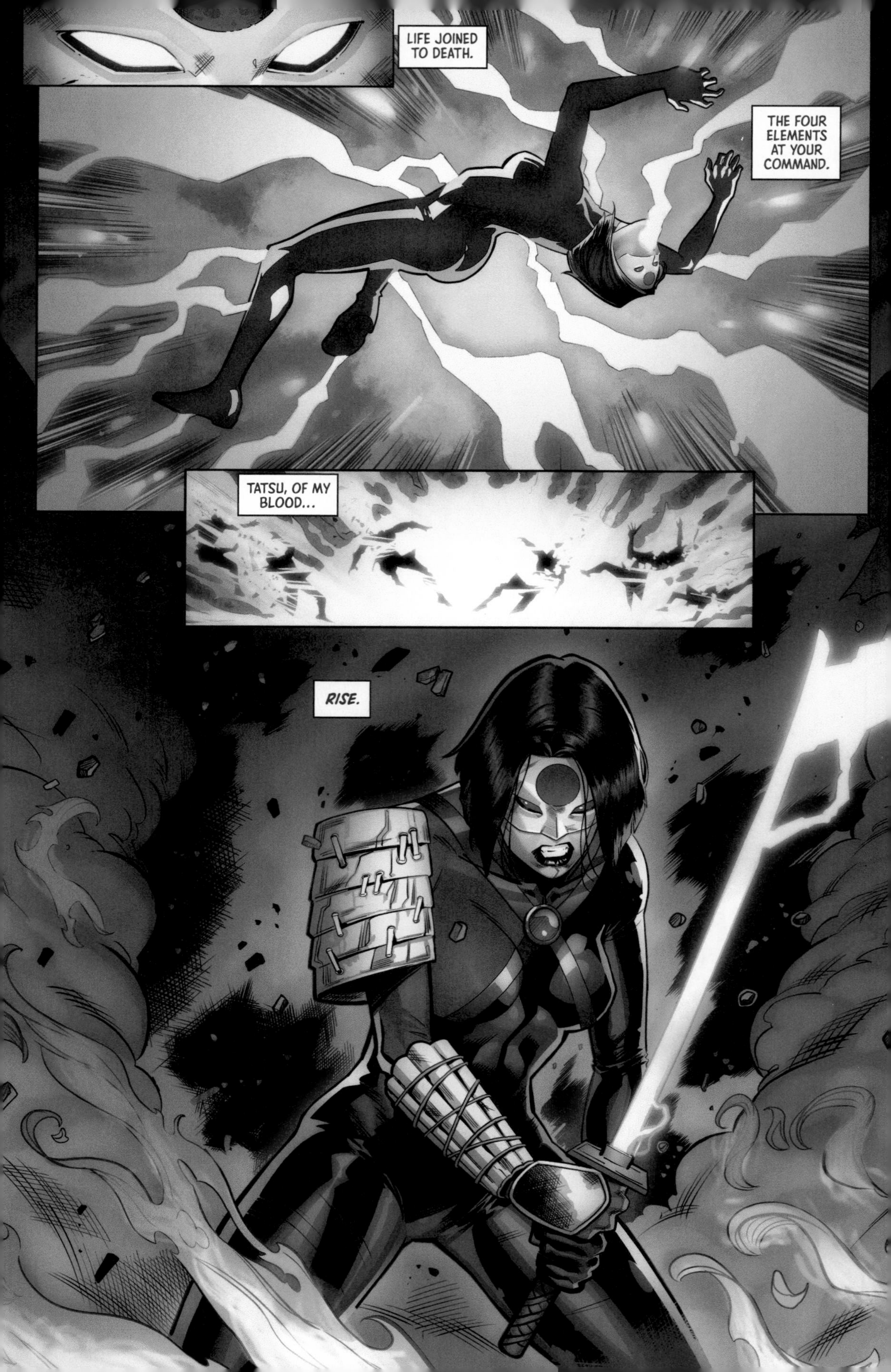
LIFE JOINED TO DEATH.
THE FOUR ELEMENTS AT YOUR COMMAND.
TATSU, OF MY BLOOD...
RISE.

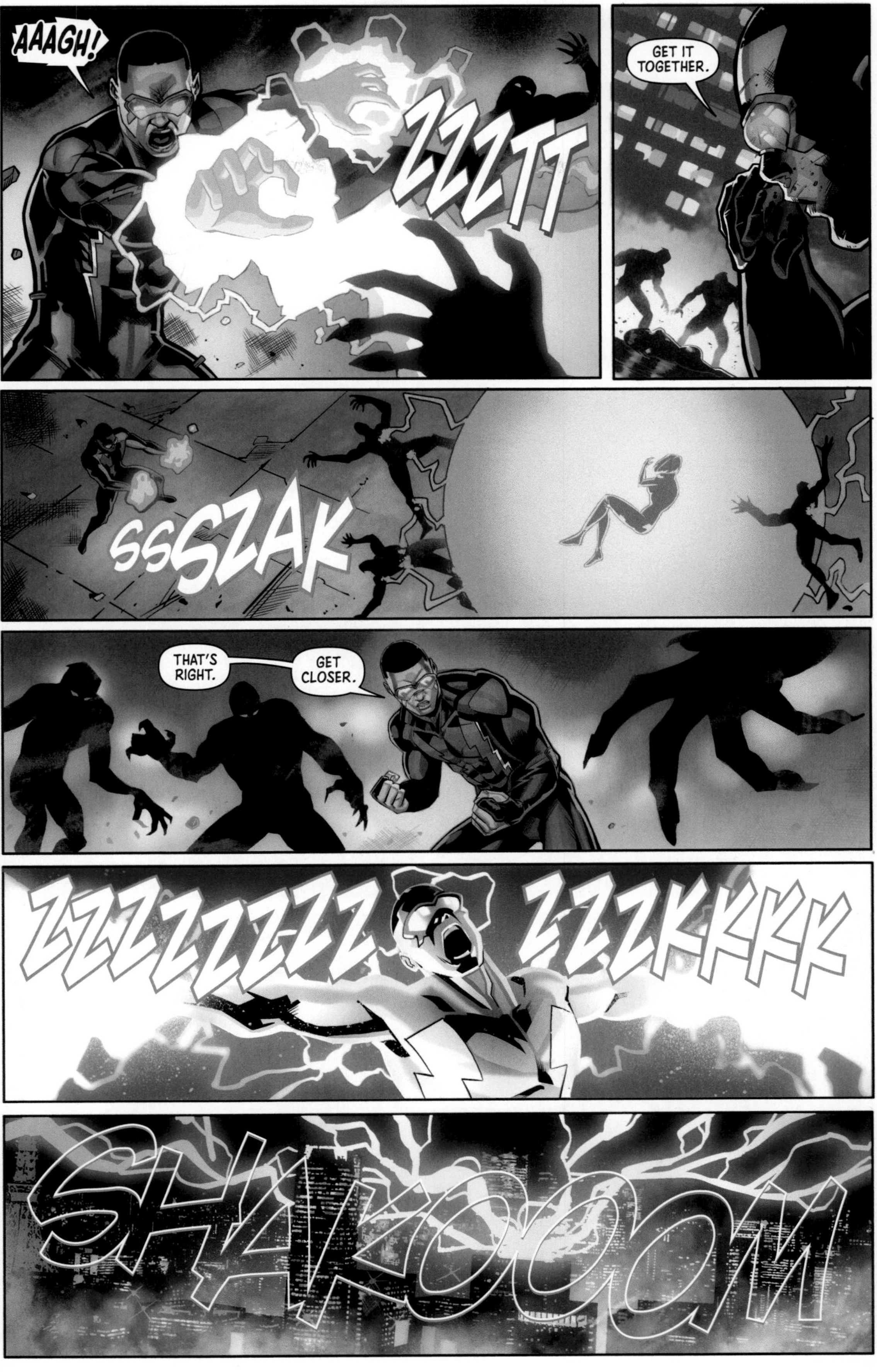
AAAGH!
ZZZTT
GET IT TOGETHER.
SSSZAK
THAT'S RIGHT.
GET CLOSER.
ZZZZZZZZ
ZZZKKKK
SHAKOOOM

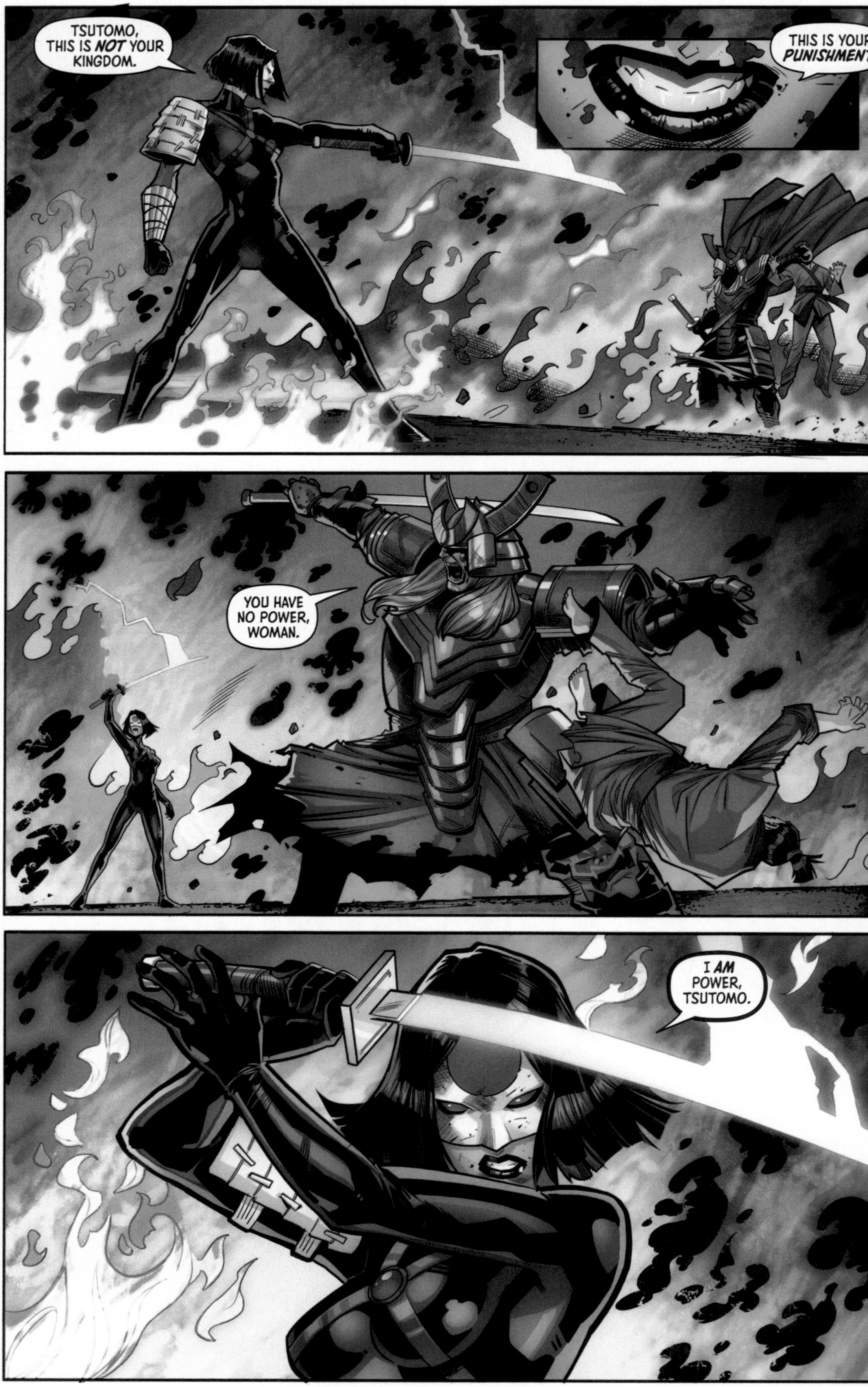
TSUTOMO, THIS IS NOT YOUR KINGDOM.
THIS IS YOUR PUNISHMENT.
YOU HAVE NO POWER, WOMAN.
I AM POWER, TSUTOMO.

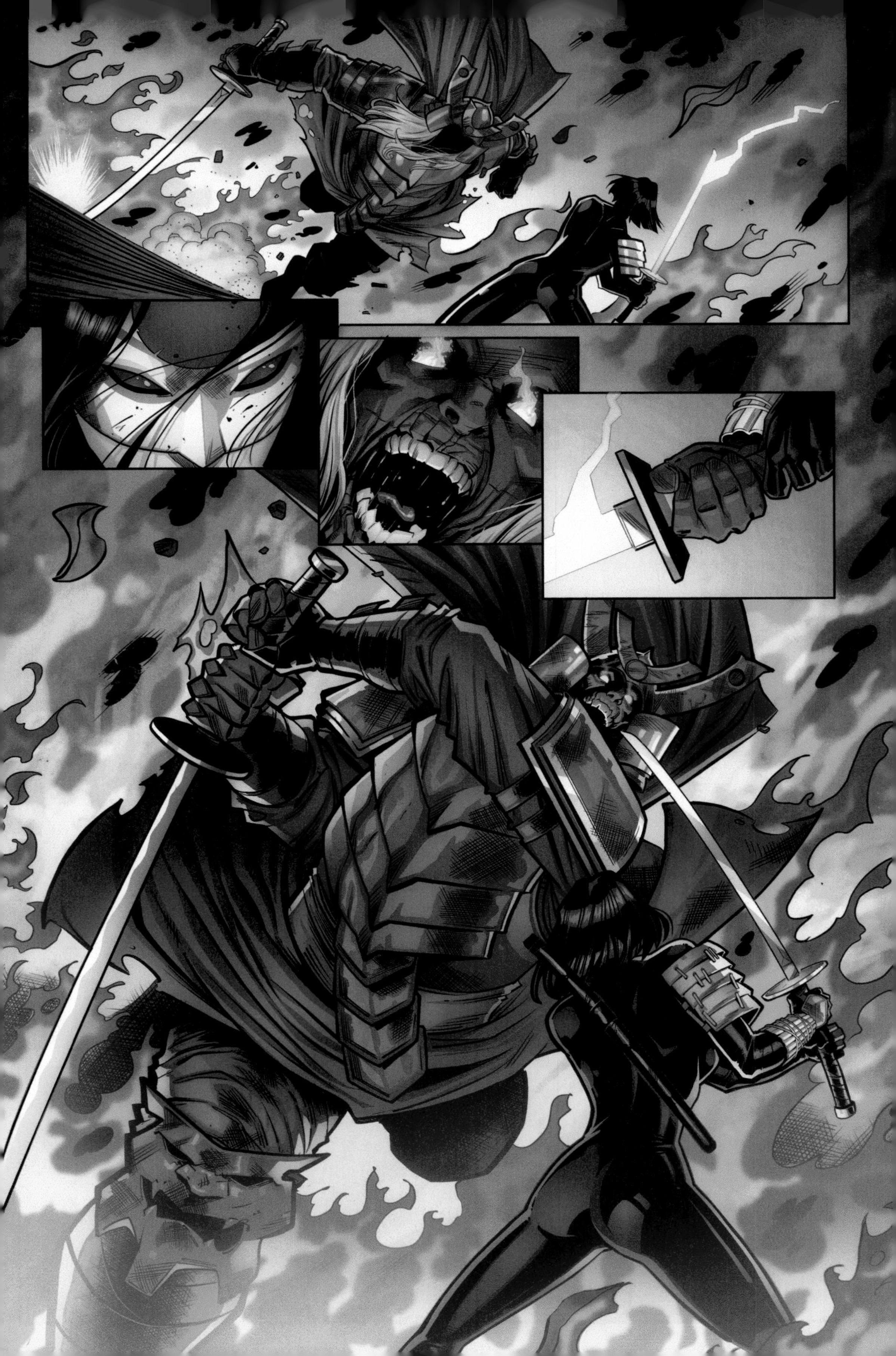

SHHKK

TATSU.

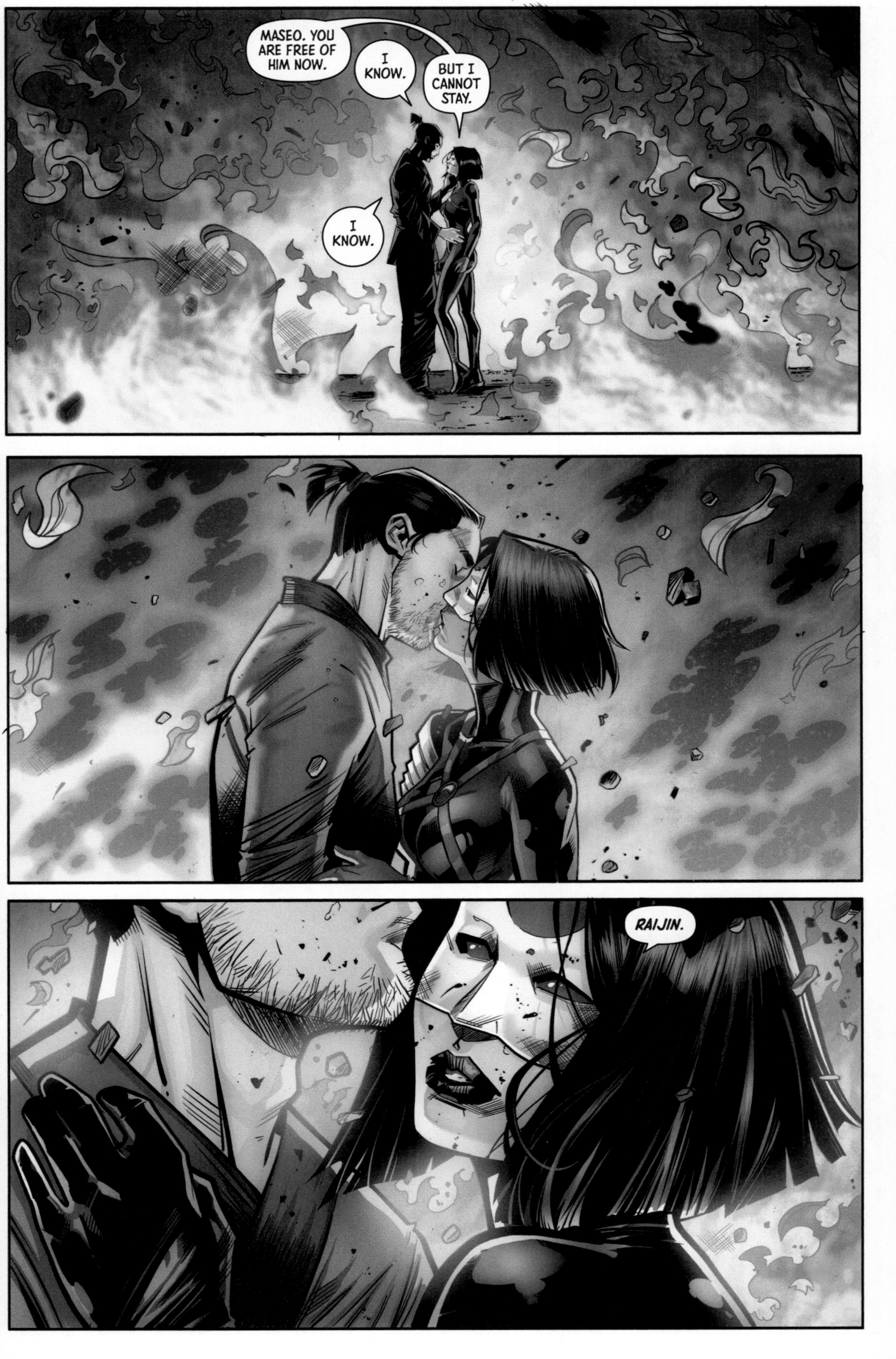
MASEO. YOU ARE FREE OF HIM NOW.
I KNOW.
BUT I CANNOT STAY.
I KNOW.
RAIJIN.

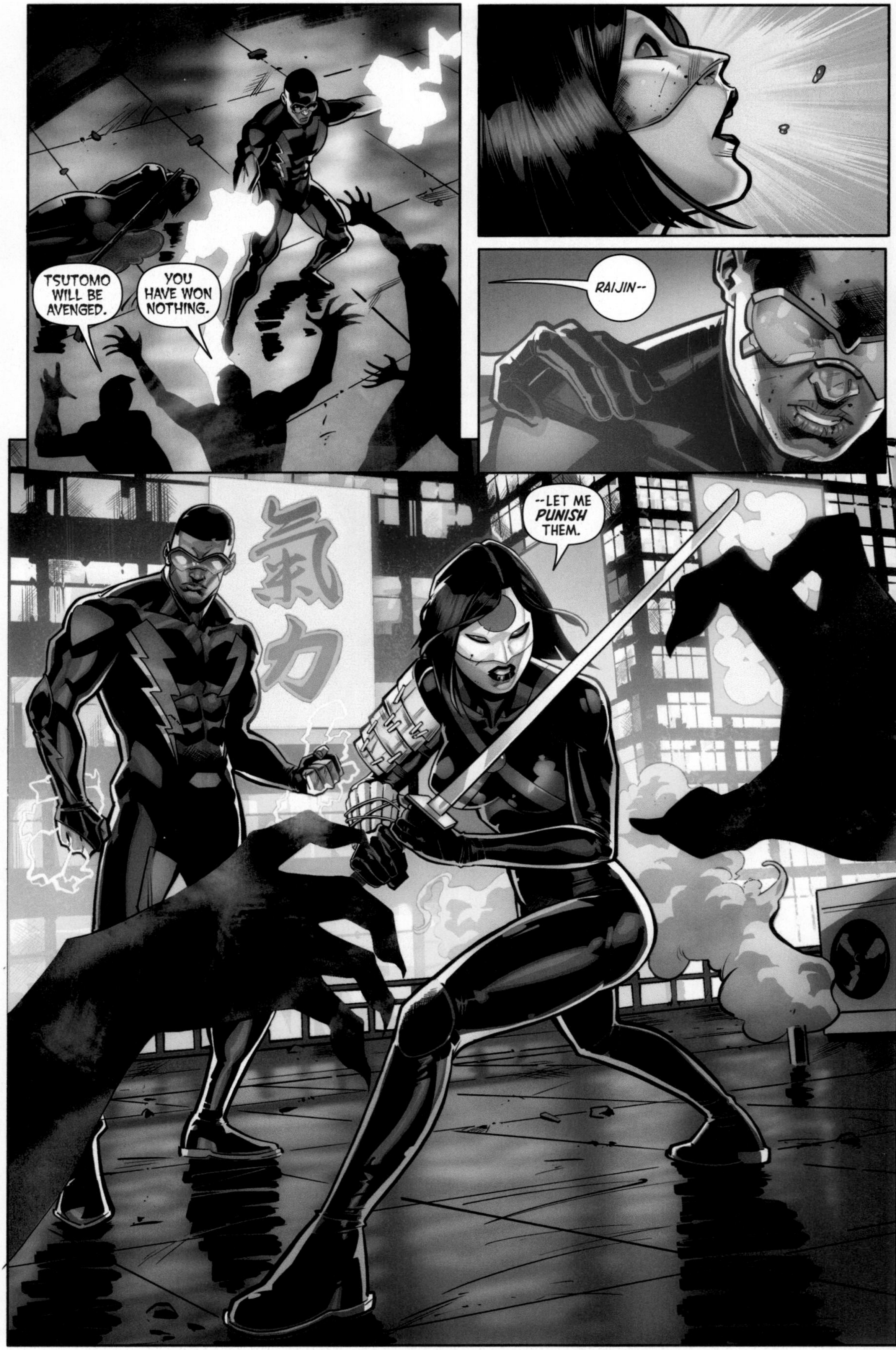
TSUTOMO WILL BE AVENGED.
YOU HAVE WON NOTHING.
RAIJIN--
--LET ME *PUNISH* THEM.

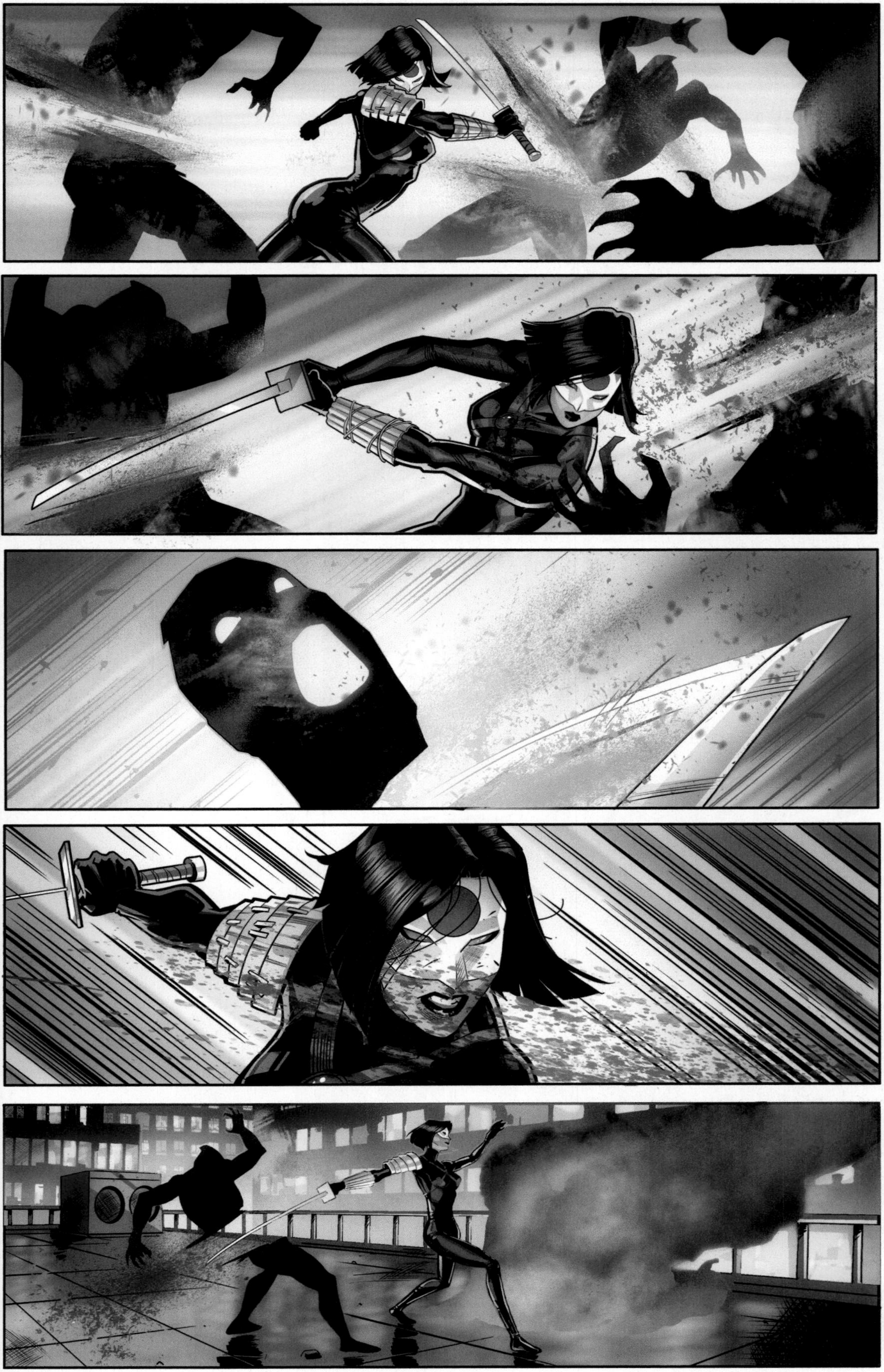

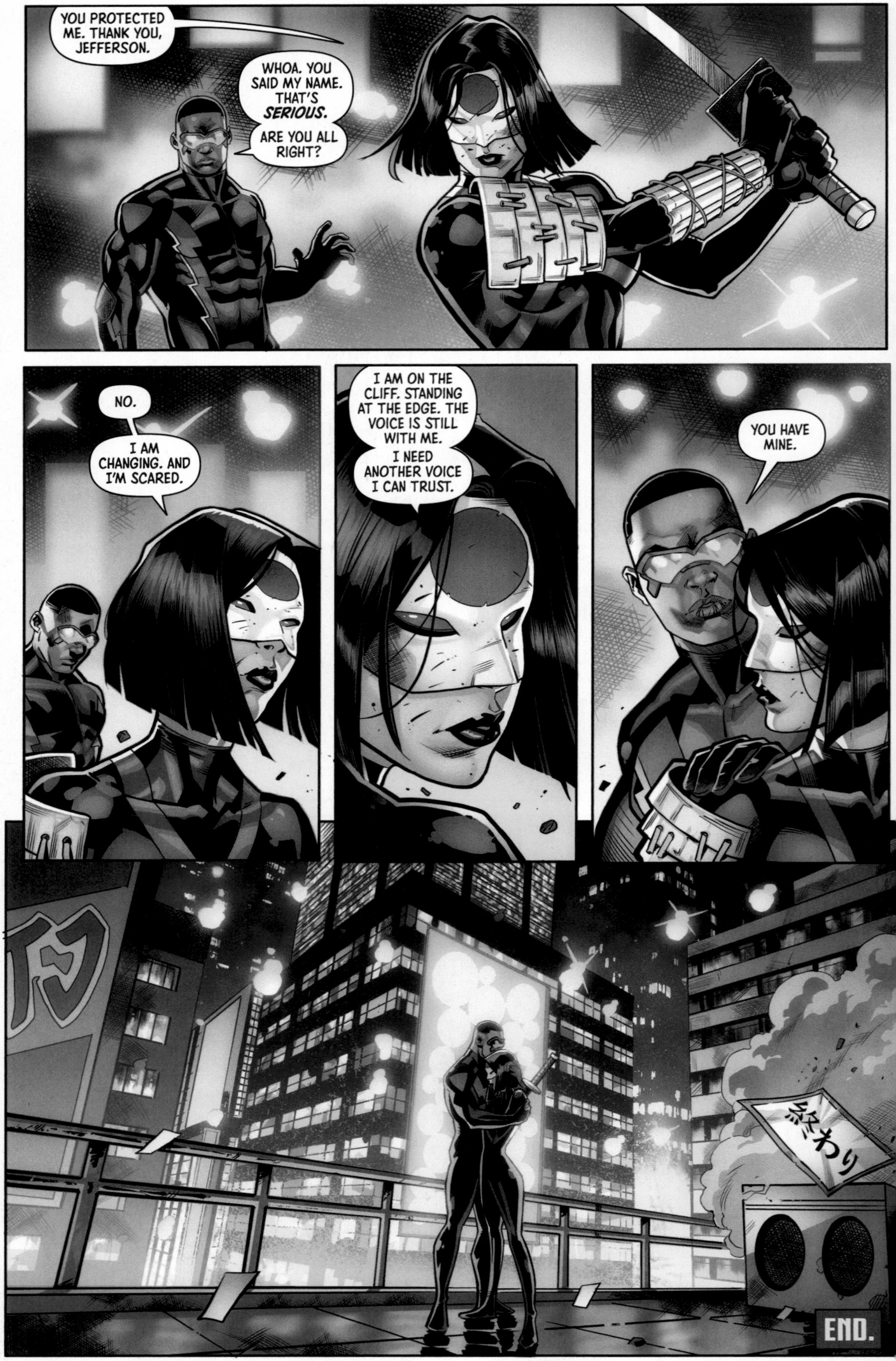
YOU PROTECTED ME. THANK YOU, JEFFERSON.
WHOA. YOU SAID MY NAME. THAT'S *SERIOUS.*
ARE YOU ALL RIGHT?
NO.
I AM CHANGING. AND I'M SCARED.
I AM ON THE CLIFF. STANDING AT THE EDGE. THE VOICE IS STILL WITH ME.
I NEED ANOTHER VOICE I CAN TRUST.
YOU HAVE MINE.
終わり
END.

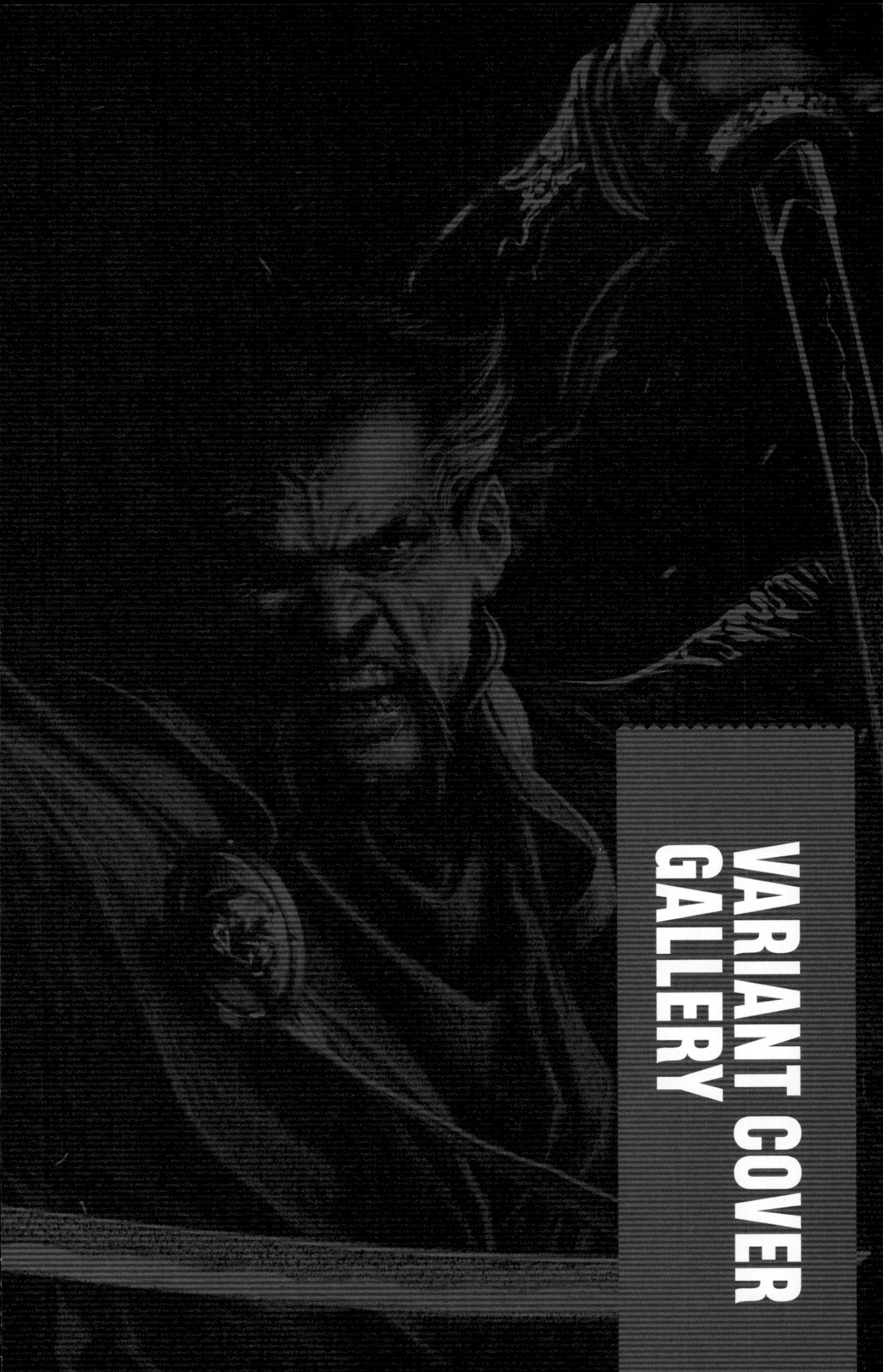

VARIANT COVER GALLERY

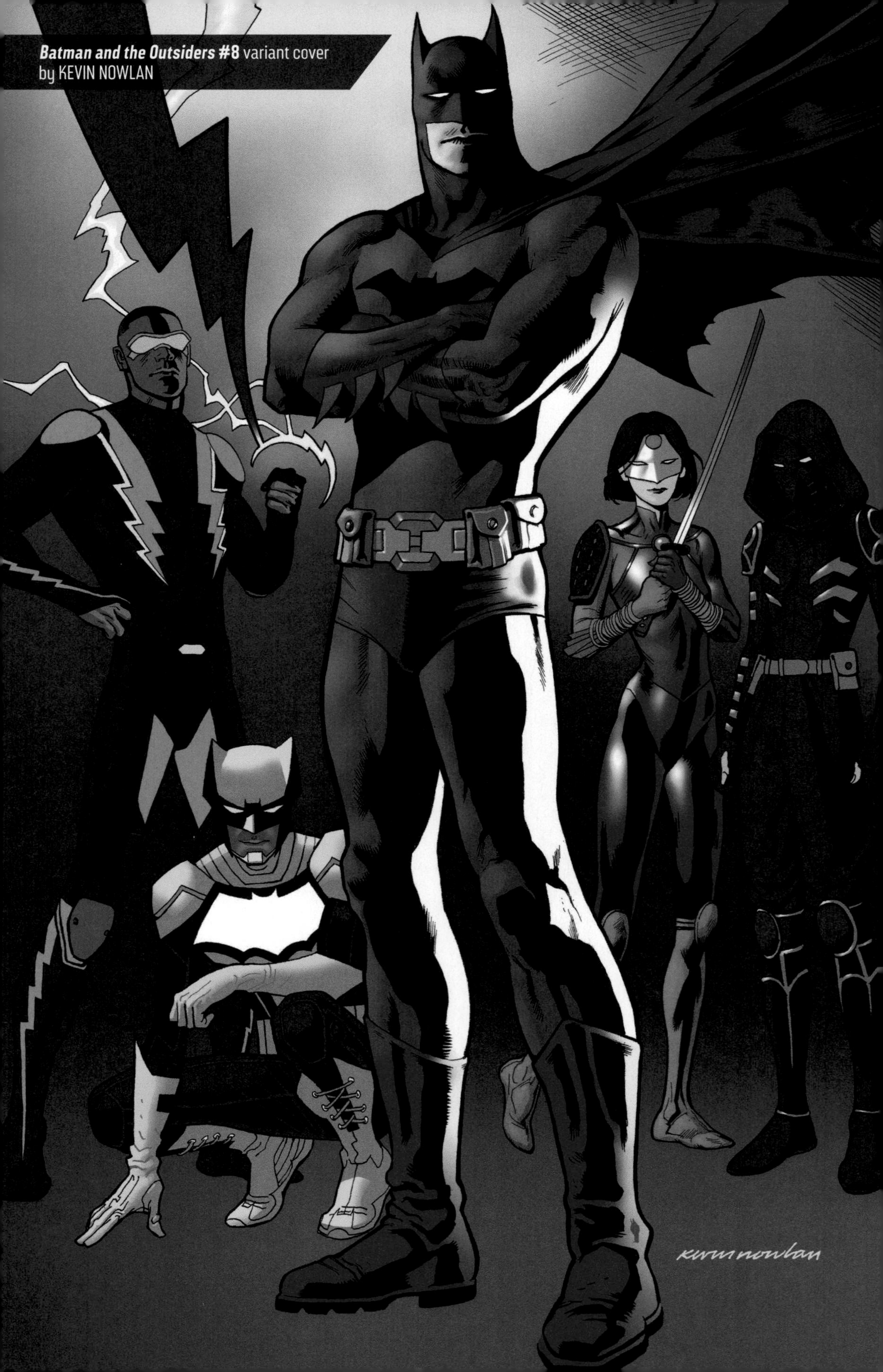
kevin nowlan

Batman and the Outsiders **#8** variant cover
by KEVIN NOWLAN

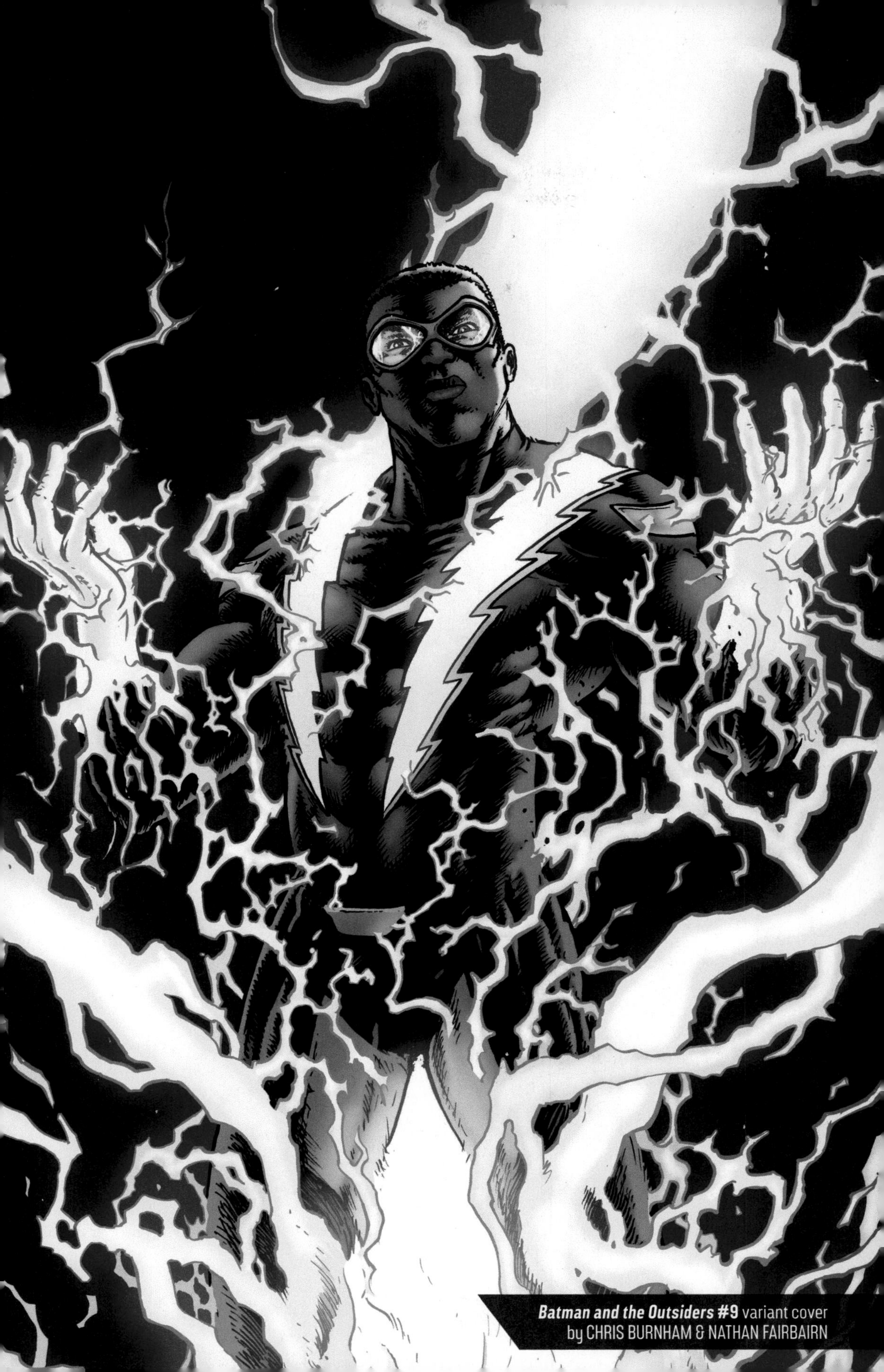

***Batman and the Outsiders* #9** variant cover
by CHRIS BURNHAM & NATHAN FAIRBAIRN

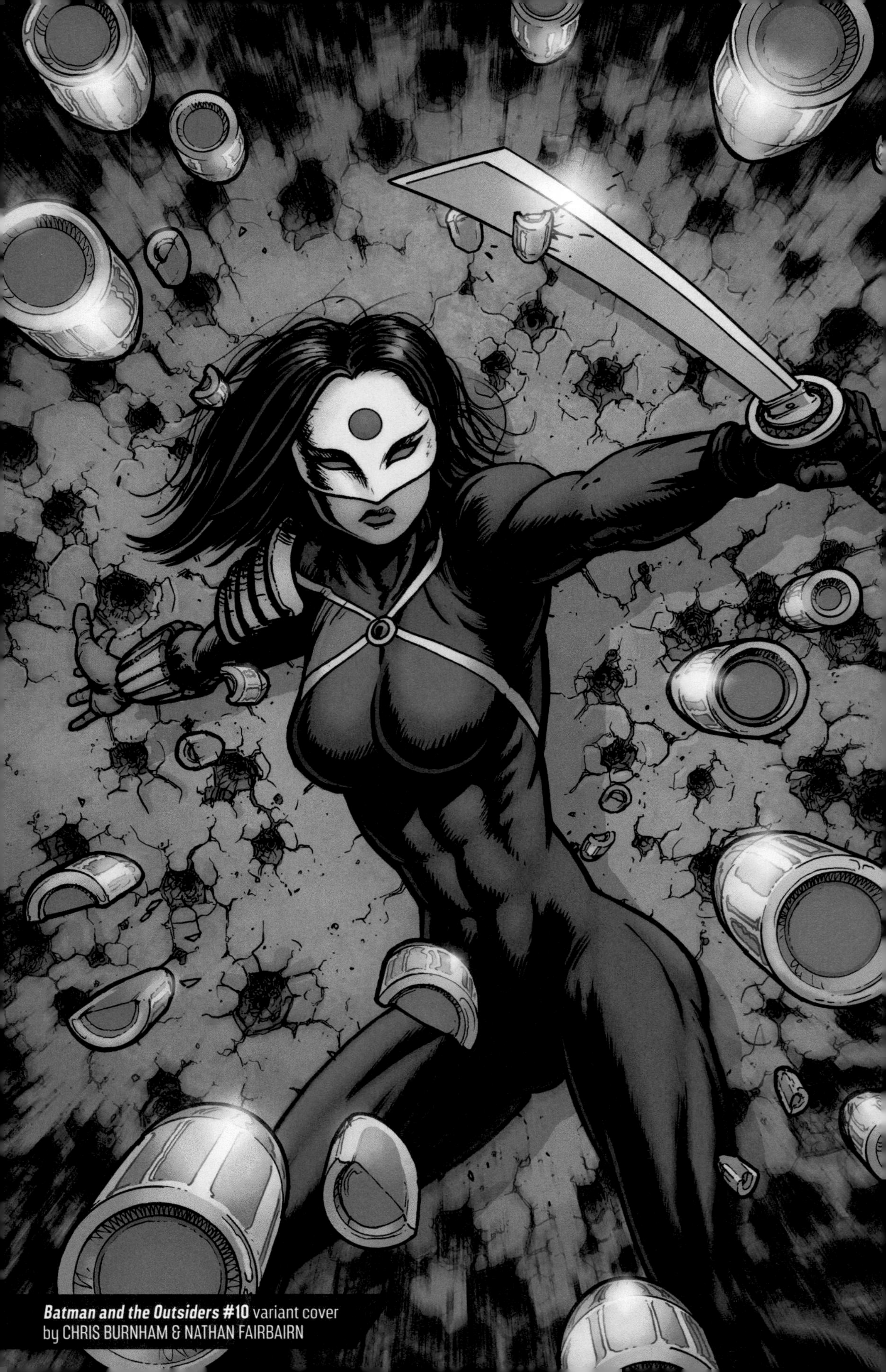

***Batman and the Outsiders* #10** variant cover
by CHRIS BURNHAM & NATHAN FAIRBAIRN

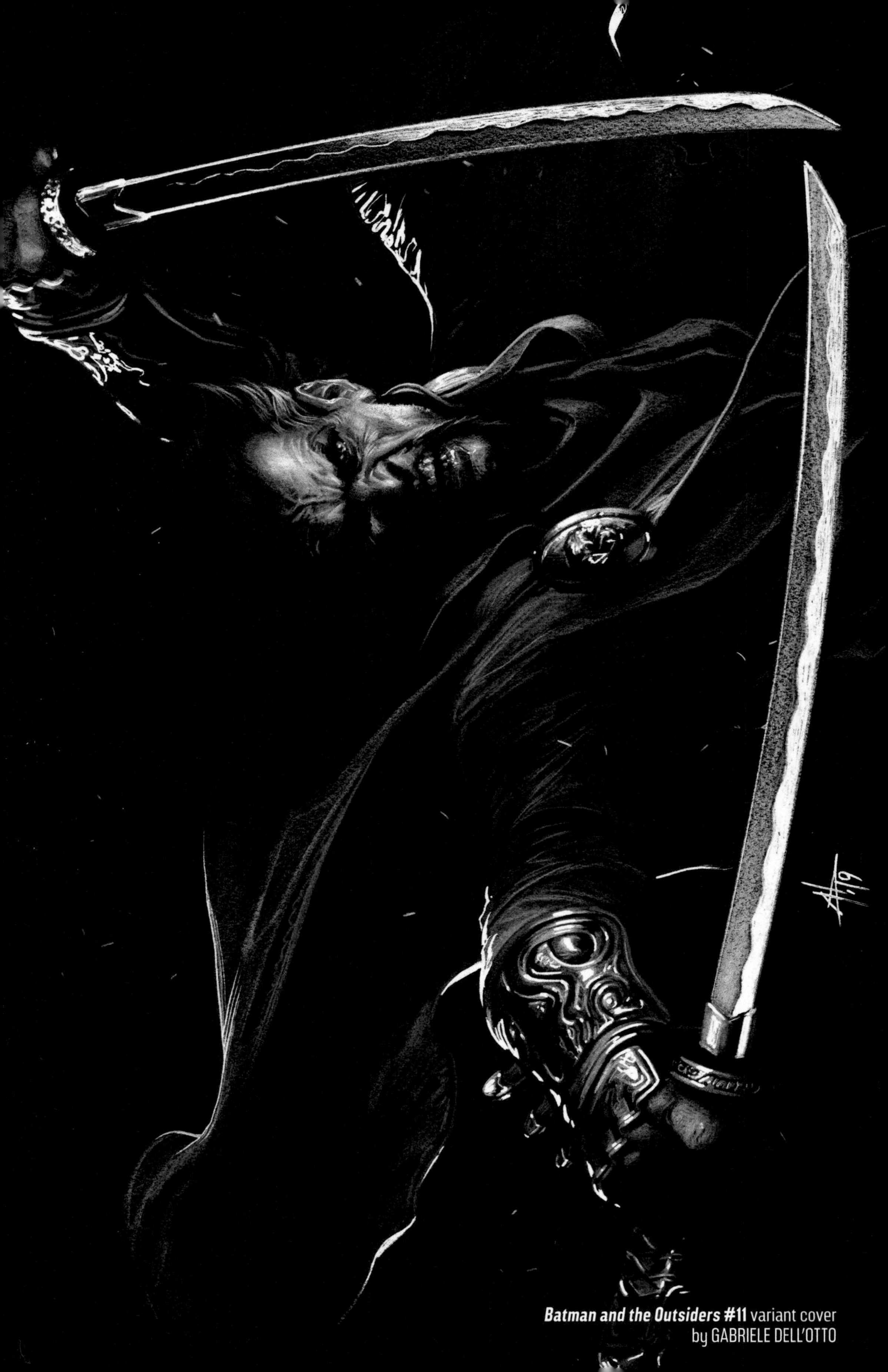

***Batman and the Outsiders* #11** variant cover
by GABRIELE DELL'OTTO

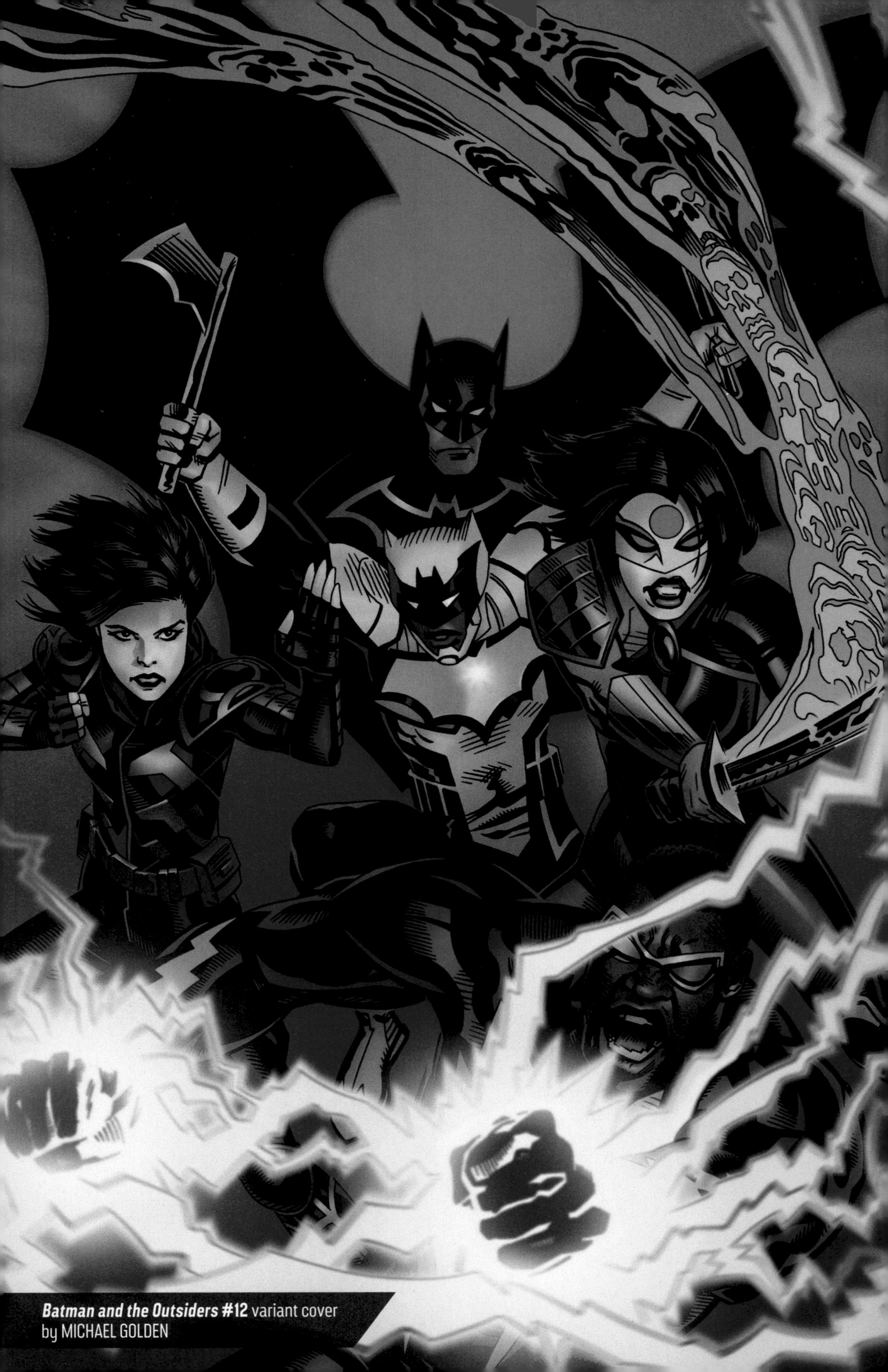

***Batman and the Outsiders* #12** variant cover
by MICHAEL GOLDEN